ART + FASHION

COLLABORATIONS AND CONNECTIONS BETWEEN ICONS

BY E. P. CUTLER AND JULIEN TOMASELLO

CHRONICLE BOOKS
San Francisco

Library of Congress Cataloging-in-Publication data available.

ISBN: 978-1452-1-3869-5

Manufactured in China

Page 222 constitutes a continuation of the copyright page.

Design by Sara Schneider

10 9 8 7 6 5 4 3 2 1

Chronicle Books LLC
680 Second Street
San Francisco, CA 94107

www.chroniclebooks.com

TO MY BROTHER, CLARK:
OUR RELATIONSHIP IS MY
LONGEST-RUNNING AND
BEST COLLABORATION.

— EPC

TO THE MRS. T'S: EISA,
DOROTHY, ANGELINA,
PAULINE, AND JULIETTE,
WITH ENDLESS LOVE
AND GRATITUDE FOR
YOUR INSPIRATION.

— JT

CONTENTS

JACKSON POLLOCK	+	CECIL BEATON
ALEX PRAGER	+	BOTTEGA VENETA
CINDY SHERMAN	+	CHANEL
JAMES NARES	+	COACH
MATT GROENING	+	COMME DES GARÇONS PLAY
ANDY WARHOL	+	DIOR
MELVIN SOKOLSKY	+	*HARPER'S BAZAAR*
RICHARD ANUSZKIEWICZ	+	JACQUES KAPLAN
JOHN CHAMBERLAIN	+	MARY KATRANTZOU
MERCE CUNNINGHAM	+	REI KAWAKUBO
NAN GOLDIN	+	JAMES KING
PETER SAVILLE	+	LACOSTE
JEFF KOONS	+	STELLA McCARTNEY
DAMIEN HIRST	+	ALEXANDER McQUEEN
NICK CAVE	+	RAYMOND MEIER
YASUMASA MORIMURA	+	ISSEY MIYAKE
ELMGREEN & DRAGSET	+	PRADA
WING SHYA	+	RODARTE
PIET MONDRIAN	+	YVES SAINT LAURENT
SALVADOR DALÍ	+	ELSA SCHIAPARELLI
STERLING RUBY	+	RAF SIMONS
TIM ROELOFFS	+	VERSACE
THE CHAPMAN BROTHERS	+	LOUIS VUITTON
TIM BURTON	+	TIM WALKER
KEITH HARING	+	VIVIENNE WESTWOOD

ACKNOWLEDGM

Every book is a collaborative effort. E. P. would like to thank Arianna Funk, Brenna Barks, and Sara Idacavage for your tireless, no-page-unturned help with research, as well as Alexandra King, Mariah Woodruff, Jacky Kuper, and Ilana Winter. Thanks to Maike Papenkort and Arezu Rahimi for your help with German translation. As always, the help of Shawn Waldron and Pamela Griffiths at the Condé Nast Archives was invaluable. Thank you to Abigail Sebaly at Walker Art Center for your help and the introduction to wonderful *Scenario* dancer Jennifer Goggans. I am appreciative of the help of Lauran Rothstein at Jeff Koons LLC and Simon Freschard at the Foundation Pierre Bergé–Yves Saint Laurent. Thanks to Jes Guns for pointing me to the fashion insights of John Waters, and Matthew Pandolfe for your willingness to look into anything! Christine L. Mace, you are gem! Ayesha Pande, you are a divine agent. Julien, your work is always stunning. Bridget, you're an outstanding editor. And Christine Rodriguez—your emotional support is my foundation.

Julien extends his deepest gratitude to the following for their trust and participation in this project; their contributions have immeasurably enriched this labor of love: Richard Burbridge, Tim Burton, Nick Cave, Jake & Dinos Chapman and White Cube, the Merce Cunningham Trust, Waddington Custot Gallery, Michael Elmgreen & Ingar Dragset and Galerie Perrotin, Alexander Englert at BlackFrame for Rodarte, Kai Z. Feng, Jérôme Gautier at Christian Dior Couture, Josh Gaynor at Bottega Veneta, Nan Goldin, Timothy Greenfield-Sanders, the Keith Haring Foundation, Damien Hirst, Hongyi Huang at Alexander McQueen, Pierre Jouhaud, Albright-Knox Art Gallery, Maciek Kobielski, Jeff Koons and Gagosian Gallery, Gia Kuan & Daphne Seybold at Comme des Garçons, the Estate of George Platt Lynes, Raymond Meier, Jacques Moatti, Yasumasa Morimura and Luhring Augustine Gallery, Kate & Laura Mulleavy of Rodarte, James Nares and Paul Kasmin Gallery, the Irving Penn

NTS

Foundation, the Pollock-Krasner Foundation, Alex Prager and Lehman Maupin Gallery, Hilary Richardson at HCR International for the Piet Mondrian Trust, Tim Roeloffs, Alex Sainsbury, Peter Saville, Martin Schoeller, Cindy Sherman and Metro Pictures, Wing Shya, Austin Smedstad at Lacoste, Claire-Aude Staraci at Coach, Jaspar Stephane at Stella McCartney, Melvin Sokolsky, Solve Sundsbo, Mario Testino, PR consulting for Versace, Tim Walker, the Andy Warhol Foundation, Vivienne Westwood, and Zevs and De Buck Gallery. Julien also wishes to thank his fellow art and photography colleagues for their tireless assistance and shared love of beautiful and powerful imagery: Alamy, Jessica Alamonte & Lorraine Goonan at The Image Works, Alan Baglia & J'Aimee Cronin at Artists Rights Society, Lyndsay Black at FirstView, Jennifer Belt & Peter Rohowsky at Art Resource, Nikki Brauton at Museum of London, Tricia Gesner at AP Images, Anna Gibson at Advertising Archives, Nancy Glowinski at Reuters, Thomas Haggerty & Wendy Zieger at Bridgeman Images, Tess Hines at Mary Evans Picture Library, Malick Kane at Corbis, Kimberly LaPorte at Art + Commerce, Stephanie Levine at Newscom, Joanna Ling at Sotheby's Picture Library, Guy Marineau & Yannis Vlamos at Fashion Anthology, Melissa Marra at the Museum at FIT, Katherine Marshall at Sotheby's Picture Library, Leigh Montville at Condé Nast Licensing, Rosemary Morrow at Redux, Alice Moschetti at V&A Images, Shonn Sanchez at Getty Images, Julie Schilder at VAGA, Greg Spencer at Art Partner, Dan Terry at August Images, and Billy Vong at Trunk Archive. And finally, Julien gives special thanks to the brilliant E. P. Cutler for sharing this wonderful journey, to Ayesha Pande of Pande Literary for her wisdom and guidance, and to the delightful Bridget Watson Payne of Chronicle Books for her incredible vision and leadership—thank you for making my experience with Chronicle Books so amazing.

INTRODUCTION

In the 21st century, art and fashion have risen to "It couple" status, stealing headlines and engaging audiences, but their long, entangled courtship has been unnecessarily complicated. Rather than focusing on the beauteous symbiosis possible between art and fashion, critics have pitted the two against each other—as if art and fashion were rambunctious siblings trying to best one another. Setting up a needless faux wrestling match between the two prevents them from becoming the unstoppable team they could be.

The antagonistic relationship between art and fashion is seen at its most aggressive when considering Cecil Beaton's 1951 *Vogue* shoot with fashion-clad models in front of Jackson Pollock paintings. Teeth-baring, vitriolic art criticism followed. Screams bellowed that Beaton disturbingly denigrated Pollock's brilliant work, transforming the modern marvel into merely obscured wallpaper. Critic T. J. Clark preached that associating Pollock's abstractions in any way with Cecil Beaton "blackened" them.[1] Paul Mattick boasted that by the 21st century, Pollock's work would be found in the museums, while the ball gowns photographed by Beaton were relegated to "the dust bin."[2] In 2002, Linda Nochlin haughtily echoed the sentiment, noting that "the paintings have long since triumphed culturally and economically over the fashions and the photographs."[3]

In *Fashion and Art*, Adam Geczy and Vicki Karaminas countered the unforgiving art criticism, arguing that Cecil Beaton's spread, disseminated to thousands of *Vogue* readers, gave Pollock a newfound visibility and raised his profile in a new market. While the points they made were true enough, the very act of making that argument allowed Geczy and Karaminas to become entranced by this debate, where art and fashion are placed in inherent opposition. By engaging in the two-sided debate, they needlessly furthered it.

The primary problem with this dialectic is that there is simply no need to attribute a hierarchy to art or fashion. Society is not up against a wall to choose one over the other. Museums are large enough to feature fashion exhibitions without throwing out their Monets or shattering Majiayao pottery. Andy Warhol once prophesied, "All department stores will become museums, and all museums will become department stores."[4] This is not an apocalyptic warning of impending doom, but the musings of an artist about the shifting relationship between art and consumerism. If, indeed, Warhol's words truly came to life, well . . . society has weathered worse.

Hundreds of pages (perhaps thousands) are dedicated to debating or denigrating Cecil Beaton's four-page Jackson Pollock shoot. Why? The authors desperately try to situate the cultural importance of art and the value (or lack thereof) of fashion, and determine a pecking order between the two.

Attempts to determine where art fits in society often place it stepping on fashion, which in turn is referenced as a lower placeholder. This "art versus fashion" argument is tired. It is reminiscent of the question "Is photography art?" Once rigorously debated, that question is now not only moot but also laughable. Similarly, it is likely future generations will look back with amusement on this frenzied intellectual tête-à-tête of fashion versus art as frivolous and irrelevant.

Boiled down, the argument is essentially that art is more important, value-filled, and enduring than fashion is. Fashion theorists and critics agree, but quietly coo that fashion is still important. When Cecil Beaton began his book *The Glass of Fashion*, he stated, "When we talk about fashion or the minor arts, we really mean the whole art of living."[5] Without indicting Beaton's important observation, it is key to explore it a little further. By referring to fashion as a minor art, it is easy to raise the question "How much of an art *is* fashion?" Yet by doing so, one inherently places art and fashion in opposition, all the while elevating art by using it as the measuring stick.

Yes, the disciplines of art and fashion are different, and solid arguments can be made for keeping a line in the sand between the two. Firstly, tackling one discipline alone for either a creator or a member of the intelligentsia can take a lifetime to perfect. Secondly, both fashion and art benefit humanity, albeit in different ways and through different methods. Designers themselves struggle with being called artists, rarely referring to themselves as such. They often rebuke the title and go to great lengths to explain why. At the opening of a exhibition about Jean Paul Gaultier at the Brooklyn Museum of Art, Gaultier stressed, "I don't speak about fashion as an art," and no one challenged the couturier with the inherent irony of the statement given his location.[6]

This is not a call for anarchy. But when society creatively benefits from blurred lines, why not enjoy the indulgence? While undoubtedly imperfectly, this book attempts to rise above the fray and remove itself from dichotomous, prejudiced value-based thinking. As fashion historians, we have used fashion as the prism, so fashion bias likely emerges in the text.

This book looks at twenty-five of our favorite fashion and art collaborations—an appetite-whetting sliver of convergence from 1935 to 2015. This is not to say that fashion and art collaborations did not exist before 1935. They did. Parisian couturier Paul Poiret tapped artist Raoul Dufy to design fabric for him in 1911. Alexandre Vassiliev's *Beauty in Exile* teasingly references French designer extraordinaire Jeanne Paquin's 1913 collaborations with Léon Bakst of the Ballets Russes, which begs to be researched more. From 1903 to 1932, the Wiener Werkstätte—which did not attempt to narrowly define design by restricting it to one medium—produced stunning textiles by Maria Likarz, Gustav Klimt, and Dagobert Peche, in addition to glorious furniture, lighting, sculptures, paintings, cutlery, and jewelry. But when considering where to begin chronologically, we wanted to start with a bang, and the collaboration between surrealist artist Salvador Dalí and couturier Elsa Schiaparelli is explosive.

Over the past decade collaborations between fashion figures (designers, photographers, models, and magazines) and artists have increased exponentially, in a manner never seen before in history. This work primarily focuses on recent art and fashion collaborations—attempting to capture the raw, exciting energy buzzing in the air. They are so cutting edge that they might draw blood.

While this book features well-known collaborations, at times it favors the lesser-known underdogs. Under the creative direction of Marc Jacobs, Louis Vuitton's womens wear spearheaded fashion and art collaborations: Takashi Murakami, Stephen Sprouse, Richard Prince, and Yayoi Kusama. Since the vast and undeniable global impact of these projects has been much discussed elsewhere, we opted to feature instead the underappreciated collaboration between Louis Vuitton menswear designer Kim Jones and the irascible Chapman Brothers. This is also an attempt to appropriately represent the exciting events in men's fashion, which all too often takes second chair to women's.

This book uses the term "collaboration" fluidly throughout the text; fanatics of literalism may disapprove. But to exclude inspired work based on the narrow confines of a definition seemed as shortsighted, purposeless, and self-defeating as separating art and fashion. Piet Mondrian did not create neoplastic work on mod dresses alongside Yves Saint Laurent. But, Saint Laurent's Mondrian dress is iconic, often referenced as a fashion and art endeavor, and repeatedly used as fashion inspiration.

The collaborations featured vary from garments to public art installations, film to photography editorials. The hope is that all the examples featured can be seen as representative of the larger reality, as well as illustrative of the plethora of forms collaboration can take.

How creative people come to collaborate can be mysterious. The romanticism of cities like New York and Paris comes from the exciting geographic overlap of the world's best creators. Crammed together in urban environments, massive cosmopolitan areas magically create neighborhoods and give birth to hot-spot hideaways. The greatest cities in the world create an air of possibility, and the energy in the air seems to lead shining people toward each other. In his autobiography, Christian Dior refers to fevered Parisian nights in the 1920s when likeminded people were simply drawn together. Dior recollects: "If I were asked: 'How did you come to meet your friends?'—I should answer that since we came from quite different backgrounds we met purely by chance, or rather in obedience to those mysterious laws which Goethe called elective affinities. . . . Strange evening parties were held in our home. Sitting on the floor in the regulation semi-darkness of that date, we would play modern music of a kind that sent our elders into fits of horror."[7] A few years later, likely in a similar manner, Schiaparelli met Dalí, although neither divulge how in their autobiographies. There is something almost spiritual about the coming together of brilliant people. Yves Saint Laurent referred to his 1970s Parisian posse as "*faiseurs de feux*" (fire-makers), as they emanated a creative heat. It's as if they were magnetically drawn to each other. These luminaries who burn brighter than the rest find others like a beacon.

Schiaparelli and Dalí are at one end of our chronology, and at the other we find the hands-on endeavor of designer Raf Simons and artist Sterling Ruby, who created a new dual-named menswear label for Autumn/Winter 2014-2015. Using globalization and technology to their advantage, the pair relied on constant communication during time-zone overlaps to bridge the geographic gap between Simons, in Belgium and Paris, and Ruby, in Los Angeles. Though "Raf Simons/Sterling Ruby" is supposed to be a one-season-only label, fashion fingers are crossed that it will be revived in the future.

The heart-stopping brilliance of collaborations comes when two extraordinary people combine to make something greater than the sum of their parts. This synergy defies the nature of mathematics, allowing for 1+1=3. It is these types of collaborations that we feature in this book.

ENJOY!

QUOTES

"I don't speak about fashion as an art."

JEAN PAUL GAULTIER

"Some of the greatest works of art were done on commission."

ALEX PRAGER

"I suddenly had this intuitive feeling that it could become dancers' clothes as well."

REI KAWAKUBO

"I may work with artists, but what I do is make things to be used, not looked at, like a picture or a sculpture. You can't use art."

ISSEY MIYAKE

"I treat the dress as a canvas. . . . I want to create wearable art."

MARY KATRANTZOU

"There is no day that I am not looking at art."

RAF SIMONS

"My work is an amalgamation of both fashion and art, and I exist within their fluid interface."

NICK CAVE

"Art is about something being seen, whether it is absorbed by the eyes of people in the subways or of people in galleries."

KEITH HARING

COLLABORATIONS

JACKSON POLLOC

K + CECIL BEATON

THE MARCH 1, 1951 *VOGUE* featured a four-page spread of photographs by Cecil Beaton. The "Spring Ball Gowns" were modeled by Irene and Sophie in front of Jackson Pollock's works from 1950: *Lavender Mist (Number 1)*, *Number 27*, *Number 28*, and *Autumn Rhythm (Number 30)*, then on display at the Betty Parsons Gallery. The American-made but Paris-inspired gowns were available for order at New York's top department stores: Henri Bendel, Milgrim, Lord & Taylor, and the Salon Moderne at Saks Fifth Avenue.

Featuring artists in fashion magazines was by no means a new phenomenon. Profiles and artist studio visits have long been segments in fashion publications. *Harper's Bazaar* had name-dropped Jackson Pollock (1912–1956) in its April 1944 issue, with a double-page spread dedicated to American painters. However, Brit Cecil Beaton (1904–1980) ventured further, using Jackson Pollock's work in a fashion spread, not an artist profile. Numerous art critics saw Beaton's actions as drastically overstepping. This *Vogue* editorial caused a commotion that continues to this day because Cecil Beaton visually compared the dusky blue of the Bianchini silk dress to the drips of color found in Jackson Pollock's *Lavender Mist*, the perky pink of Henri Bendel's silk paper taffeta day dress and the warm browns in Pollock's *Autumn Rhythm*. The bold line in the sand between the disciplines of art and fashion was blurred. From the debate, one would think riots ensued. How dare Beaton compare high art with fashion, a lower art—if an art at all! The models obstructed Pollock's "genius" work![8] Pollock's art matters more than *Vogue* fashions! Vociferous objection!

Yet, for those not mired in the hundreds of pages of dense, often snarky art theory and criticism, the spread illustrates a beautiful cultural confluence. The same societal realities that birthed modernism produced indulgent post–WWII New Looks. What's more, with this fashion spread, women in search of the perfect frock were educated not just on the new trends but also on high society's new obsession: Jackson Pollock and his "dazzling and curious" creations. As *Vogue* wrote, Pollock's works had been purchased by "the most astute private collectors and museum directors in the country," among them people affiliated with the Museum of Modern Art in New York, the San Francisco Museum of Modern Art, and Yale University, as well as Pollock's first agent, Peggy Guggenheim.[9]

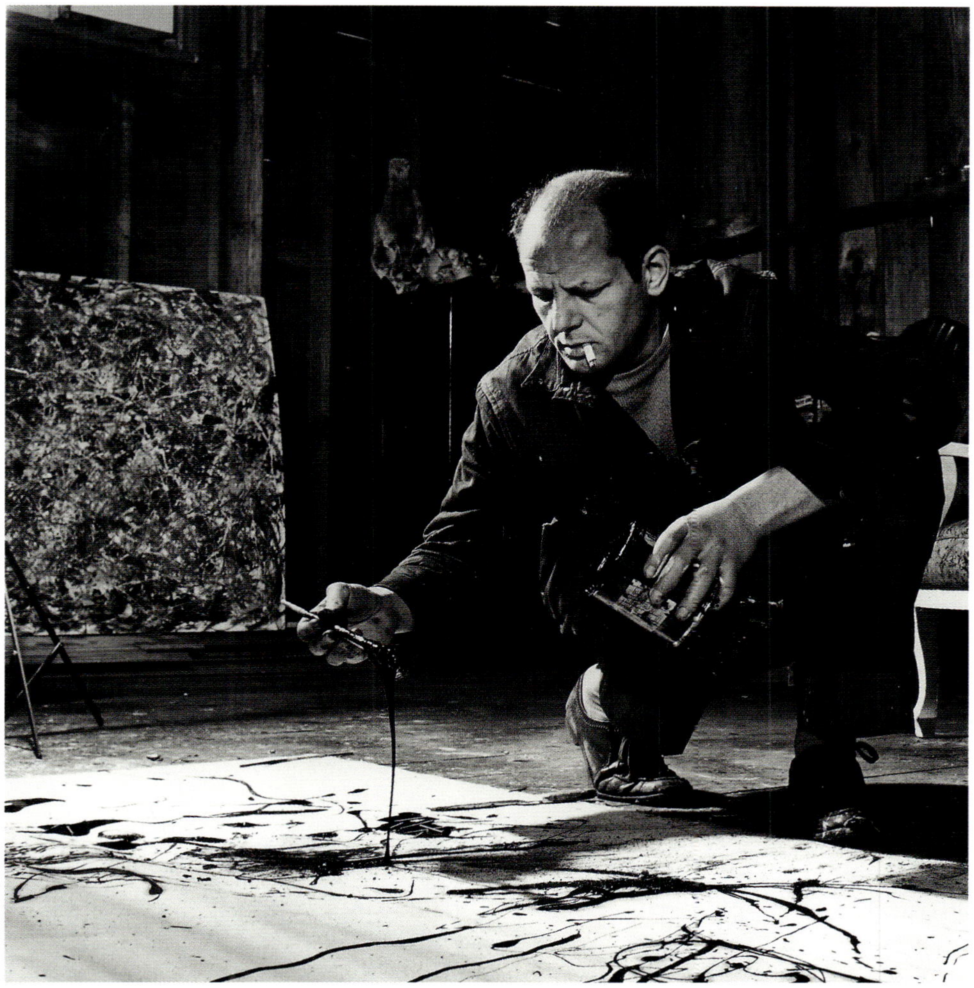

JACKSON POLLOCK

Vogue viewed Jackson Pollock in a positive light when Pollock's paintings were barely selling—the Betty Parsons Gallery only sold one Pollock, *Lavender Mist*, during the exhibition—and critics were finding new ways to disparage his work. Venice-based critic Bruno Alfieri had mused a year earlier that Jackson Pollock's work represented "absolutely nothing" other than perhaps "chaos, absolute lack of harmony; complete lack of structural organization; total absence of technique; once again, chaos."[10]

While it seems unlikely that Pollock was contacted for permission regarding the shoot beforehand, he was happy to be in *Vogue*, writing to his friend that "the issue of *Vogue* has three pages of my paintings (with models of course). Will send a copy."[11]

So, what's all the fuss about?

> *THE NEW SOFT LOOK* FEATURING A PAINTING BY JACKSON POLLOCK | CECIL BEATON FOR *VOGUE*, 1951

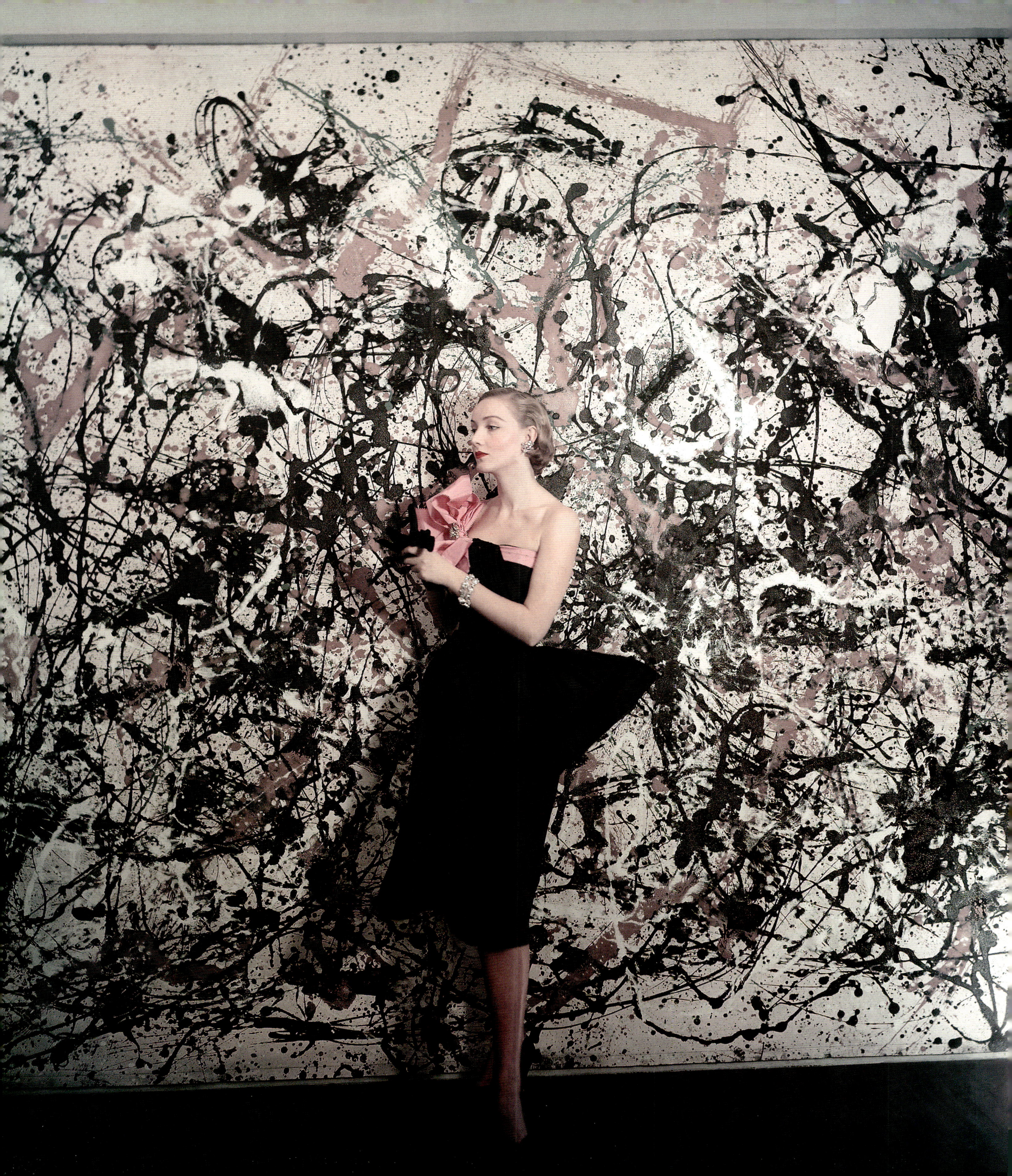

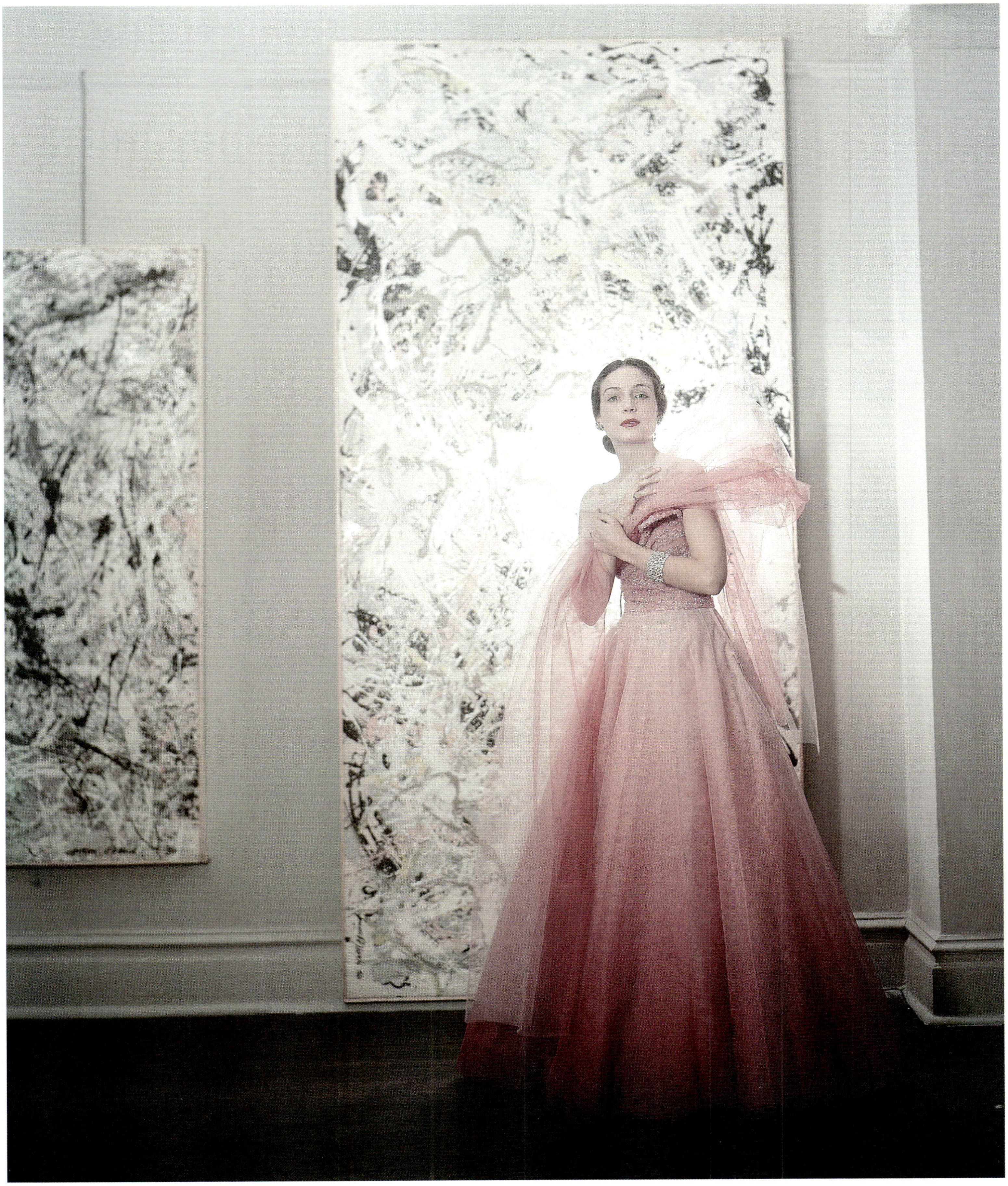

THE NEW SOFT LOOK FEATURING PAINTINGS BY JACKSON POLLOCK | CECIL BEATON FOR *VOGUE*, 1951

ALEX PRAGER

BOTTEGA VENETA

DON'T UNDERESTIMATE

the power of shoes. In 1974, William Eggleston photographed bedraggled wingtips under a bed. Art critic Hilton Kramer was less than impressed, smirking that if he ever wanted to see that, he'd go home and look at his own. Yet, twenty-five years later, the stark, poignant simplicity of Eggleston's work inspired then-directionless Alex Prager (b. 1979) to buy a camera on eBay. Her beginnings were less than glamorous: "For the first seven years, I was being turned down by galleries and anyone involved in the official art world. So, I would rent out little spaces. . . . There was a show I had in a motel for three hours because [the owner] had his regular customers that rented by the hour."[12] By 2010, the art world had changed its tune and Prager's work was featured in the Museum of Modern Art's *New Photography* exhibition. The following year, despite participating in a group exhibition entitled "*No fashion, please!*" at the Kunsthalle Wien in Vienna, Prager collaborated with Italian fashion house Bottega Veneta on its Spring/Summer 2011 campaign.

Birthed by Michele Taddei and Renzo Zengiaro in 1966, the Venetian atelier was reborn in 2001 when the Gucci Group bought the brand and named German-born Tomas Maier as creative director. Maier, educated at the Chambre Syndicale de la Haute Couture, brought to the table decades of combined fashion experience at Guy Laroche, Sonia Rykiel, and Hermès. He immediately resurrected Bottega Veneta's 1970s anti-logo campaign, "When Your Own Initials Are Enough," crafted the nonchalant *luxe* "Cabat" shopper, and began hunting down the world's best photographers to capture his Bottega Veneta collections through their lenses. Maier nabbed the likes of Lord Snowdon, Annie Leibovitz, and Robert Longo before tapping Alex Prager. Tomas Maier was drawn to Prager's cinematic, hyper-real work, which had been featured in *Art in America* and is permanently housed in the collections of the San Francisco Museum of Modern Art, Kunsthaus Zürich, and Moderna Museet in Stockholm.

While Alex Prager rattles off inspirations ranging from photographer Diane Arbus to the band Wilco, her Spring/Summer 2011 Bottega Veneta campaign is clearly an ode to Alfred Hitchcock's films *North by Northwest* (1959) and *The Birds* (1963). Prager's editorial shoot involved some finagling; in addition to wrangling models Karolína Kurvová and Santiago Montero, Tomas Maier had to deal with cages of messenger pigeons in the hot Miami sun. The

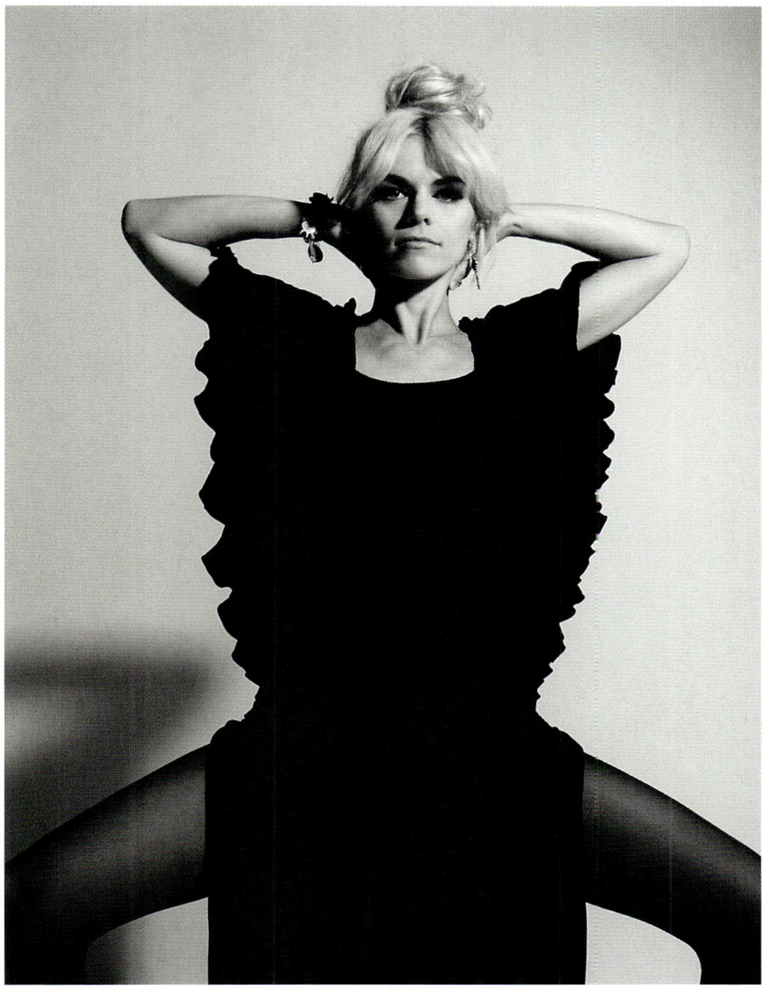

ALEX PRAGER

final product shows Kurvová in a state of unease. It's as if an accompanying orchestra is coming to a crescendo. Bottega Veneta's *intrecciato* bags fit seamlessly into Prager's shots, a perfect understated accessory for a leading lady.

Prager, who notes that "some of the greatest works of art were done on commission,"[13] welcomes projects from outside the art world: "If the commercial world assigns me a project that interests me a lot, or excites me, or I feel challenges me in some way, then I am absolutely going to take it on because their budgets and their larger audience is absolutely something that is interesting to me. But if it means that I have to water down my work to where it is no longer recognizable, then it is not interesting to me."[14]

BOTTEGA VENETA SPRING/SUMMER 2011 PRINT CAMPAIGN | ALEX PRAGER, 2011

BOTTEGA VENETA SPRING/SUMMER 2011 PRINT CAMPAIGN | ALEX PRAGER, 2011

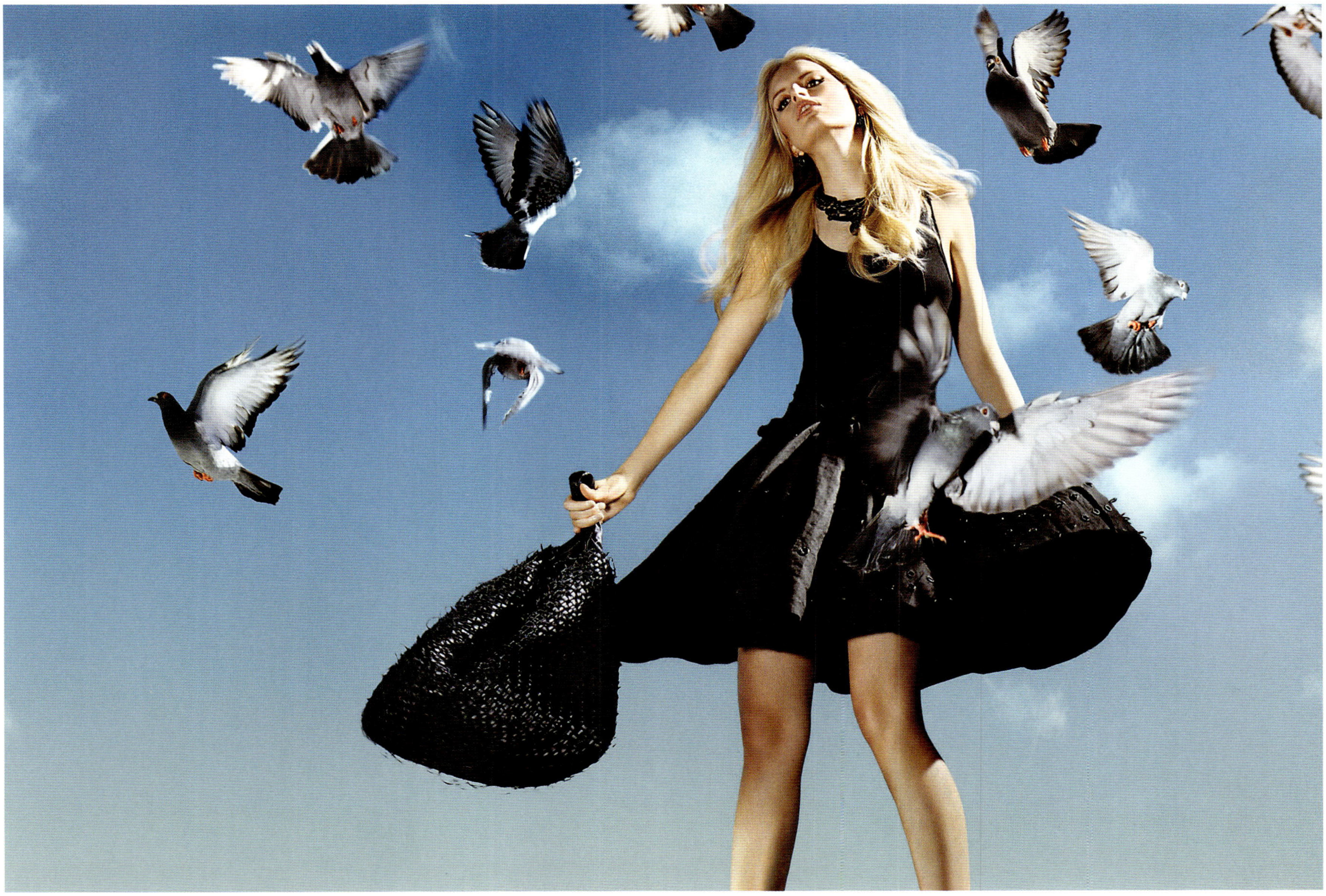

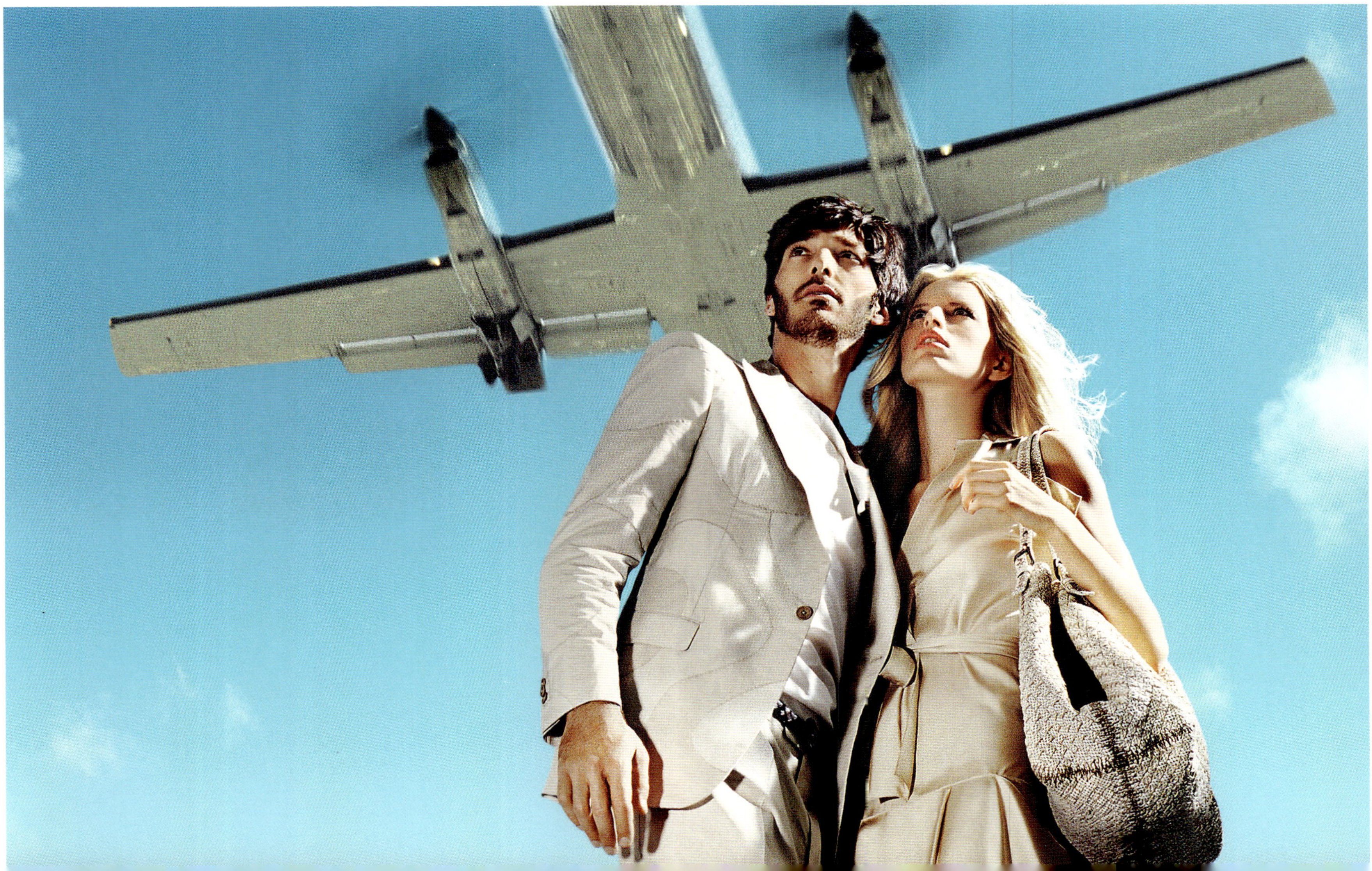

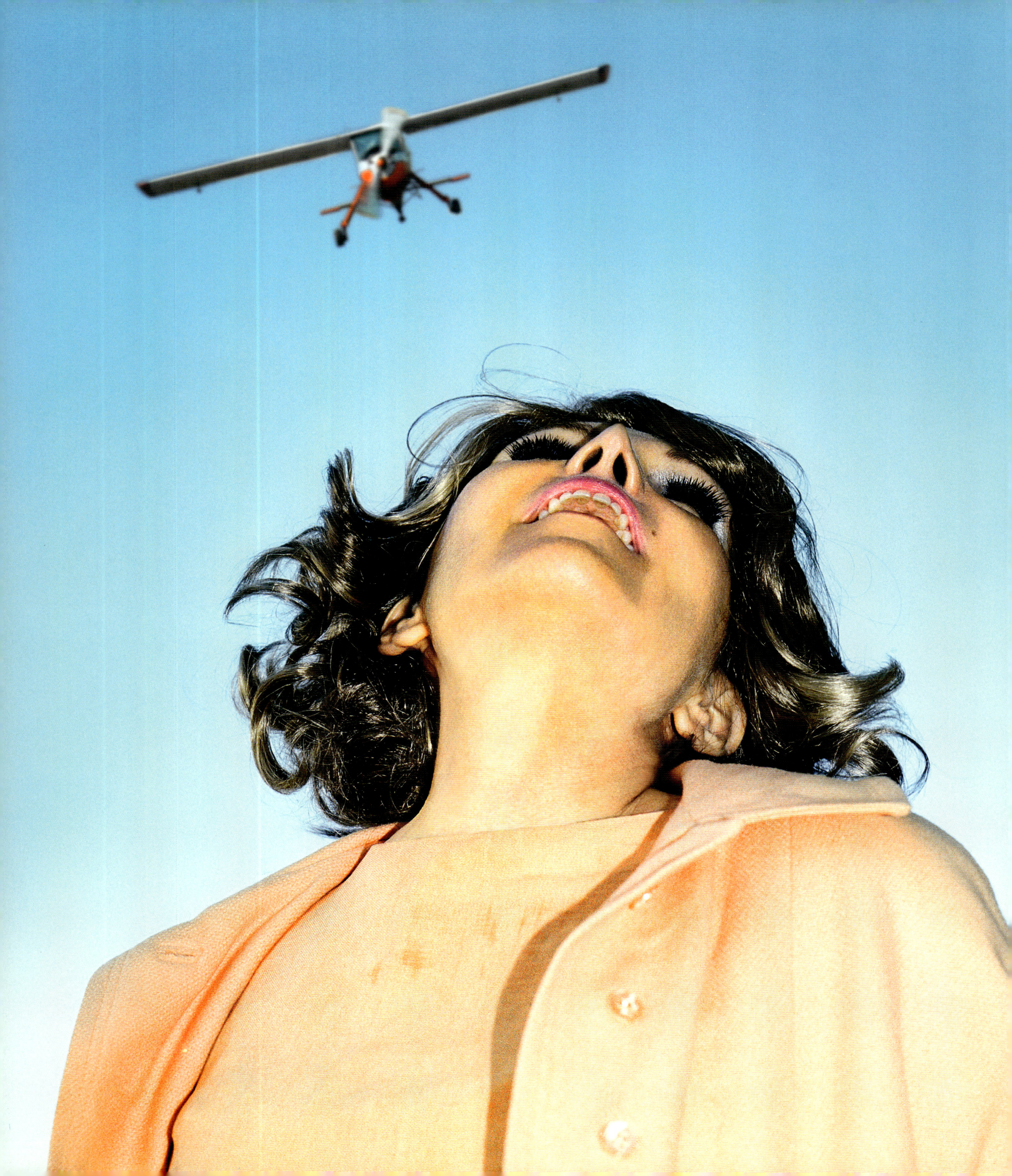

< *BEVERLY* | C-PRINT | ALEX PRAGER, 2009

V BOTTEGA VENETA SPRING/SUMMER 2011 PRINT CAMPAIGN | ALEX PRAGER, 2011

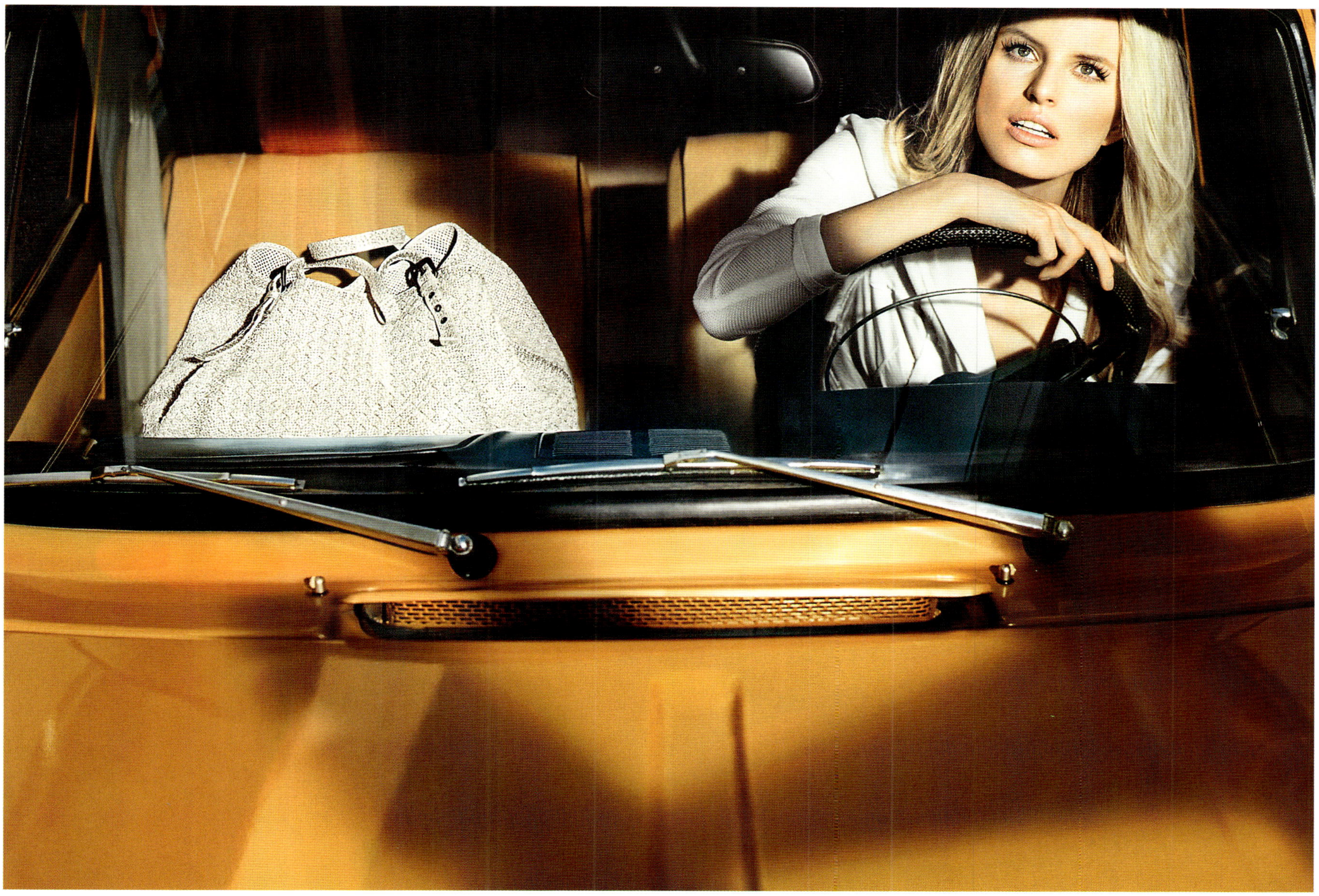

CINDY SHERMAN

CHANEL

ENIGMATIC, ICONIC, and misunderstood, Gabrielle "Coco" Bonheur Chanel was repeatedly redefined over the course of her lifetime (1883–1971), and continues to be into the 21st century. Some see her a feminist before feminism, some the epitome of chic. Others focus on her complex negotiation of WWII, calling her anti-Semitic in response both to her attempt to steal "her" perfume empire away from its Jewish owner, Pierre Wertheimer, and to her liaison with a German officer, Baron Hans Günther von Dincklage. Chanel's questionable collaboration with the Nazi party justifiably overshadows all else, including her collaborative fashion endeavors with Jean Cocteau, Igor Stravinsky, Samuel Goldwyn, Salvador Dalí, the Ballets Russes, and Jean Renoir. The attempt to determine all that Chanel was and was not will likely be an enduring effort by historians and academics. Of course, all women have many faces—which photographer Cindy Sherman portrays in her work.

Cindy Sherman was born in 1954, the same year Gabrielle Chanel made her post-WWII comeback after shuttering her business during the Occupation. Sherman moved to New York in 1976 and began her series Untitled Film Stills (1977–1980), in which she photographed herself as different B-movie characters in intriguing and emotional moments. In 1983, Sherman's costumes, integral to her creations, were elevated to couture. Dianne Benson, owner of four New York City avant-garde boutiques, commissioned her to contribute to a fashion campaign. Sherman outfitted herself in Comme des Garçons and Jean Paul Gaultier for the spread, which ran in *Interview*.

While Sherman is adamant about not mocking the women she portrays, her 1983 notebook contradicts that stance. Sherman's approach to the Dianne B. campaign was to "attack clothes" by juxtaposing an "ugly person (face/body)" with the "fashionable clothes" for the "pseudo-fashion shots" of "stupid looking model types."[15] Sherman explained, "A lot of that came out of a response to the clothes. I felt forced to use these clothes. . . . Some of it was a retaliation against fashion."[16]

In 2010, Russian art world "It Girl" and *Pop* magazine's then–editor in chief Dasha Zhukova (b. 1981) invited Cindy Sherman to team up on a fashion editorial. The House of Chanel loaned

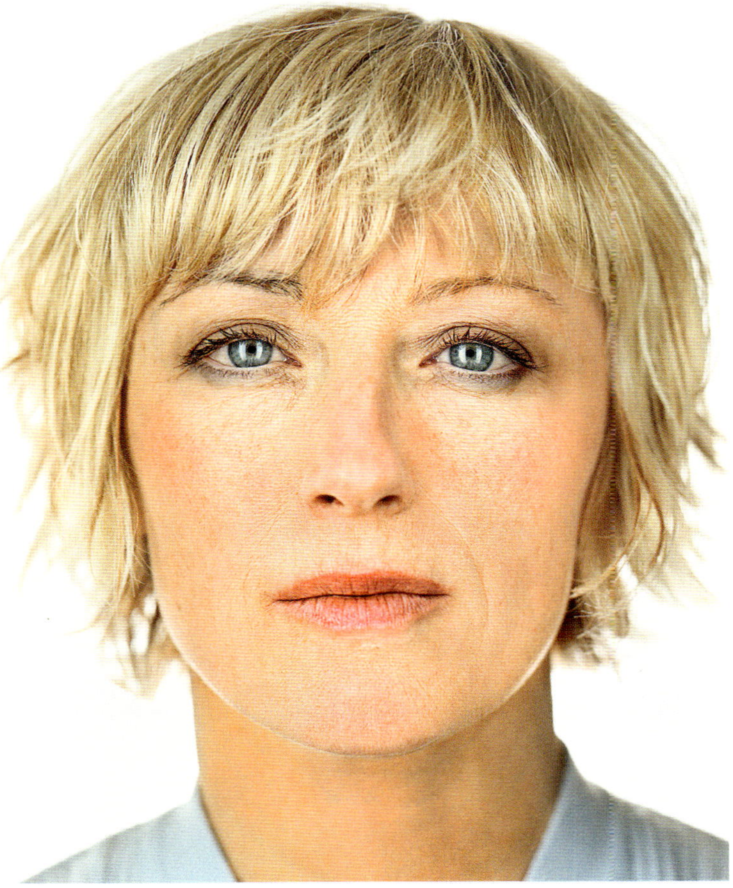

CINDY SHERMAN

Sherman pieces from its archives: 1920s–1950s couture by Mademoiselle Chanel, and Chanel by Karl Lagerfeld circa 1983–2010. Characteristically, Sherman's photographs oppose that of a typical fashion shoot. Outfitted in the Holy Grail of fashion, Sherman looks like she's wearing "*misérabilisme de luxe*," a derogatory phrase bandied about when Chanel's streamlined, easy garments in unorthodox materials first appeared.[17] Sherman exacerbated this idea by using photoshopped backdrops of Iceland (during the apocalyptic volcanic eruption of 2010), Capri, Stromboli, and Shelter Island, New York. Sherman's bizarre-looking, bedraggled, and aged characters seem trapped in a "landscape of solitude," not aspirat onal living.[18]

While Gabrielle Chanel is known for drastically departing from the corsetry and frills of the Belle Époque to create "comfortable" clothing for the modern woman of that era, in 2010, Sherman was not impressed by the garments' ease. "The dresses were so unbelievably tight on me—normally I wear a size four, but these were like size zero. . . . Some of the scowls that are on my face were also because I was just so pissed off that these goddamn designers make things so small that even a normal-sized woman can't fit into them."[19] Chanel changed the definition of comfort, and her visionary feminist ideology set the groundwork for Sherman's 21st-century irritation at fashion and its relationship with the female body.

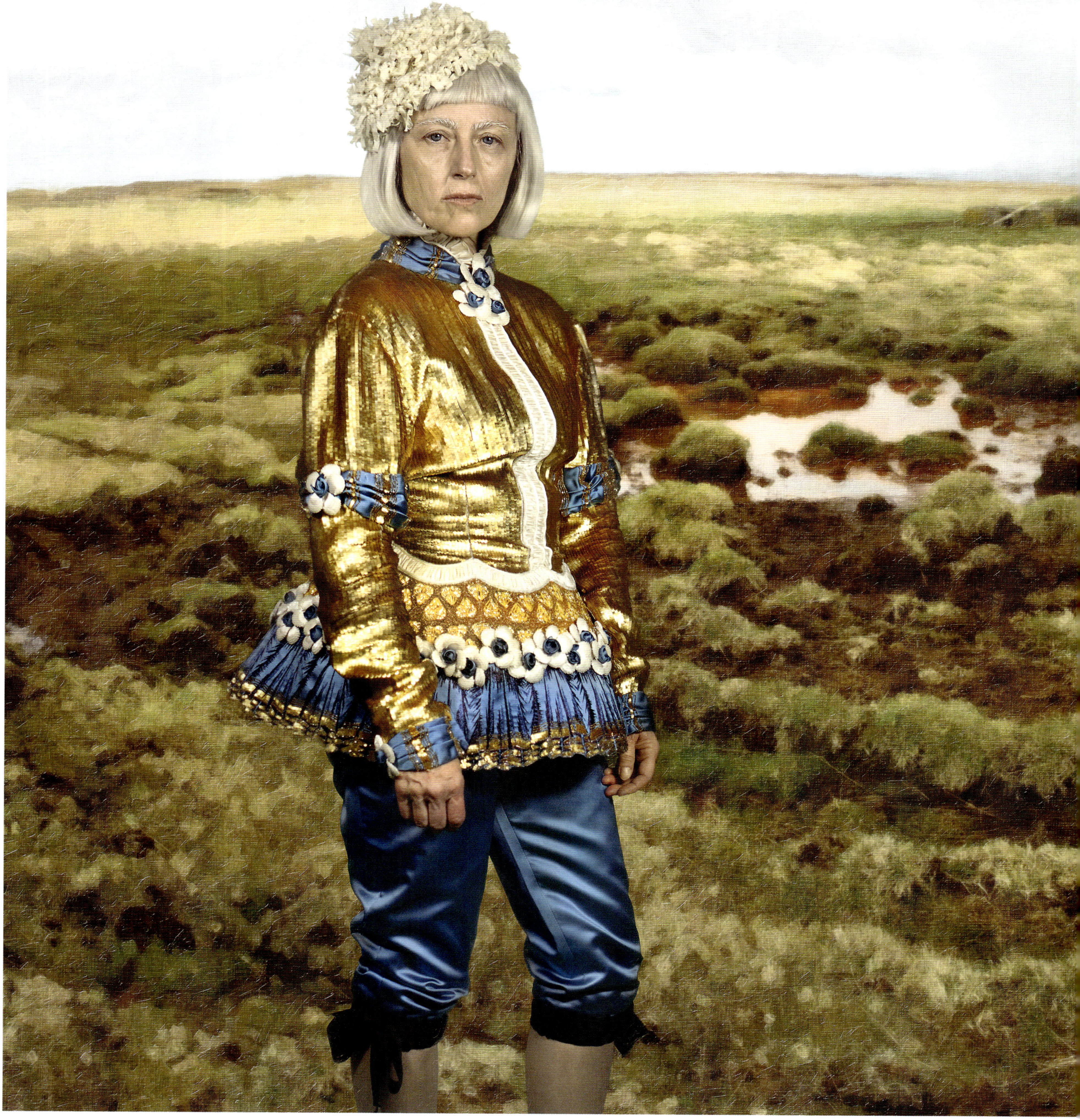

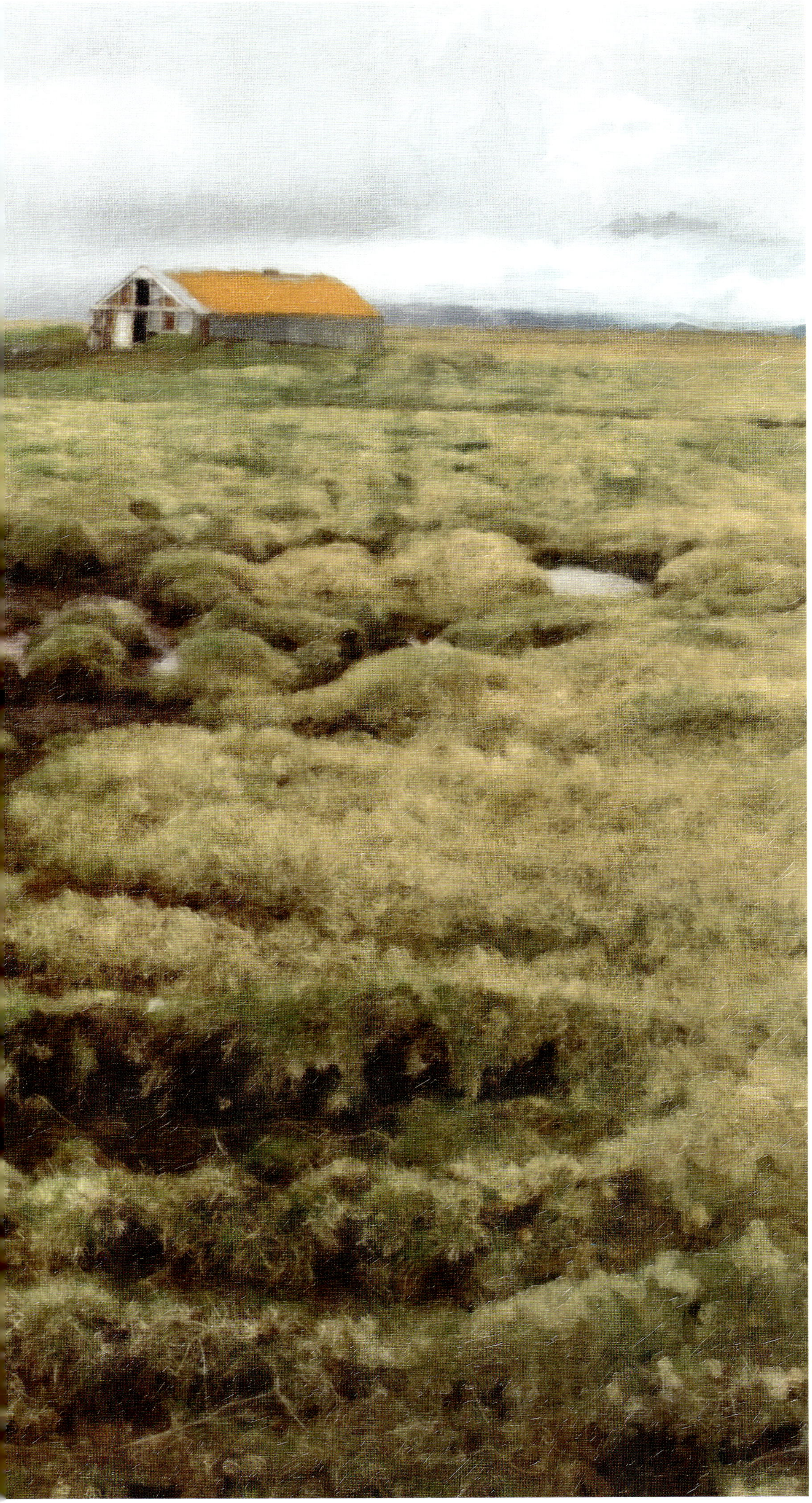

< UNTITLED | CHROMOGENIC COLOR PRINT | CINDY SHERMAN, 2010/2012

> UNTITLED | CHROMOGENIC COLOR PRINT | CINDY SHERMAN, 2010/2012

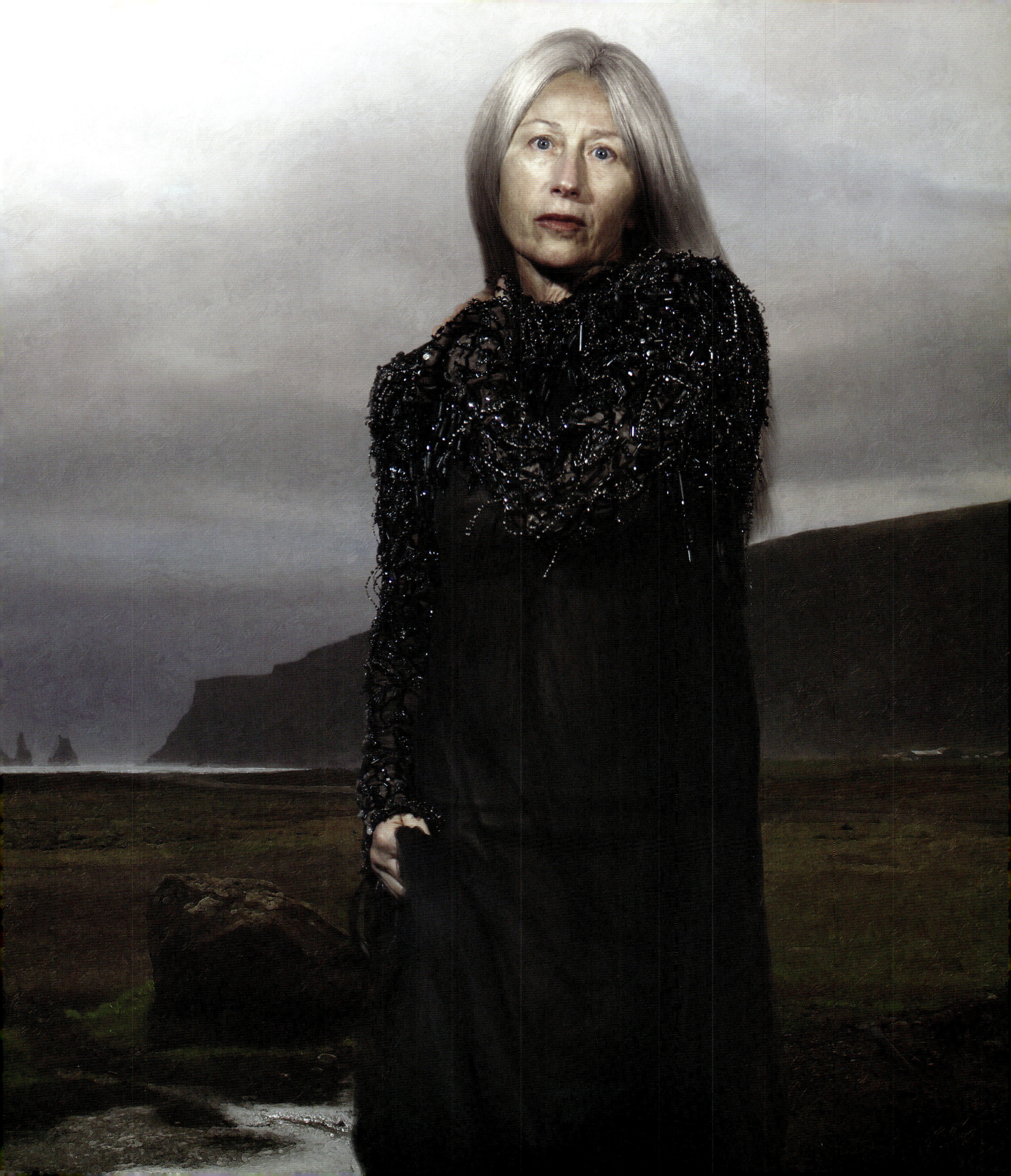

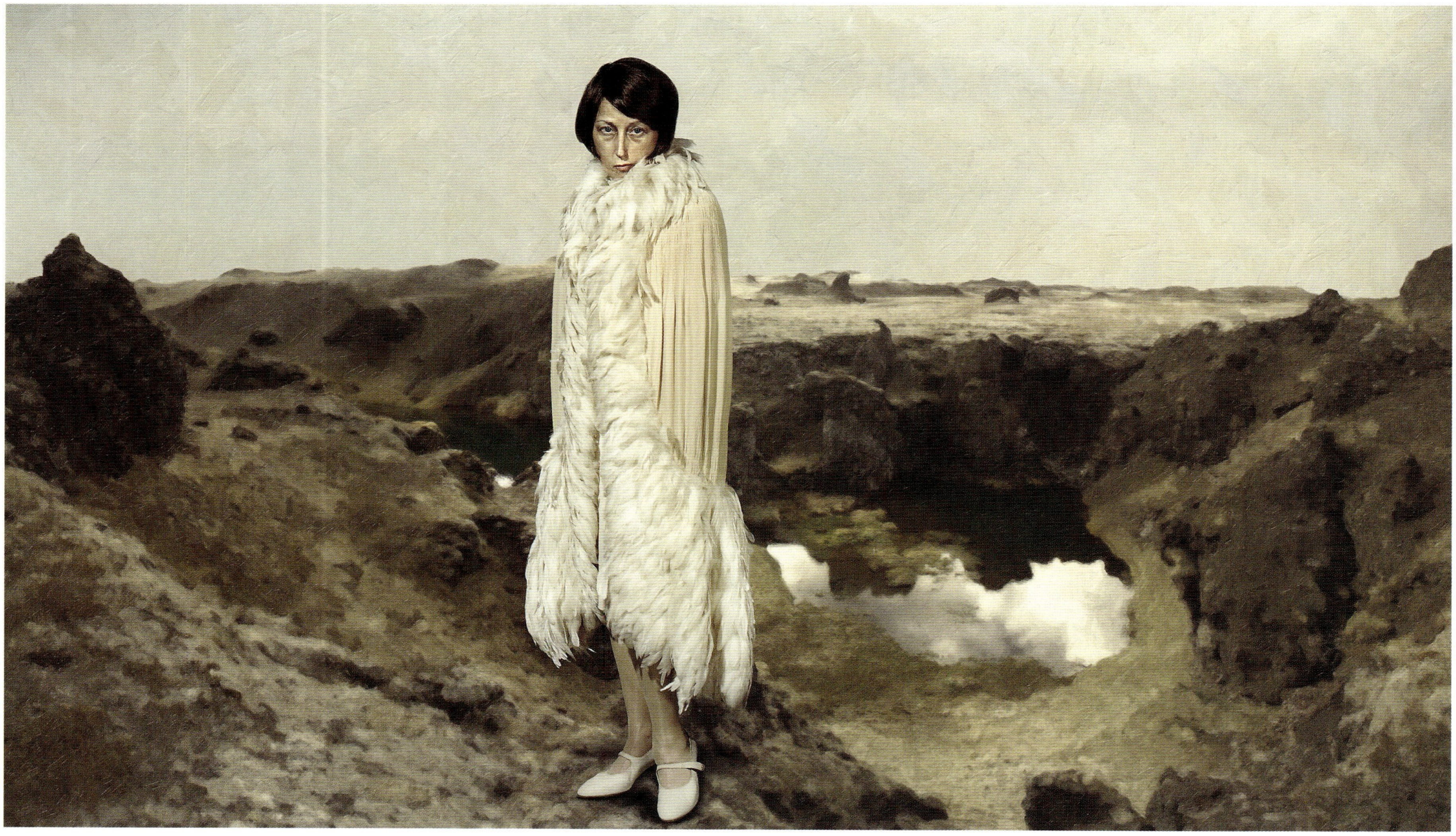

UNTITLED | CHROMOGENIC COLOR PRINT | CINDY SHERMAN, 2010/2011

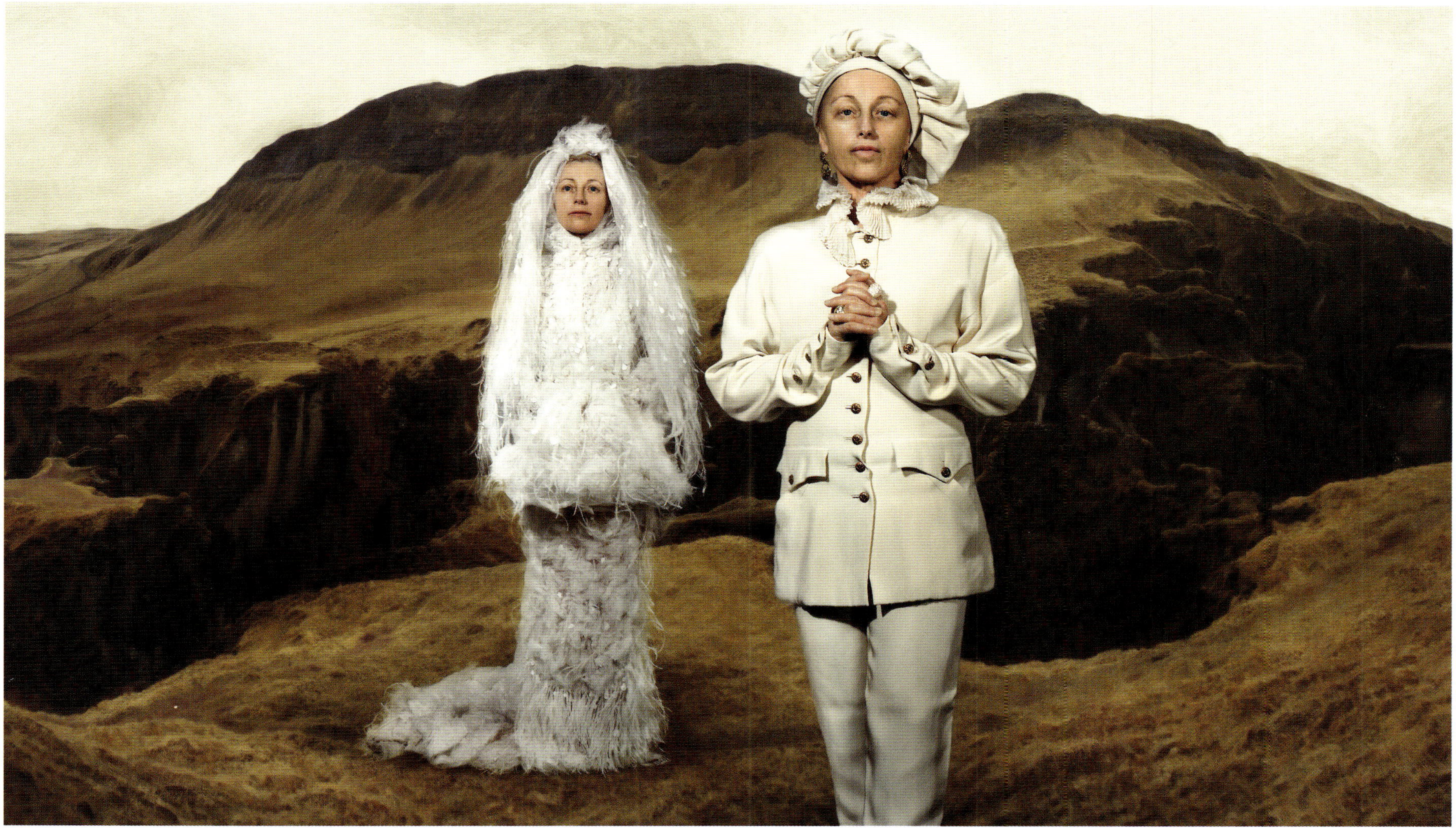

UNTITLED | CHROMOGENIC COLOR PRINT | CINDY SHERMAN, 2010/2012

JAMES NARES

COACH

OCCASIONALLY LIFE

offers up beautiful ironies: James Nares, part of the 1970s No Wave music scene in New York, is now intrinsically linked to his wave-like paintings, which made their way onto Coach bags in 2012.

Educated at the Chelsea College of Art in London, with a stint at the School of Visual Arts, British-born, New York–based Nares (b. 1953) began his signature single-stroke paintings in the early 1990s. While each brushstroke may take only six seconds to make, perfectionistic Nares may make three hundred attempts before settling on his final piece. In order to capture the essence he's searching for, Nares rigs up contraptions that allow him to hang above the canvas (like a flying Jackson Pollock) and uses hybrid brushes he has personally configured for the purpose. Coach creative director Reed Krakoff (b. 1964), who helmed the label from 1997 through the end of 2013, took notice of Nares's work, which *GQ*'s Glenn O'Brien considers "so provocatively beautiful that it sticks out in the irony-obsessed, agenda-dependent art world like a gorgeous thunderstruck sore thumb."[20]

Started in a West Chelsea factory loft in 1941, Coach took off as a label when bought out by Hungarian immigrant Lillian Cahn (née Lenovitz) and her husband, Miles, in 1961. Inspired by paper shopping bags, Lillian Cahn created a must-have carryall using cowhide normally reserved for American baseball gloves. From 1962 to 1974, designer Bonnie Cashin contributed to Coach by crafting brightly hued "Cashin Carry" handbags with piped seams and convenient turnkey fobs. The brand's second coming was ushered in twenty-three years later by Parsons alum Reed Krakoff.

While Krakoff is an ardent art collector (he co-authored a book on Claude & Francois-Xavier Lalanne and published a portrait book, *Women in Art)*, he collaborated relatively little with artists during his sixteen-year tenure at the leather goods company. While small couplings occurred between Coach and fashion designer Anna Sui, illustrator Hugo Guinness, and street artist Craig Costello (better known as KR), the James Nares collaboration sent shockwaves through the fashion world, significantly raising the company's image among the elite. "When one of these bags is carried past you, you have the impression of a painting set in motion. They

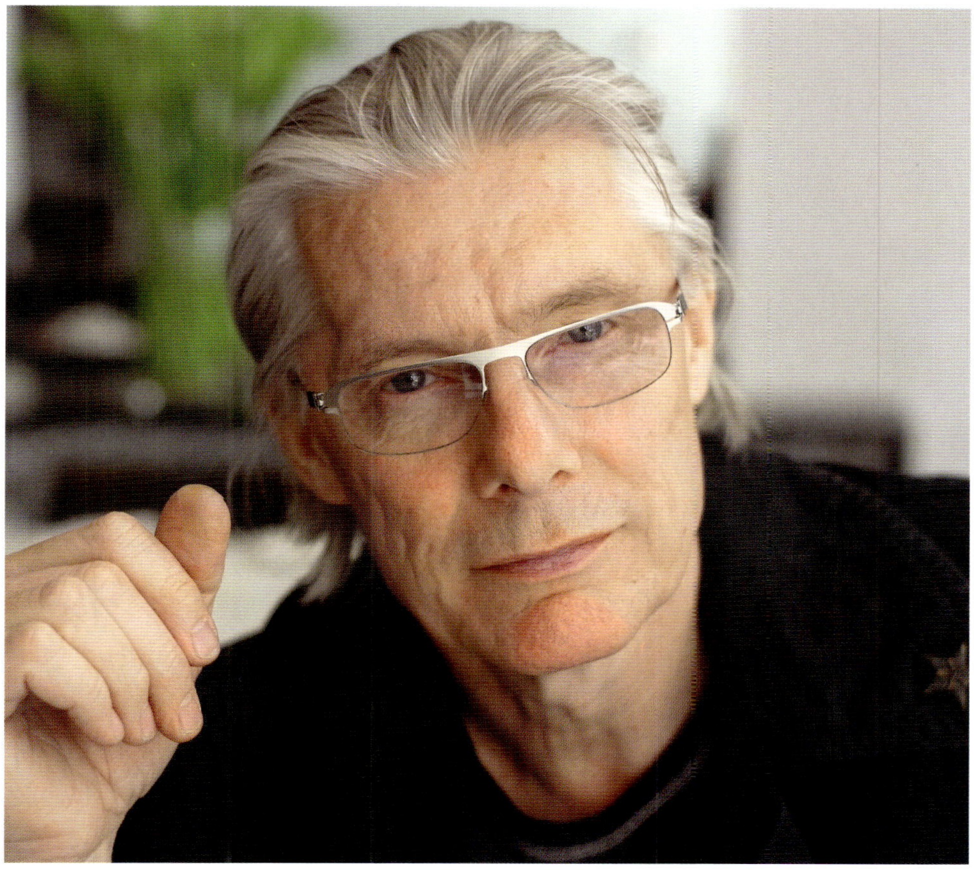

JAMES NARES

really are works of art."[21] Launched on May 1, 2012, the Coach × James Nares limited-edition collection consisted of a double-layered Italian canvas bag "brushed" with one of five colorful strokes: black, blue, green, pink, or red. Only 175 bags of each color were available. Originally retailing at $798, every one came numbered with a Coach story tag featuring James Nares's signature. Nares explained his collaboration, saying: "Coach has long been admired for its storied tradition of excellent craftsmanship and elegant design—qualities that are also important to me as an artist."[22] These qualities were also appreciated by consumers, and the collection was nearly sold out by Labor Day.

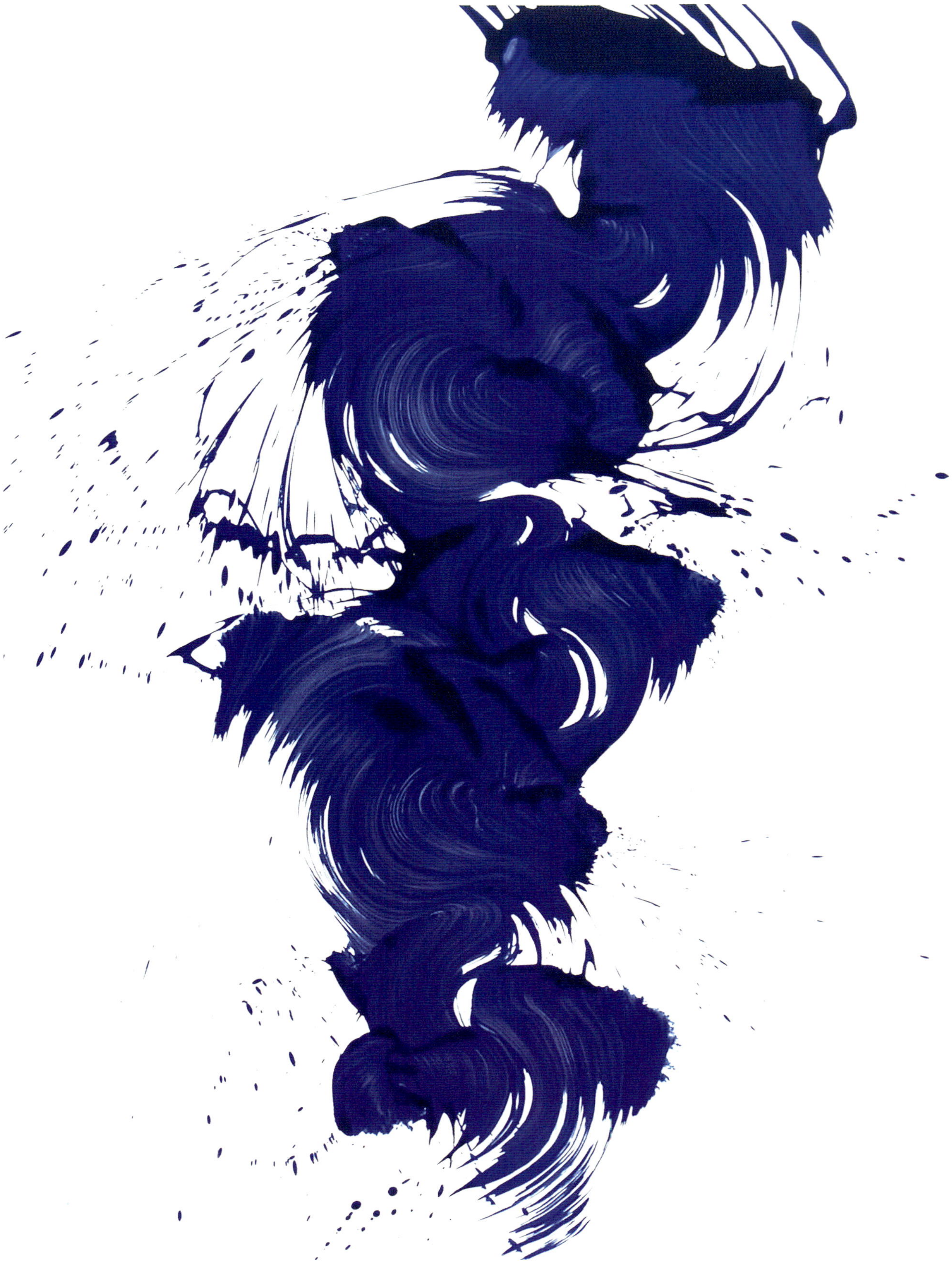

UNTITLED | OIL ON PAPER | JAMES NARES, 2011

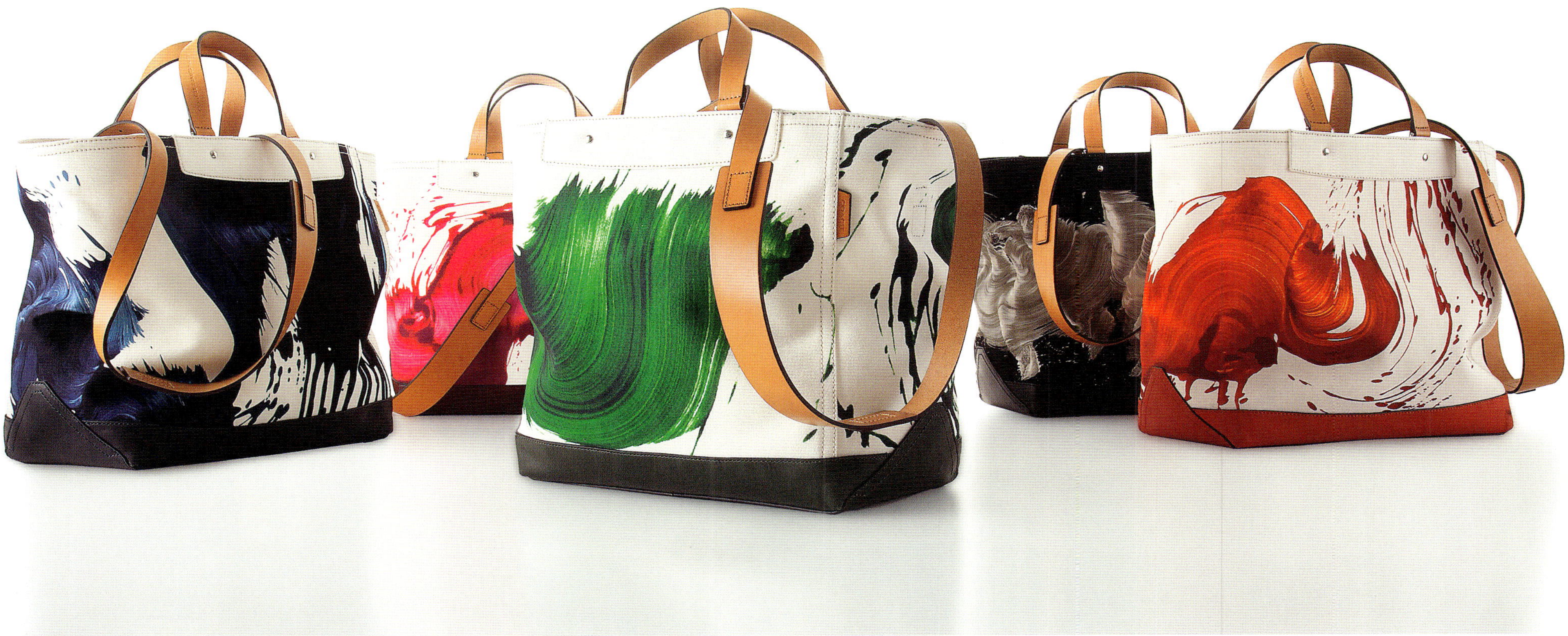

COACH *WAVE* TOTE COLLECTION | JAMES NARES, 2012

COACH *WAVE* TOTE | JAMES NARES, 2012

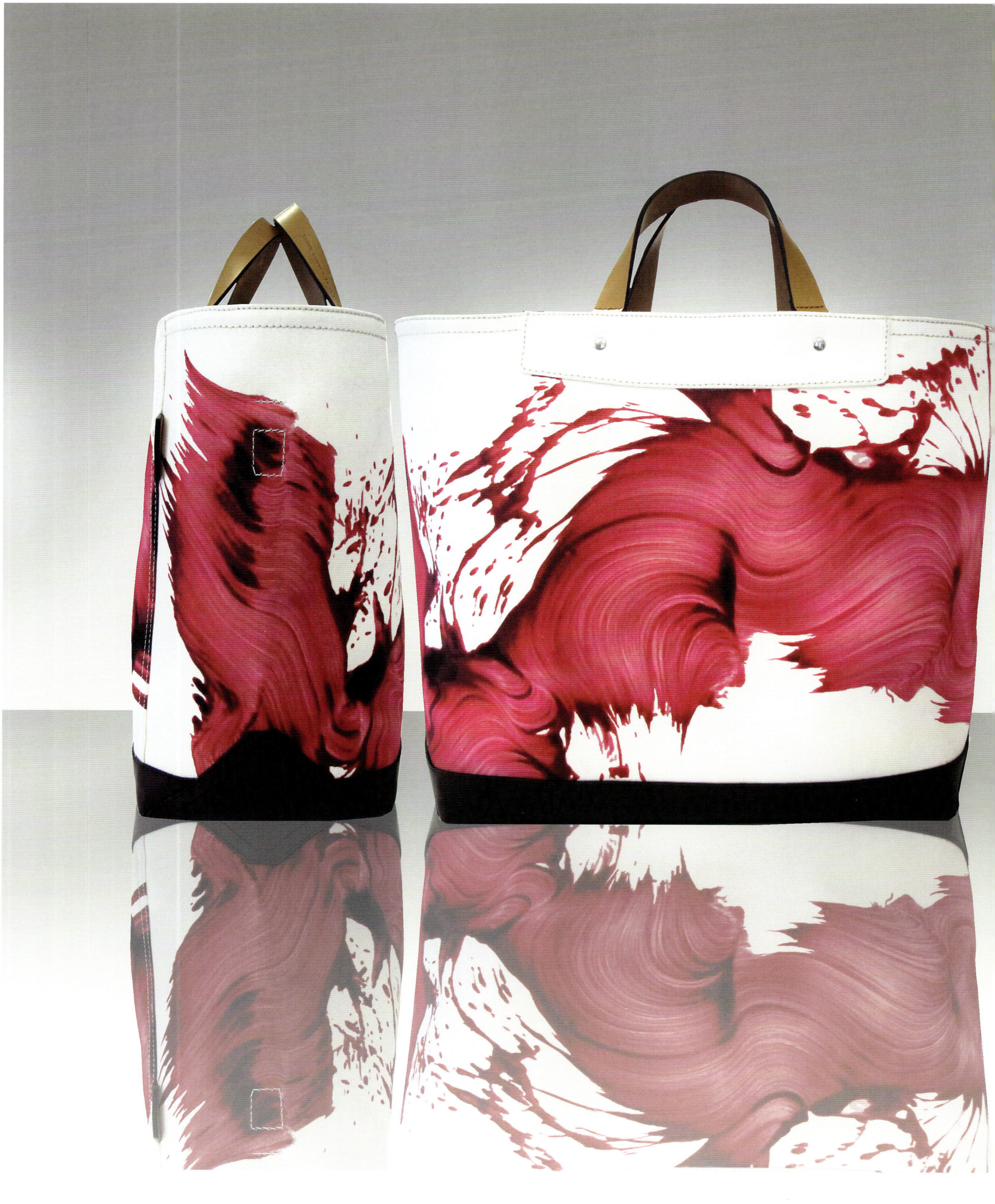

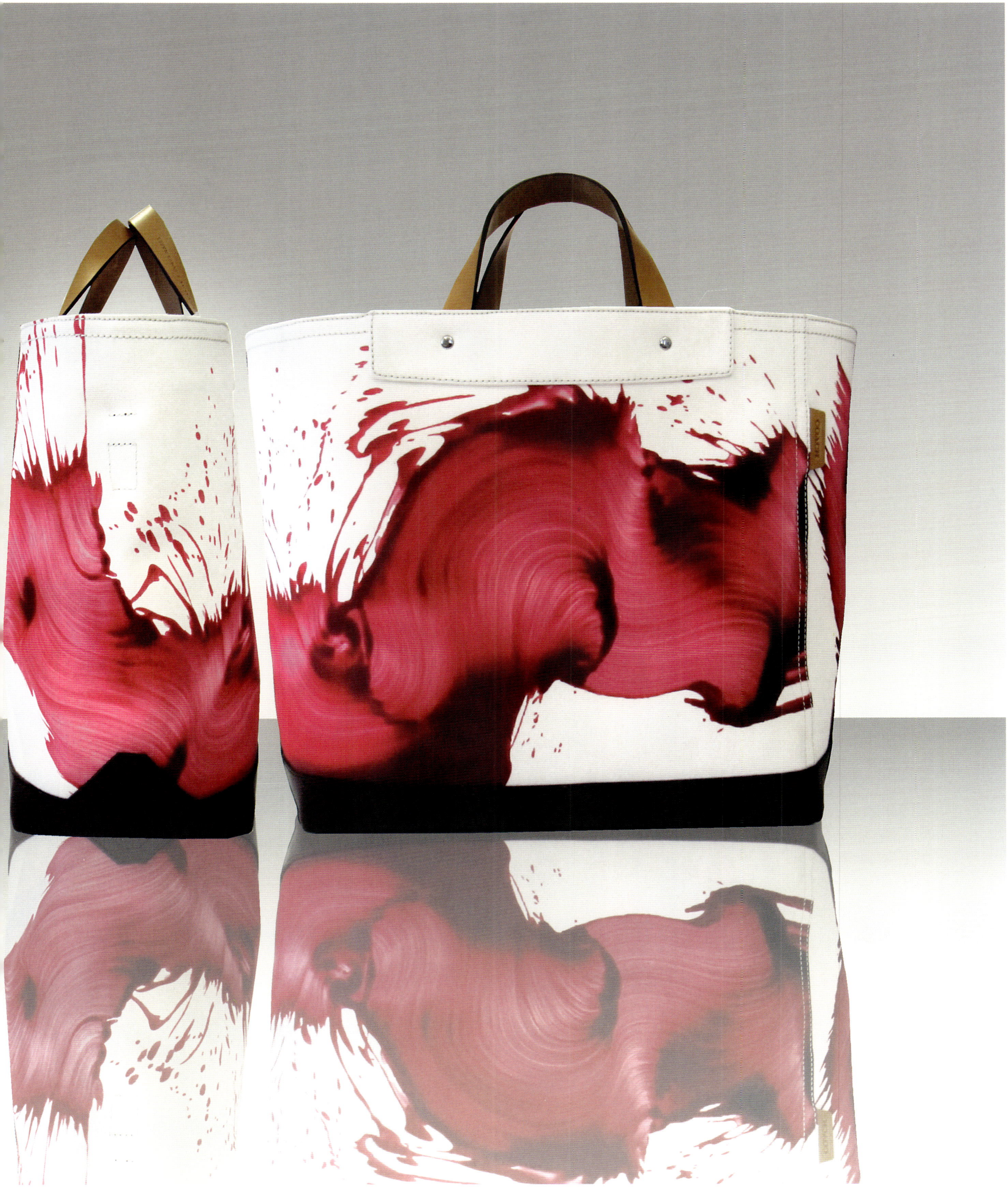

MATT GROENING + COM

IME DES GARÇONS PLAY

DESIGNER REI KAWAKUBO has long understood the power of visual communication and the vast potential of collaboration. Since Kawakubo began labeling garments "Comme des Garçons" in 1969, her brand has increasingly typified the bizarre, the controversial, and the avant-garde. The brand ideology of Comme des Garçons was further cemented between 1988 and 1991 with the semiannual publication *Six*. The large A3-size magazine relied on disparate images (from a spiral staircase by Pierre Lefebre Jahrgang to Steven Meisel's woman smoking) to convey the mood of each season's collection.

Since its inception, Rei Kawakubo has reached out to a plethora of talented people to contribute to Comme des Garçons. Untangling all of the collaborations would take at least one book in itself, as would unearthing all of the company's offshoot labels.

Here, the spotlight is placed on one of Rei Kawakubo's fifteen labels under the Comme des Garçons umbrella: Comme des Garçons PLAY. Created in 2002, CdG PLAY is specifically targeted at affluent twenty-somethings who fancy themselves "street." Hipsters from Paris's Ninth Arrondissement to Tokyo's Shimokitazawa neighborhood eagerly collect it with fervor. Comme des Garçons's PLAY brand is instantaneously recognizable by its ever-watchful heart logo, created by Polish-born, New York–based graphic designer Filip Pagowski. Pagowski began working for the label in November 1999 and was later invited to design textile prints by Adrian Joffee, husband of Rei Kawakubo and the "commercial brain behind CdG."[23]

For Spring 2011, CdG PLAY targeted an overlapping, equally voracious consumer demographic: cartoon lovers, specifically fans of illustrator Matt Groening (b. 1954). It would have been too obvious to choose Groening's most famous endeavor, *The Simpsons*, for a fashion collaboration, especially after the 2007 *Harper's Bazaar* editorial "shoot" in Paris featuring the cartoon family with supermodel Linda Evangelista.

Instead, CdG PLAY featured Groening's lesser-known first endeavor, *Life in Hell*, which Groening started in 1977 as comic doodles in letters to friends, bemoaning his new life in Los Angeles. Later picked up by an alternative L.A. weekly, the comic strip then went national, and by the 1990s it was being published in over 250 newspapers. Groening's main character,

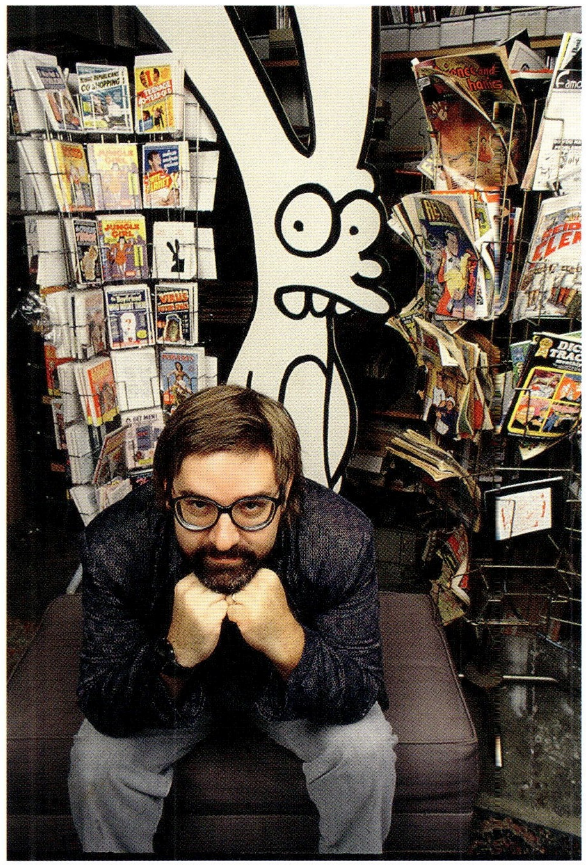

MATT GROENING

Binky, was a chronically depressed rabbit who goes to therapy to deal with his dead-end job and dreadful apartment. Binky and his existential trials struck a chord with disenchanted readers, as well as satire lovers, for a solid thirty-five years.

For Matt Groening's CdG PLAY collaboration, he contributed to an eight-piece capsule collection, primarily consisting of T-shirts and canvas totes scribbled with humorous moans like "But they told me it was decaf" and non-applicable life advice like "You can't kill a zombie." For cult consumers of CdG PLAY and ardent fans of Groening, wearing the collaborative garments or sporting CdG PLAY × Groening totes visibly expresses their affiliation with both camps.

CdG PLAY's collaboration with Matt Groening is unique. It honors the subversive, far-reaching influence of Groening's cartoon work on the culture at large. High art often distances itself from comics, which appeal to the masses. Groening's work at no point panders to a wide audience; it is dark, sarcastic, and exasperated. Yet, Groening's sense of humor and unflinching look at modern life broadly resonated. In that way, Groening melds perfectly with Comme des Garçons, which never bends to the wishes of consumers—leading, not following—but does so playfully, or at least in a manner that is tongue in cheek.

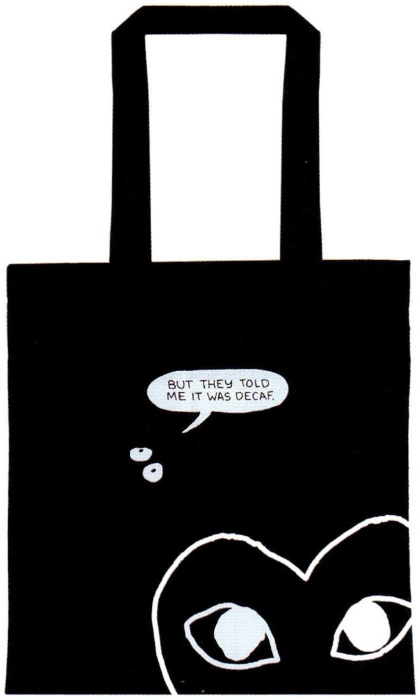

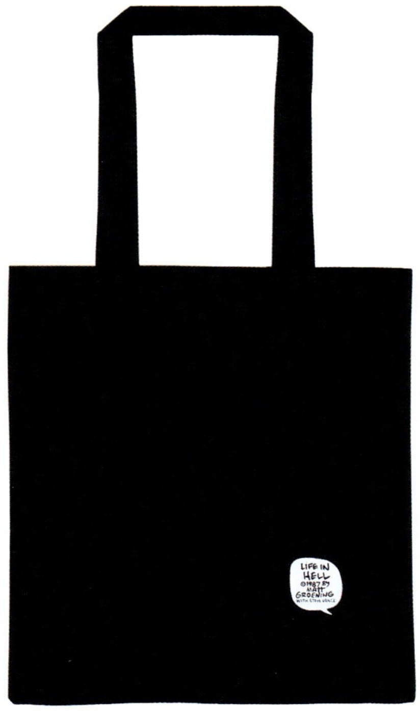

COMME DES GARÇONS *BINKY & SHEBA PLAY* TOTE | FRONT | MATT GROENING, 2011

COMME DES GARÇONS *BINKY & SHEBA PLAY* TOTE | BACK | MATT GROENING, 2011

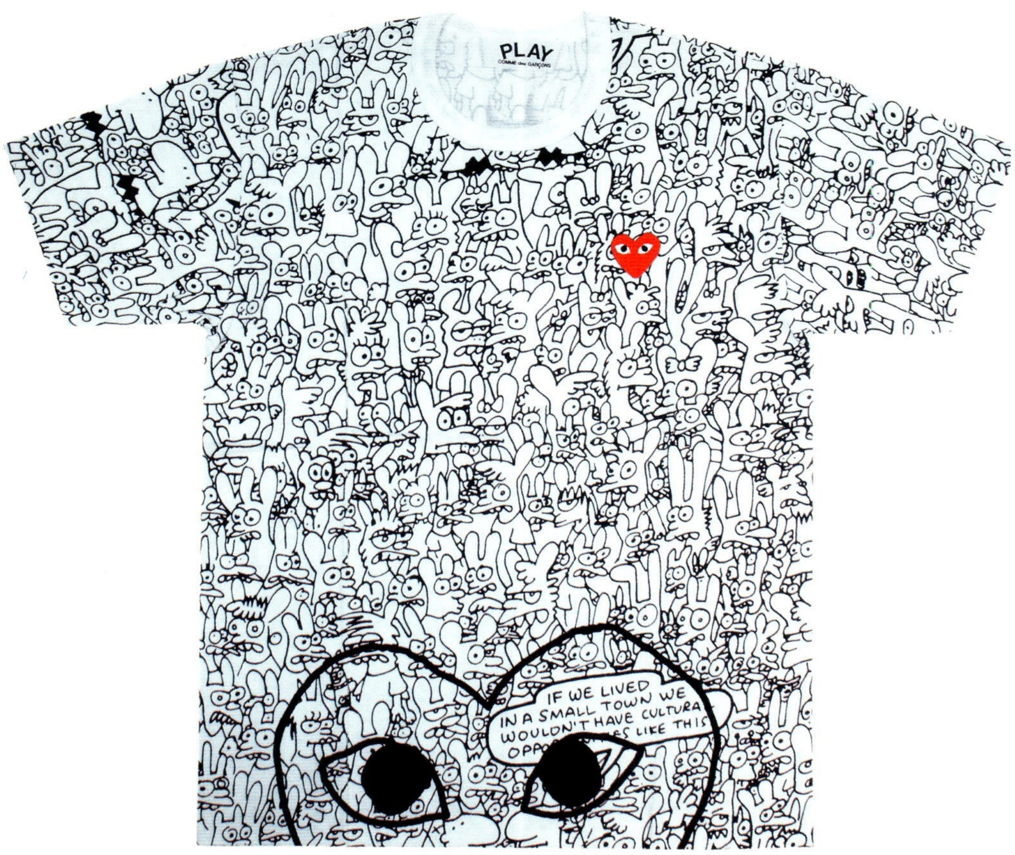

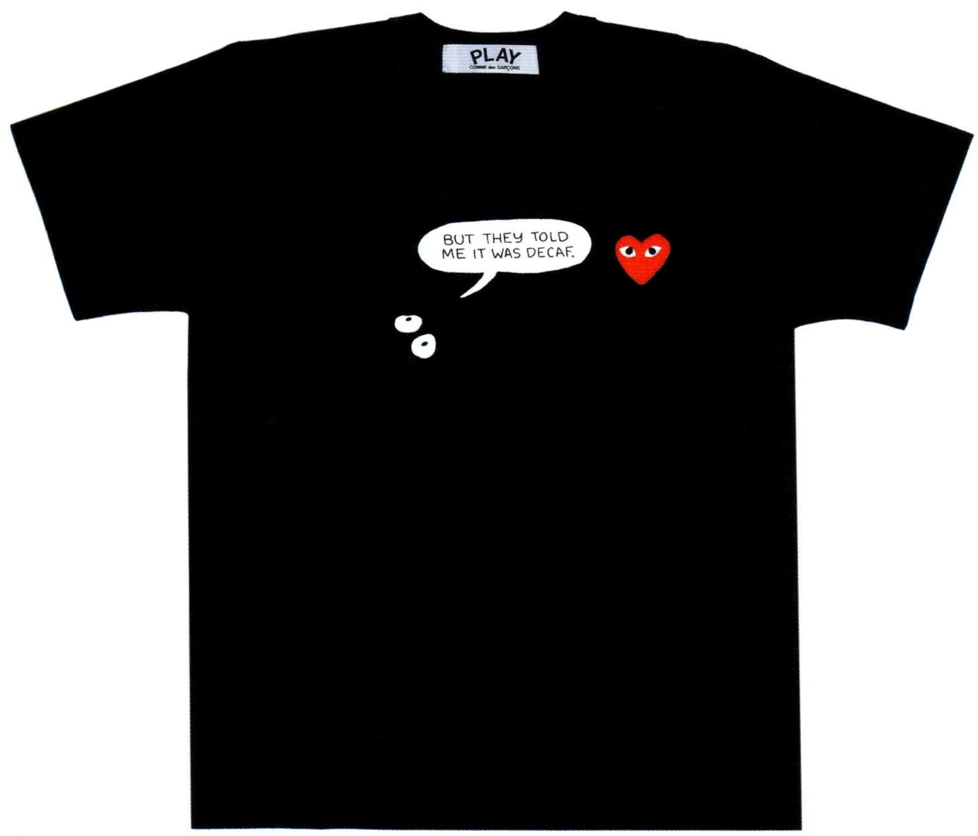

COMME DES GARÇONS *BINKY & SHEBA PLAY* SHORT-SLEEVED T-SHIRT | MATT GROENING, 2011

COMME DES GARÇONS *BINKY & SHEBA PLAY* SHORT-SLEEVED T-SHIRT | MATT GROENING, 2011

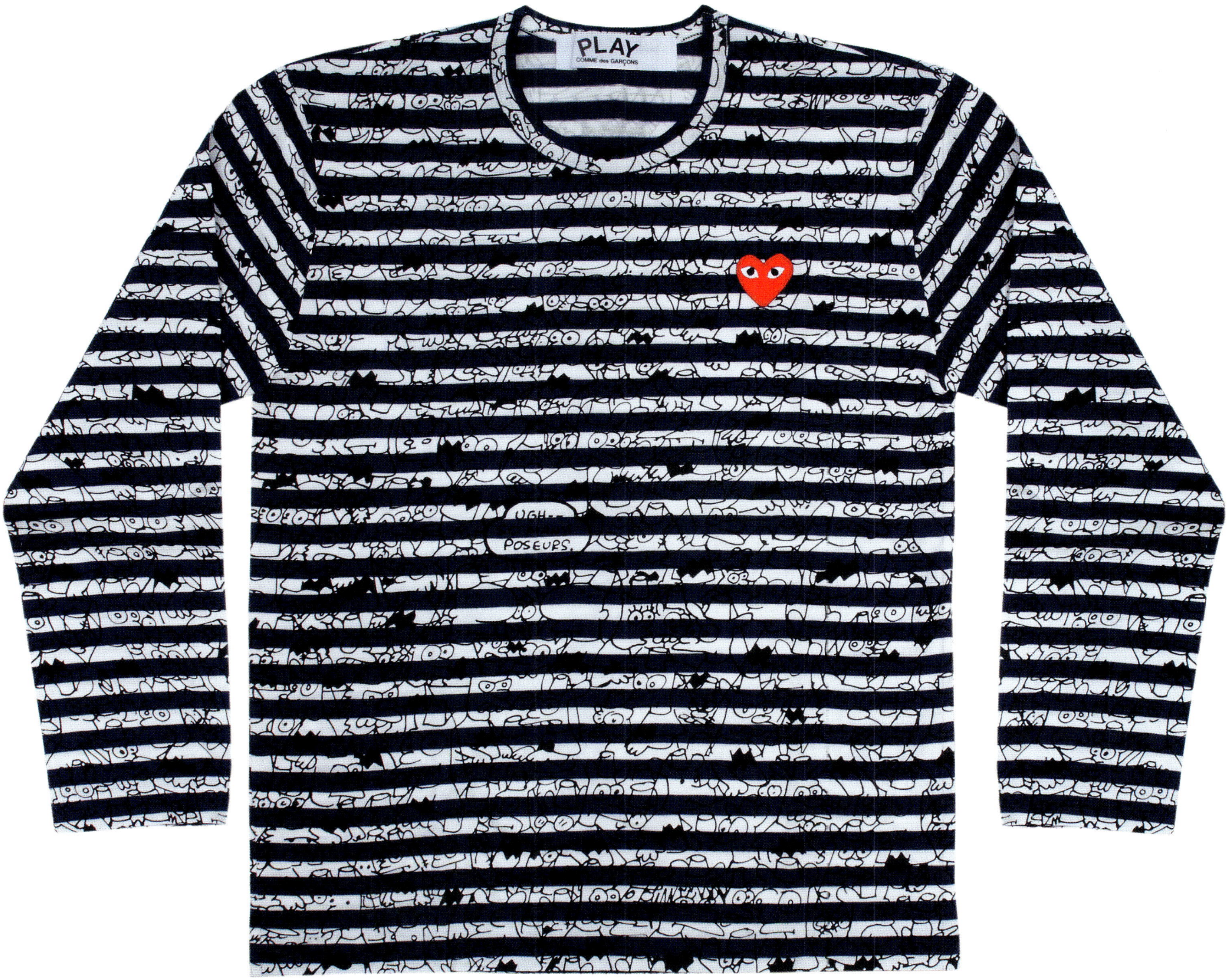

COMME DES GARÇONS *BINKY & SHEBA PLAY* LONG-SLEEVED T-SHIRT | MATT GROENING, 2011

ANDY WARHOL

DIOR

THE TALENT OF CHRISTIAN

Dior (1905–1957) as a couturier has eclipsed his early art-world beginnings. Between 1928 and 1931, young Dior partnered with his friend Jacques Bonjean to open a petit gallery: "Our ambition was to show the masters we admired the most—Picasso, Braque, Matisse, Dufy—and the younger painters we knew personally and already held in high esteem: Christian Bérard, Salvador Dalí, Max Jacob, and the Berman brothers."[24] Following the shuttering of his rue La Boétie gallery, Dior tried his hand at fashion, under the tutelage of American designer Max Kenna. Friend Jean Ozenne assisted, hawking Dior's fashion sketches to magazines, and upon selling six of them, Dior felt "my whole future was decided."[25] Christian Dior, who later became the father of the New Look, opened his eponymous *maison* (house) on Avenue Montaigne in 1946.

Andrej Varhola, Jr., better known as Andy Warhol (1928–1987), the man who would become the face of Pop Art, began his career like Dior, submitting sketches to magazines. After studying pictorial design at the Carnegie Institute of Technology in his birth town of Pittsburgh, Warhol moved to New York in June 1949. By that September, Warhol's drawing presciently accompanied an article titled "Success Is a Job in New York" in *Glamour* magazine, reaching roughly half a million American readers.[26] His illustrations made their way into *Harper's Bazaar* between 1951 and 1964, and were also featured in *Vogue*, *Mademoiselle*, the *New Yorker*, and *Life*. In 1955, Warhol landed a lucrative campaign for the I. Miller shoe store. Warhol's commercial shoe drawings were raised to art, receiving their own exhibit, *Andy Warhol: The Golden Slipper Show*, or *Shoes in America* at the Bodley Gallery from December 3 to 22, 1956. By 1960, Warhol was the highest-paid illustrator on the exotic island of Manhattan, pulling in over $70,000 annually. The majority of Warhol's drawings were of shoes, using a blotted line technique he perfected, and were accompanied by his mother Julia Warhola's spindly handwriting. Warhol attested, "Every time I draw a shoe for a job, I do an illustration of myself."[27]

For Raf Simons's second ready-to-wear line as creative director at Christian Dior, Simons embraced his own beginnings at the brand by turning to the early days of Christian Dior and Andy Warhol, prior to the breakout work they are best known for. Interested in nostalgia and recollection, Simons (b. 1968) named the Dior collection after Salvador Dalí's painting *The Persistence of Memory*, now living at the MoMA, but first displayed at Christian Dior's gallery in 1931.

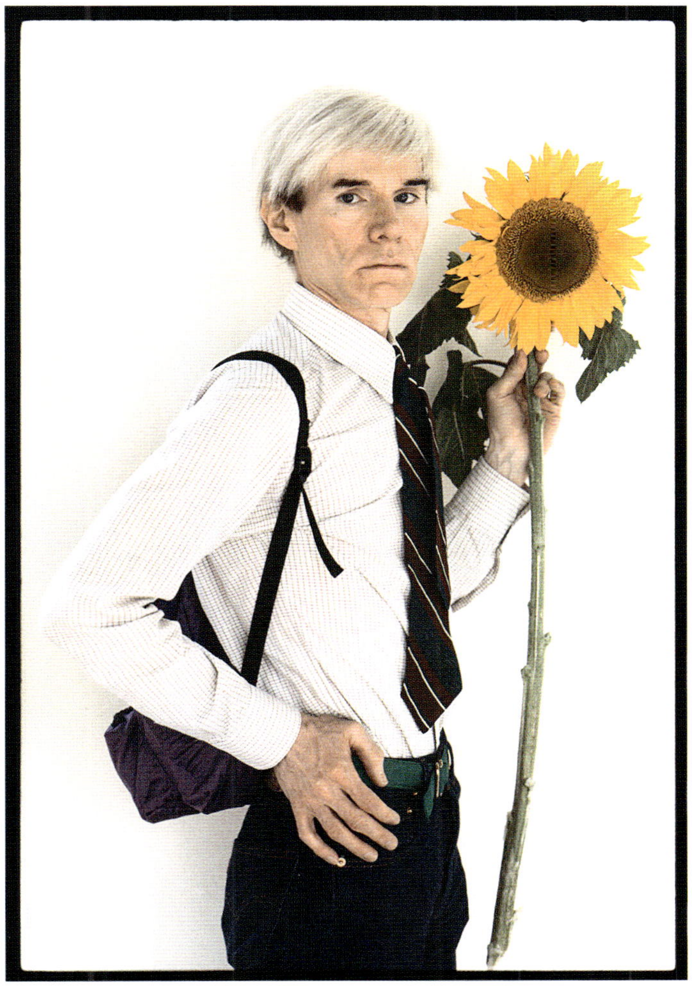

ANDY WARHOL

One in four looks on the Autumn/Winter 2013–14 catwalk featured Warhol's illustrations, which included flowers (Raf's interpretation was realized as floral houndstooth), stylish female faces, gloved hands, and shoes. Dior's best-selling handbags, Lady Dior and Diorissimo, were printed with Warholian stilettos or kitten heels. While Raf Simons and the Andy Warhol Foundation came together for the line, the ghost of Christian Dior seemed present. In a way, the final product was a collaboration between three uniquely creative men (one French, one American, and the other Belgian) that could not be stopped, two of them not even by death.

ANDY WARHOL LADY DIOR BAG | DIOR, 2013

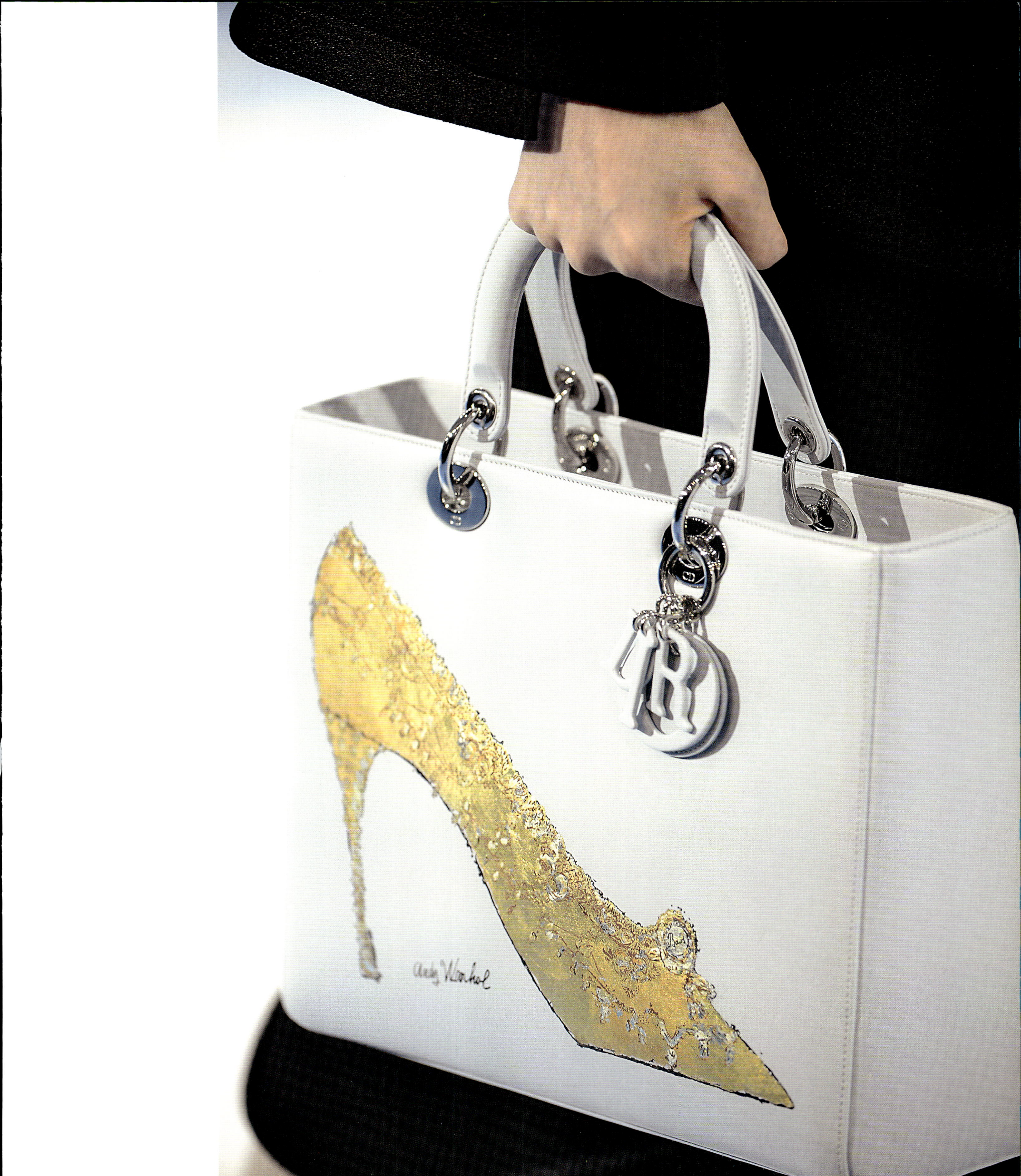
Andy Warhol

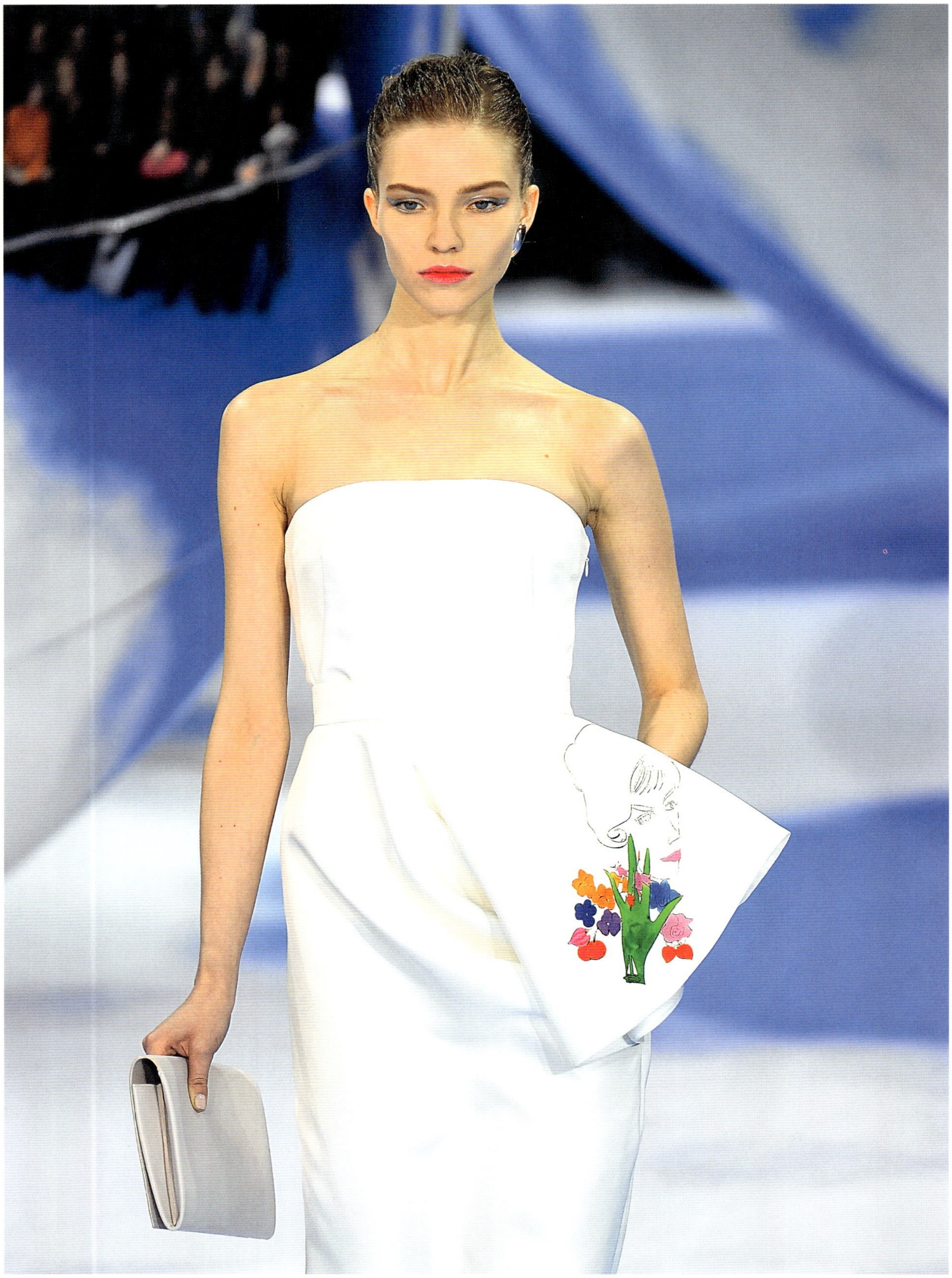

ANDY WARHOL DRESS | DIOR, 2013

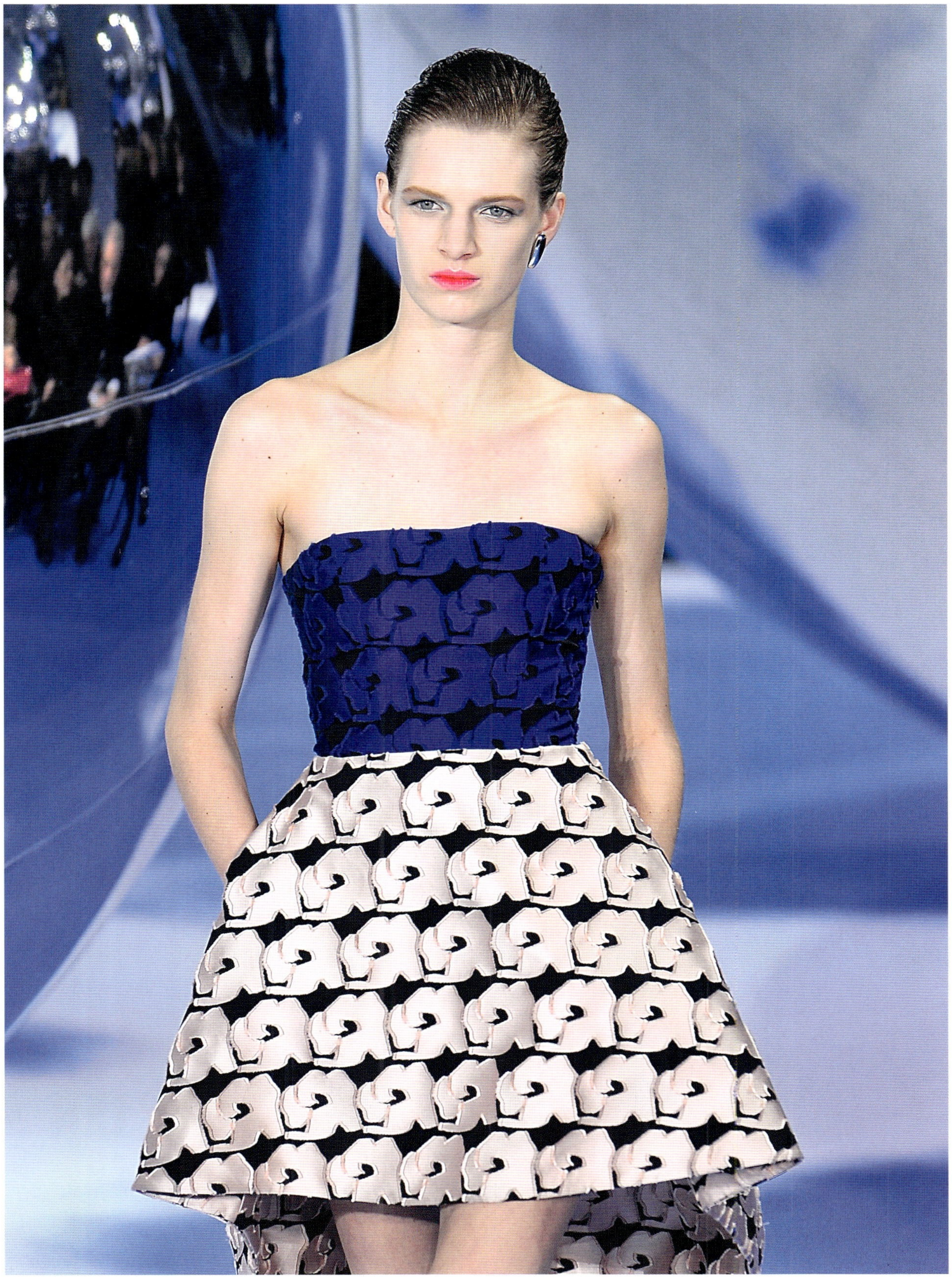

ANDY WARHOL DRESS | DIOR, 2013

MELVIN SOKOLSKY

HARPER'S BAZAAR

SINCE ITS 1867 inception, *Harper's Bazaar* has entranced viewers with its fashion, first illustrated and then—from April 7, 1888 onward—photographed. From 1958 through 1971, *Harper's Bazaar* was under the editorship of Nancy White, who wanted to surprise her readers with evocative, sometimes curious images. Unexpectedly, it was a young, self-taught photographer from the Lower East Side named Melvin Sokolsky (b. 1939) who supplied White with exactly what she was looking for.

Sokolsky began taking photographs with his father's box camera at age ten and was "educated" by visiting the city's museums as a young teenager. He received a two-day impromptu crash course in photography from a chance encounter with Martin Munkácsi at eighteen. Sokolsky joined *Harper's Bazaar* at just twenty-one. Art director Henry Wolf made it clear to him, in no uncertain terms, that Sokolsky was required to bring his own unique fingerprint to the publication. The series of images that Sokolsky presented for the March 1963 issue of *Harper's Bazaar* are undeniably his and his alone, and the photographs have since become iconic.

Sokolsky's Bubble photographs are baffling, fantastical, and otherworldly. The story of their inspiration begins with Hieronymus Bosch's triptych *The Garden of Earthly Delights* (1500–1505). Upon viewing it, Sokolsky's eye was drawn to the nude, caressing couple encased in a clear bubble. Of all the potent imagery by Bosch, the bubble idea stuck with Sokolsky—and he imagined traveling the world in it.

In 1963, Melvin Sokolsky re-created Bosch's fevered vision using a Plexiglas bubble of his own design, a ⅛-inch aircraft cable, and a very fashionable female clad in Philippe Venet and Pierre Cardin. After ensuring the deuce's safety—by using it to lift a Volkswagen Bug!—Sokolsky test shot model Simone d'Aillencourt inside the Bubble in Weehawken, New Jersey. It is this glowing color image, with New York City as a backdrop, that made the *Harper's Bazaar* cover.

Melvin Sokolsky then left for Paris with his assistant, the model-turned-actress Ali MacGraw, d'Aillencourt, and a team of six. He sent the Bubble ahead to Paris by freight. Navigating a

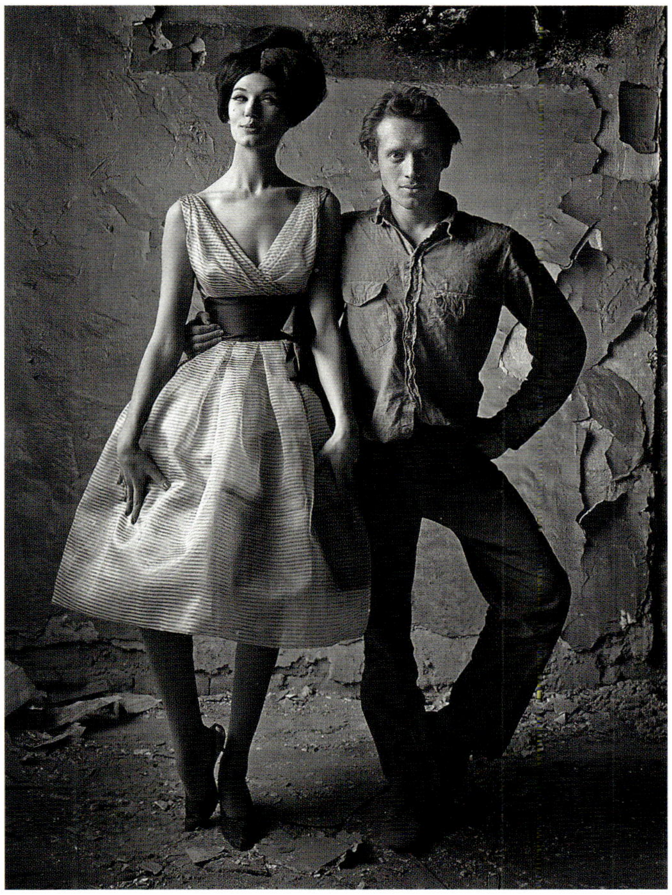

SIMONE D'AILLENCOURT AND MELVIN SOKOLSKY

crane around the city, in Saint-Germain-des-Prés, and over the Seine by the Alexandre III Bridge was an "encumbrance," but one that was eased slightly through a connection with the chief of police, who had become friendly to the project. (The husband of one of Sokolsky's model friends played cards with him!)[28] Small snafus occurred during the shoot—the Bubble was once lowered too far into the River Seine, ruining the designer shoes d'Aillencourt was modeling. When photographing around the citizens of Paris, Sokolsky would routinely shoot a few rolls to engender an "organic situation," as in his February morning shot of d'Aillencourt floating above children, police, and onlookers on a quiet street.

Faced with such impossible-seeming images, today's audience inevitably thinks: they must have been made using Photoshop! But as such a program did not exist in 1963, the only retouching of the photos was to strip the ⅛-inch cable—which was nearly invisible to begin with—out of the shot.

Sokolsky later experimented with a similar theme: making model Dorothea McGowan fly using a specially designed corset, and then lifting Erin Wasson to new heights in 2002—at the behest of *Harper's Bazaar* editor in chief Glenda Bailey. His images are available to view in *Paris 1963/ Paris 1965* (Leafcar Editions, 2011) and *Harper's Bazaar: Greatest Hits* (Harry N. Abrams, 2011)—as well as at the Victoria & Albert Museum and the Museum of Fine Arts Boston.

"OVER NEW YORK," FROM *BUBBLE* | MELVIN SOKOLSKY FOR *HARPER'S BAZAAR*, 1963

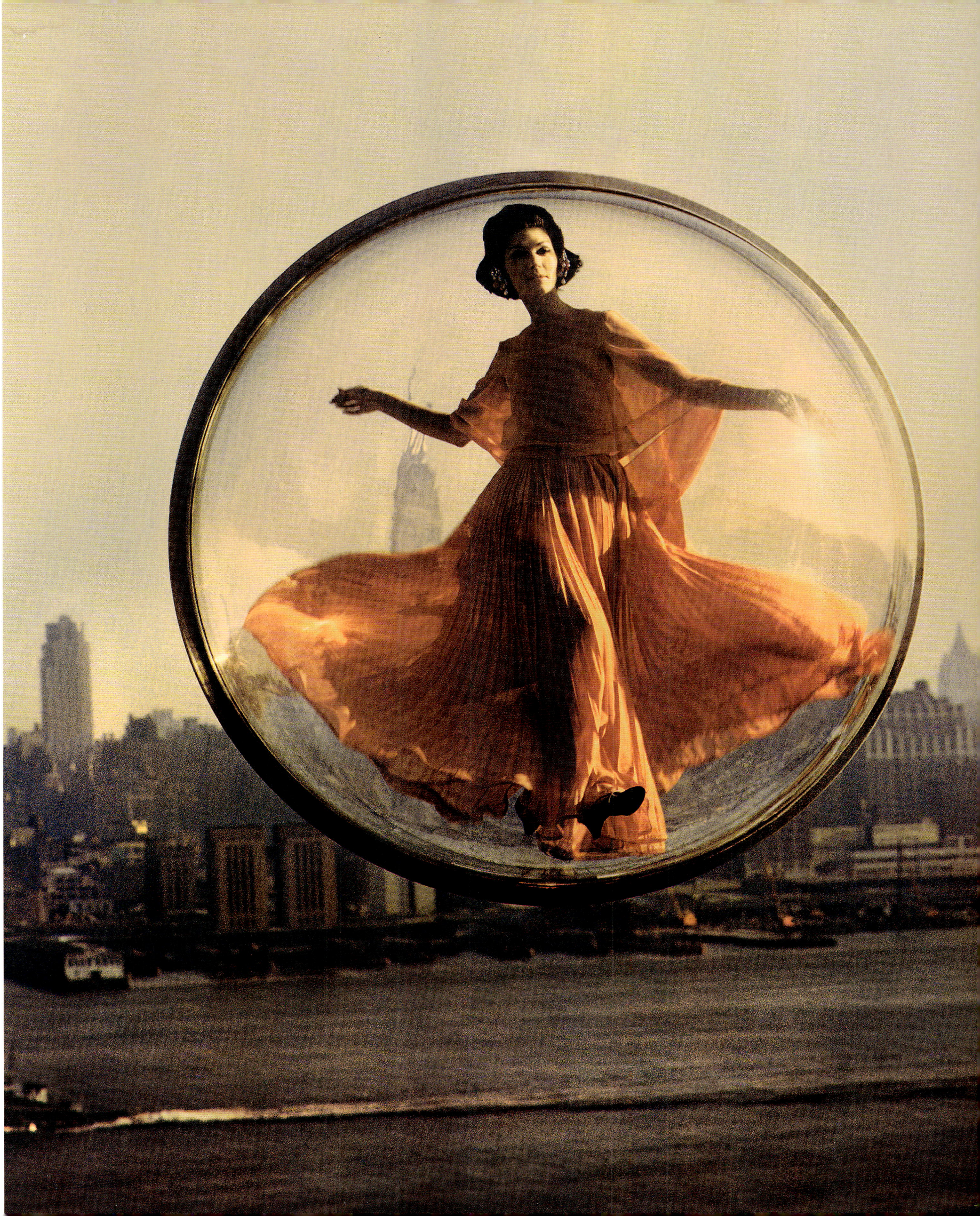

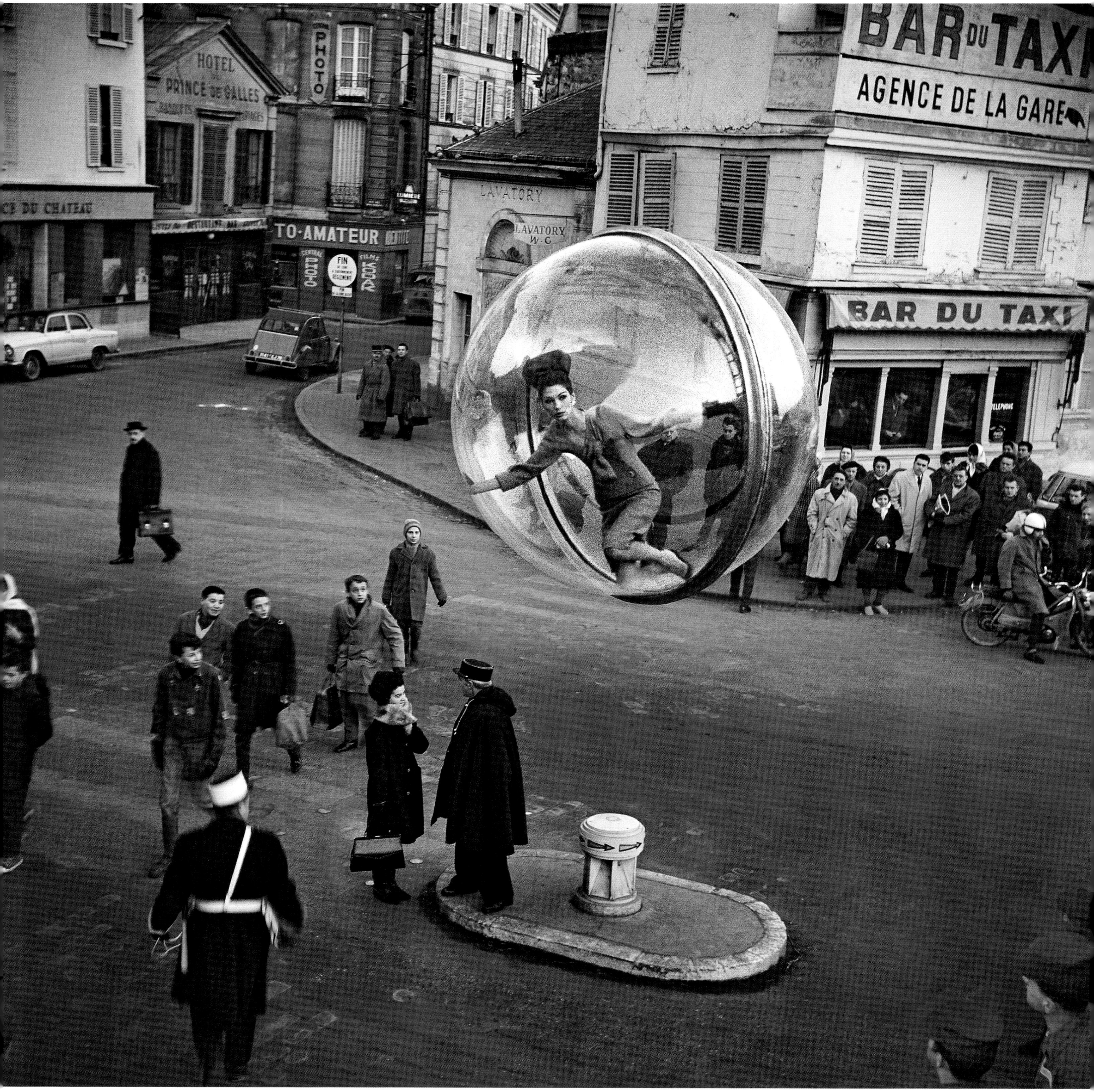
HOTEL
PRINCE DE GALLES
PHOTO
CE DU CHATEAU
TO-AMATEUR
LAVATORY
LAVATORY
W.C
BAR DU TAX
AGENCE DE LA GARE
BAR DU TAXI

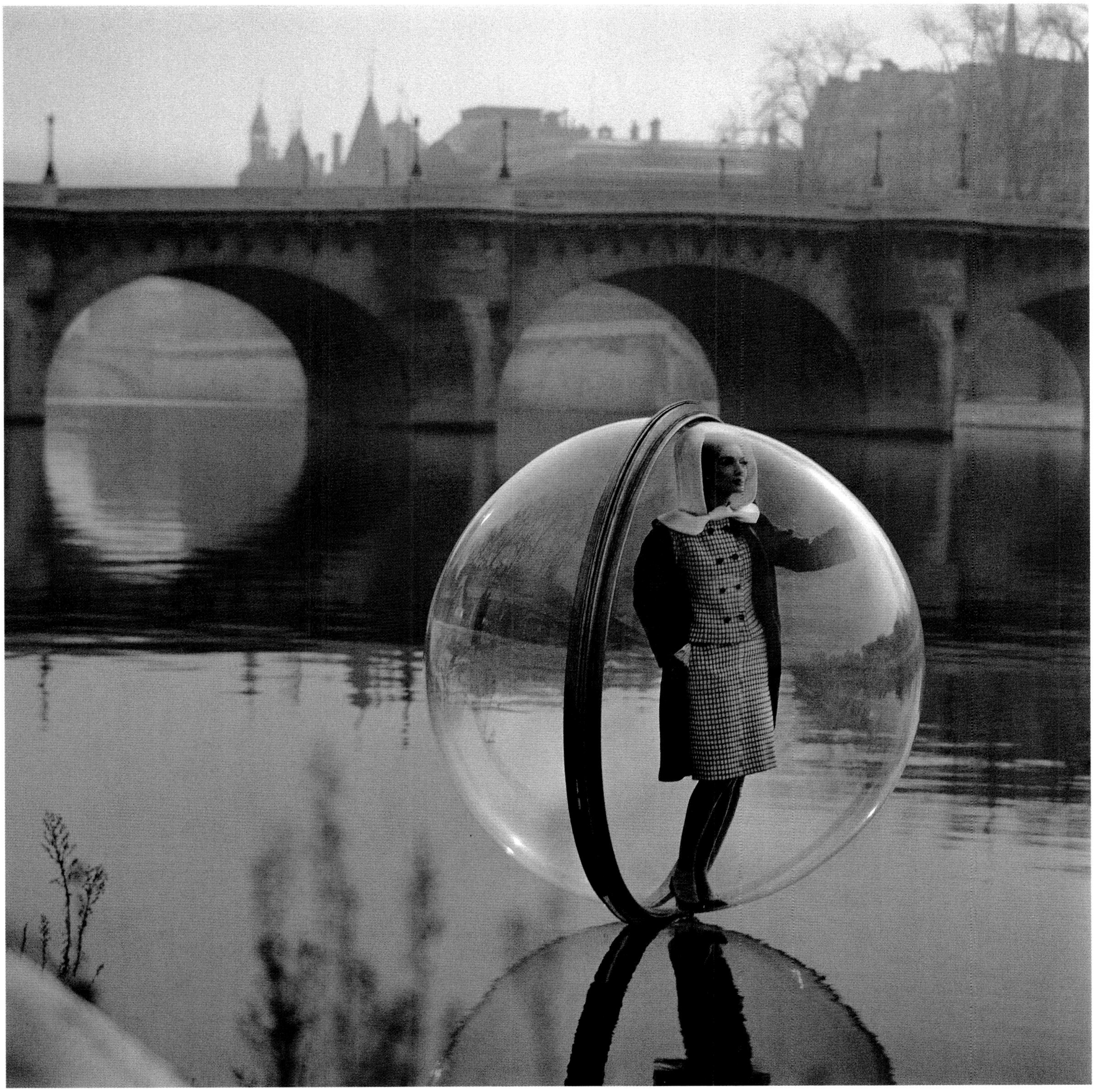

/\ "ON THE SEINE," FROM *BUBBLE* | MELVIN SOKOLSKY FOR *HARPER'S BAZAAR*, 1963

< "LUMIERE STREET," FROM *BUBBLE* | MELVIN SOKOLSKY FOR *HARPER'S BAZAAR*, 1963

RICHARD ANUSZKIEWI

CZ + JACQUES KAPLAN

FRENCHMAN JACQUES Kaplan (1924–2008) was the wild card of his family. When his father, Georges, and the rest of his family fled to the United States in response to the Nazi occupation of Paris, Kaplan went instead to England and joined General Charles de Gaulle's Free French Army. After his wartime heroics, for which he was awarded the Croix de Guerre, Kaplan attended the Sorbonne and then belatedly joined his family in New York.

In 1956, Jacques Kaplan took over his father's successful furrier business. Reluctant to join the family enterprise (his grandfather was also in the fur trade), Kaplan brought his "beatnik" attitude to the Midtown West shop.[29] In 1960, Kaplan showed his fur collection at an unusual venue: the Whitney Museum of American Art. Rather than merely using an art museum as a setting, Kaplan upped the ante in 1963, when he collaborated with top artists to make over his fur creations. Kaplan invited Jane Wilson, Maria Sol "Marisol" Escobar, Frank Stella, Theodoros Stamos, and Richard Anuszkiewicz to paint on his furs. Kaplan said with glee, "The artists had absolute freedom to do whatever they wanted, so each fur is a complete surprise to me."[30] Marisol ran rampant with that autonomy, painting a risqué female nude torso on a coat, now a part of the Metropolitan Museum of Art collection.

The work Richard Anuszkiewicz (b. 1930) made for Jacques Kaplan was significantly more modest, but still visually enticing and era-defining. A student of Bauhaus-educated color-contrast expert Josef Albers, Anuszkiewicz brought his psychedelic optical art to Kaplan's white calfskin with perspective-defying black polka dots in varying sizes. The trippy work, "somewhere between fashion, furnishings, and—just maybe—art," was created the same year Anuszkiewicz's work was featured in New York's Museum of Modern Art.[31]

Jacques Kaplan's initial fur collaborations were such a raging success that he invited sixteen artists—a flurry of Americans, French, and Belgians—to collaborate in 1964. Kaplan's furry fashions and their artistic merit were recognized around the same time; his collaborative coats received their own exhibition, *All Fur Art*, at the Allen Stone Galleries. *New York Times* critic Brian O'Doherty noted that the artists stuck to their signature styles for the project and that it was only when in close proximity that one discovered they had painted on fur. He snidely

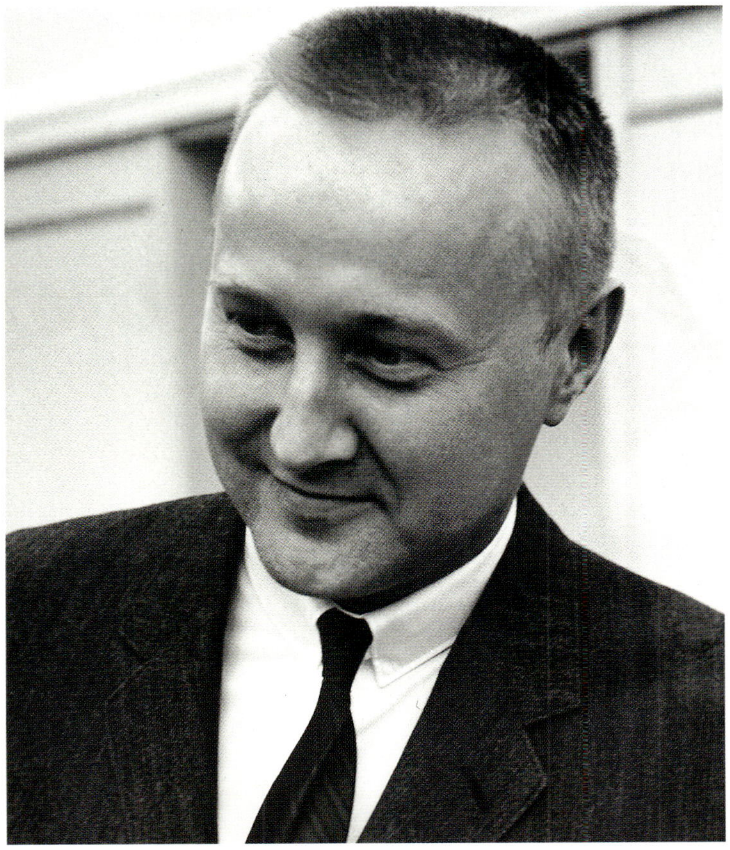

RICHARD ANUSZKIEWICZ

added, "Anuskiewicz [*sic*] and Stella sprinkle and slice their hard optical designs on a surface that splinters when the model walks, looking like some sort of locomoted attention-getting device—which after all is what some women are."[32]

While Doherty's comment meant to denigrate conspicuous fashion-following females, *Vogue* women refused to be disparaged, and embraced the accusation unapologetically! The fashion bible went "absolutely dotty," hollering that its readers should absolutely "wear polka dots bang bang bang."[33] But since the original Jacques Kaplan by Richard Anuszkiewicz sold within two hours to Mrs. Harcourt Armory, Jr., *Vogue* followers would have to use the idea as inspiration—or take paintbrushes to their own minks!

Though Kaplan shuttered his business in 1972, he set an exciting precedent for the possibilities of fur as a medium for fashion and art, one future designers will hopefully gather inspiration from. As for Anuszkiewicz, his work is housed at the Museum of Contemporary Art in Zagreb, Croatia; the Museo de Arte Moderno in Ciudad Bolivar, Venezuela; the Hokkaido Museum of Modern Art in Sapporo, Japan; and nearly fifty American museums—all keeping Anuszkiewicz's work available for viewers who need a little change in perspective.

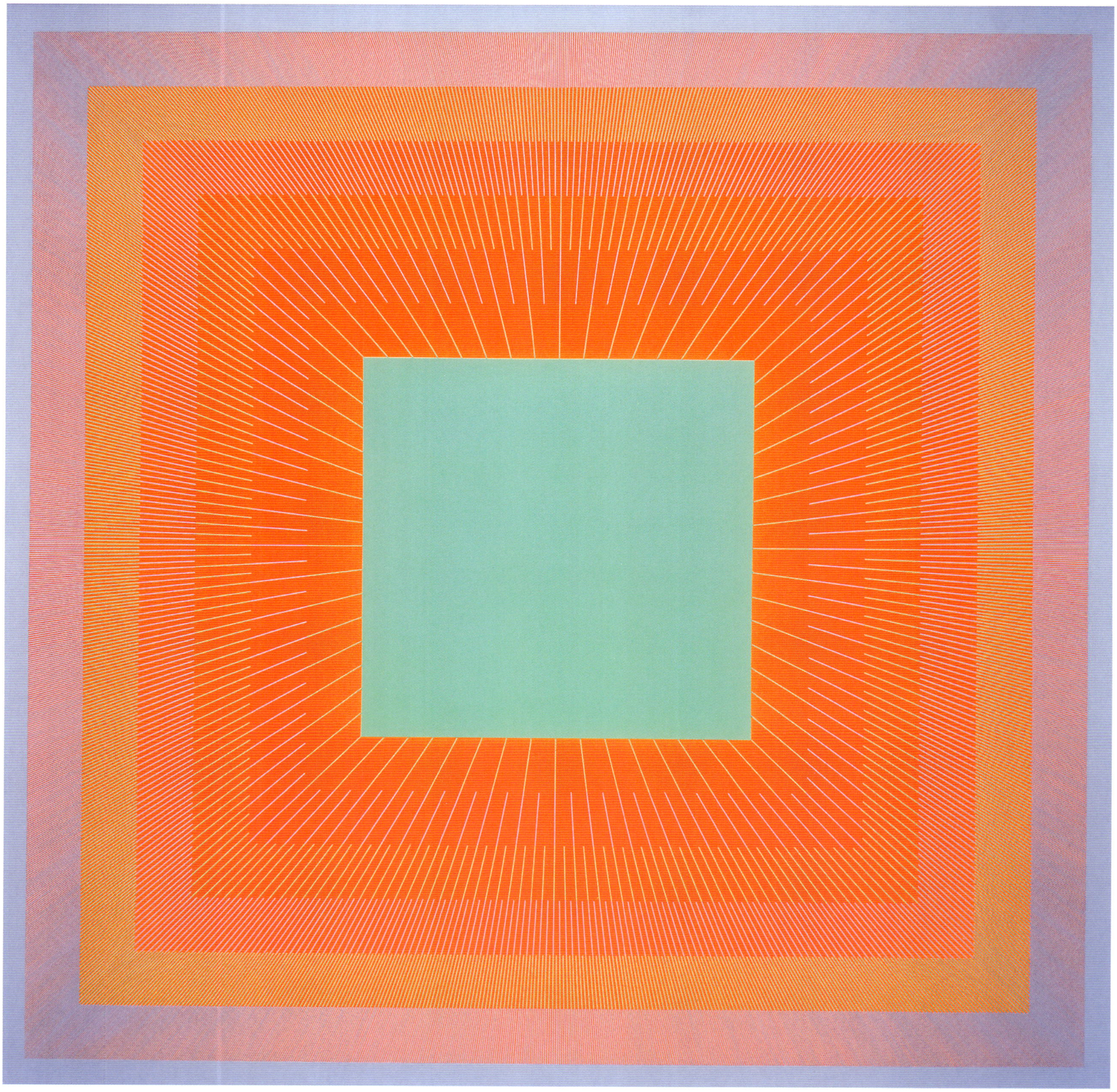

⋀ *IRIDESCENCE* | ACRYLIC ON CANVAS | RICHARD ANUSZKIEWICZ, 1965

⋗ **JACQUES KAPLAN COAT PAINTED WITH BLACK DOTS** | RICHARD ANUSZKIEWICZ, 1963

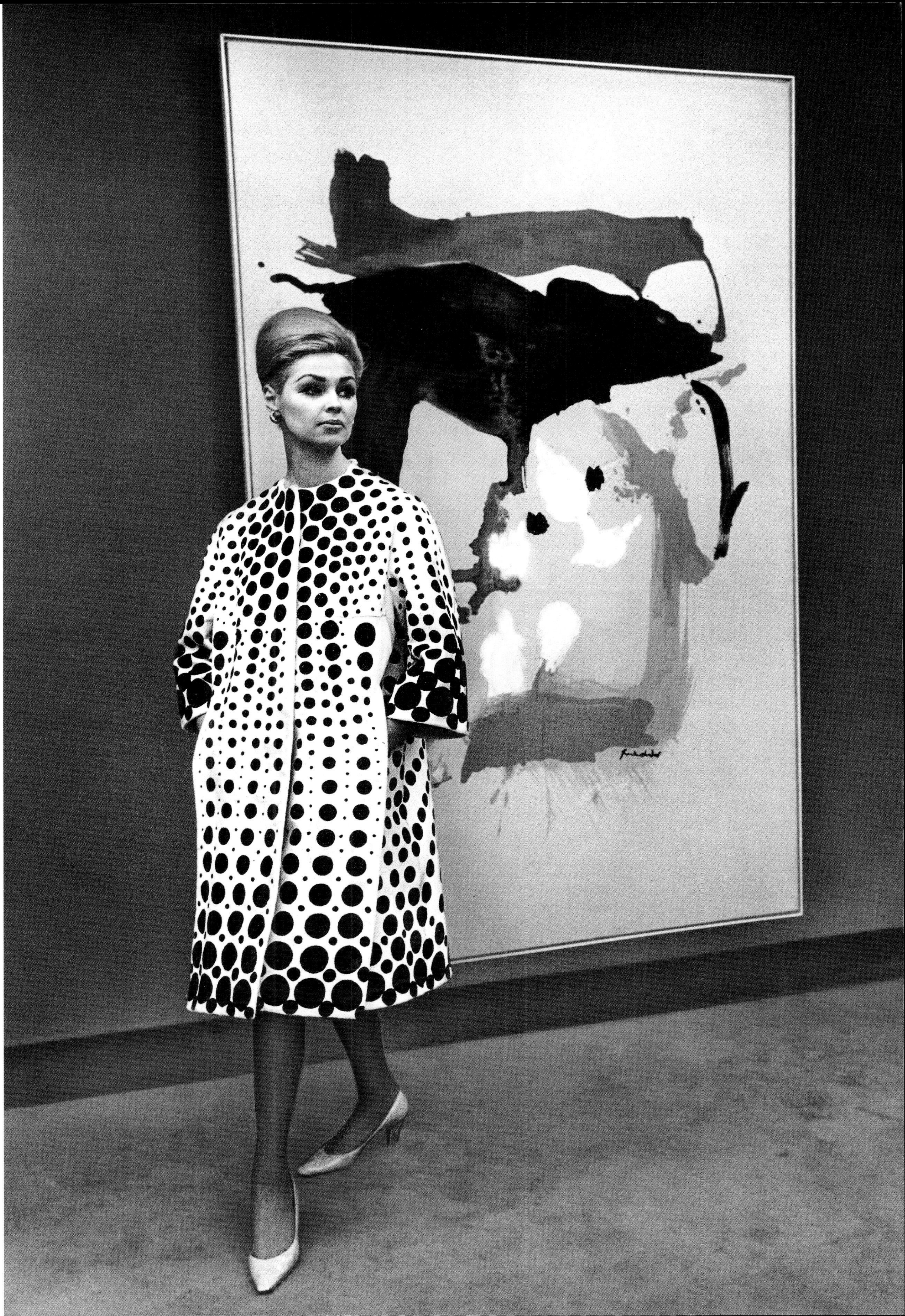

JOHN CHAMBERLAIN

MARY KATRANTZOU

"I TREAT THE DRESS

as a canvas. . . . I want to create wearable art." —Mary Katrantzou[34]

American artist John Chamberlain (1927–2011) is best known for twisting crushed automotive steel into extraordinary lacquered sculptures. Chamberlain, who had over a hundred solo exhibitions in his lifetime, was internationally exhibited in the São Paolo Bienal in 1961 and 1994, as well as at Amsterdam's Stedelijk Museum and the Staatliche Kunstsammlungen in Dresden. In 1993, Chamberlain was duly awarded the Lifetime Achievement Award in Contemporary Sculpture from the International Sculpture Center in Washington, D.C.

London-based Greek designer Mary Katrantzou (b. 1983) has reinvigorated British fashion. During her undergraduate education, Katrantzou studied architecture at the Rhode Island School of Design before transferring to Central Saint Martins (University of the Arts, London) to study textile design. She continued her studies at the renowned school, receiving her master of arts in fashion in 2008. Her graduate collection used *trompe-l'oeil* prints to brilliant effect, giving her subjects the appearance of wearing outrageously large jewelry rather than garments. Katrantzou furthered this idea in later collections, pushing the boundaries of digital ink-jet printing to unprecedented heights.

The best in fashion took immediate note, and Mary Katrantzou's garments can now be found in the world's top shops, namely Joyce in Hong Kong, Colette in Paris, Selfridges in London, and Barneys New York.

For Spring/Summer 2012, Katrantzou was inspired by the career of John Chamberlain, debuting the collection in September 2011, three months prior to the esteemed sculptor's death. The line included twenty-seven looks, primarily cocktail dresses, gowns, and suits. Each striking ensemble was a feat of technology: glorious Photoshop collages printed onto textiles with such realism that they appeared to be made out of materials straight from John Chamberlain's studio. While the finale gown was indeed made of cans, and others were appliquéd with finishing touches of metal, the majority only appeared to be constructed from crumpled metallic junkyard finds.

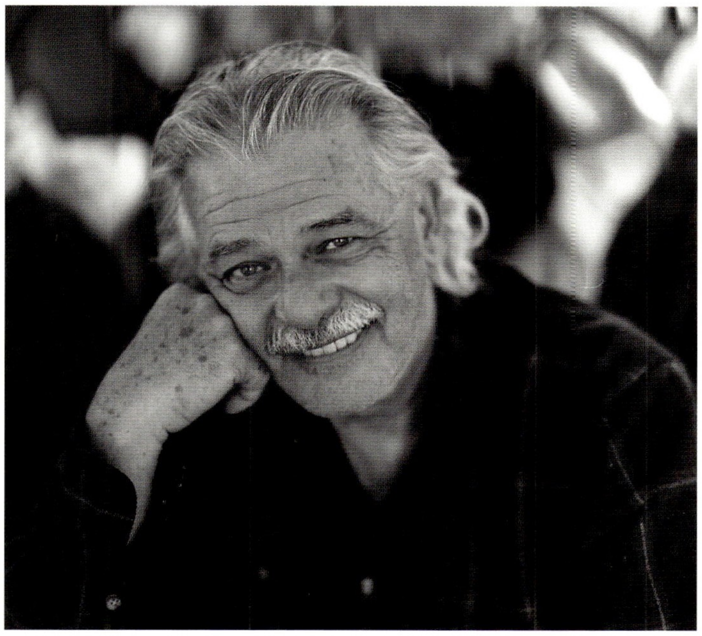

JOHN CHAMBERLAIN

Arguably, fashion begins to die the minute it hits the catwalk. And, as fashion has sped up faster and faster like an out-of-control merry-go-round, designers are forced to ruminate on the lifecycle of their creations. So, with a certain poignancy, Mary Katrantzou set her eye-tricking collection down a runway lined with flowers. As the audience gazed over the line, they were beckoned to ponder the unflinching reality of time. Despite the supposed immortality of art, Katrantzou's vision reminded viewers that even once-impressive technological marvels, like glorious new cars, are ultimately turned to scrap, and that nature will, in the end, prevail. In this way, Katrantzou's collection further enunciated the complex themes of creation versus destruction and technology versus Mother Nature that John Chamberlain's work inherently implies.

Companies have been chomping at the bit to tap ludicrously talented Mary Katrantzou for collaborative endeavors, and the already long list will undoubtedly grow to epic proportions. She teamed up with Adidas Originals in 2014 for a capsule collection, *Wallpaper** magazine for a bespoke dress, Topshop for shared lines, Longchamp for bags, Current/Elliott for denim, Moncler M for fashionable puffy coats, and more.

For Spring/Summer 2014, Mary Katrantzou joined up with SHOWstudio, a fashion website founded by Nick Knight that offers a window into creativity in real time. For a unique, site-specific project, Katrantzou used hundreds of chrysanthemums to adorn a lampshade skirt made from welded metal. John Chamberlain would have been proud.

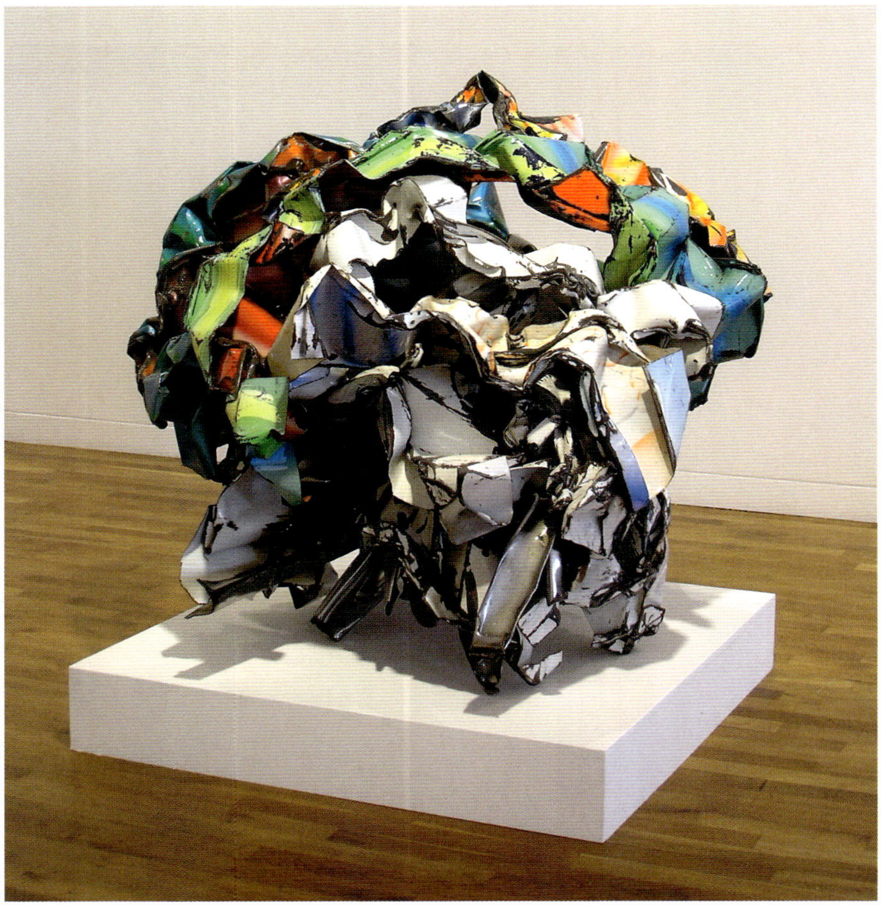

SILKY WILKIE | PAINTED AND CHROMIUM-PLATED STEEL | JOHN CHAMBERLAIN, 1994

JOHN CHAMBERLAIN-INSPIRED GOWN | MARY KATRANTZOU, 2012

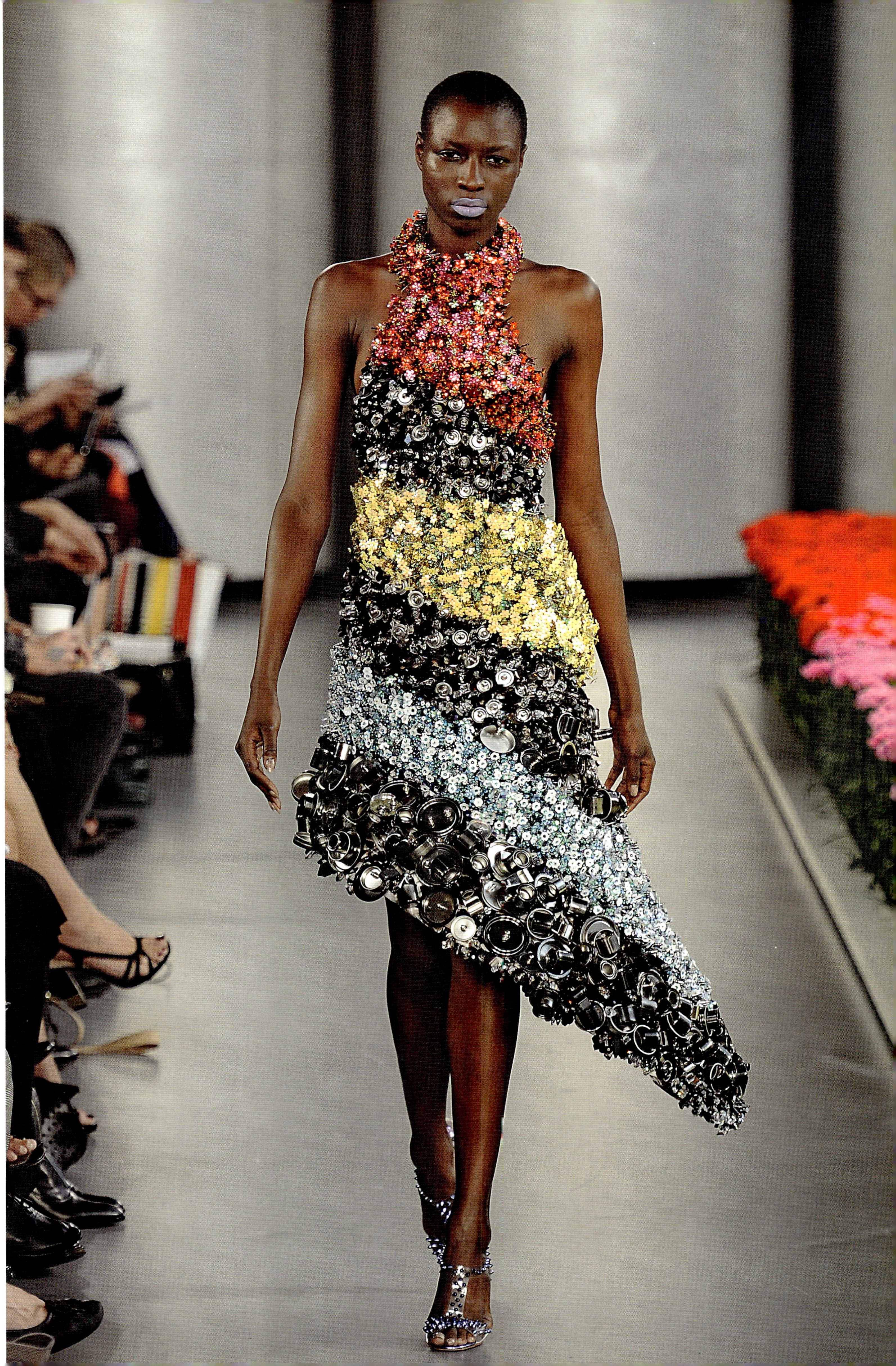

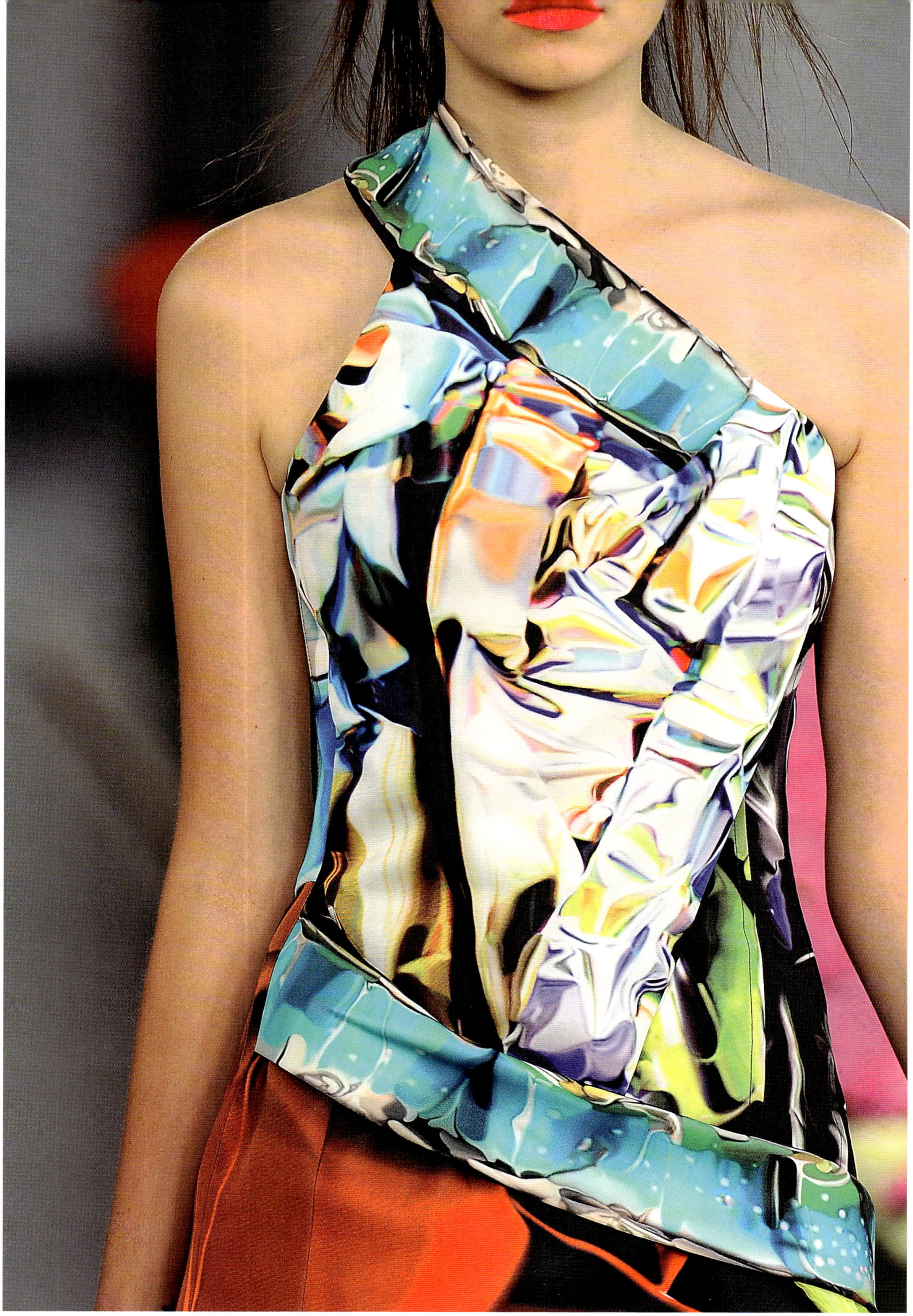

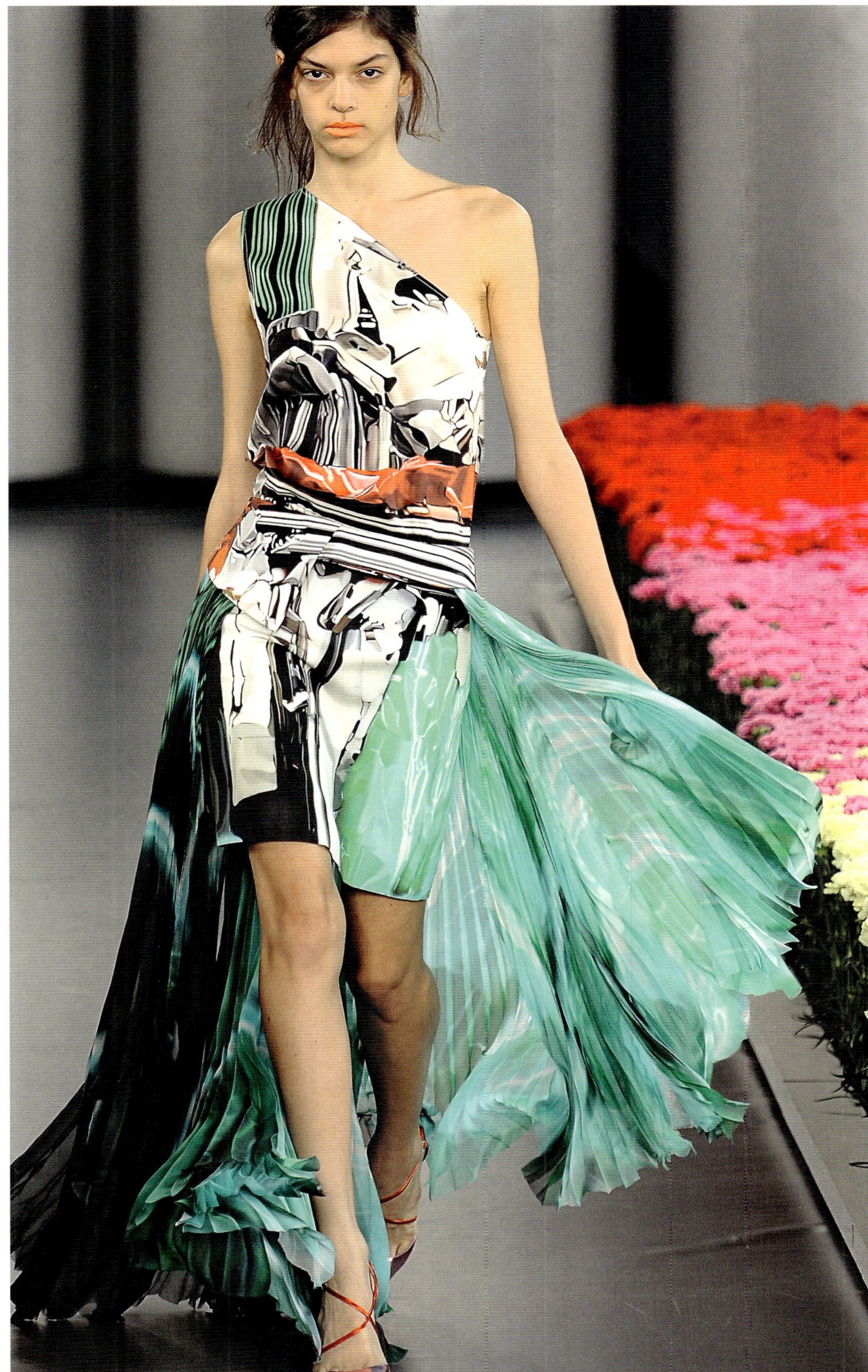

JOHN CHAMBERLAIN–INSPIRED DRESS | MARY KATRANTZOU, 2012

JOHN CHAMBERLAIN–INSPIRED DRESS | MARY KATRANTZOU, 2012

MERCE CUNNINGH

M + REI KAWAKUBO

BOTH THE DANCES

of Merce Cunningham and the garments of Rei Kawakubo tend to induce violent reactions of either feral devotion or perplexed revulsion. Understandably, their 1997 collaboration, which premiered at the Brooklyn Academy of Music, where Kawakubo designed costumes for Cunningham's dance *Scenario*, only intensified these divergent reactions.

Mercier "Merce" Philip Cunningham (1919–2009), a soloist in Martha Graham's dance company during the early 1940s, created his own company in 1953 and with it a type of dance best described simply by his name. Annoyed by inauthentic emotions attached to dance movements, which in turn were intrinsically chained to a soundtrack, Merce Cunningham created over 150 original dances that dissociated movement from sound. Like playwright Harold Pinter, Cunningham recognized the opportunity inherent in silence. He freed dance. Cunningham's work could, in the course of a minute, range from awkward to delicate, frenetic to pacifying. Were it not for the camaraderie of the fifteen dancers and occasional symbiosis of their movements, a Cunningham dance could appear as anarchy . . . or genius.

Merce Cunningham had previously collaborated with artists including Frank Stella (*Scramble*, 1967), Jasper Johns (*Walkaround Time*, 1968), and Andy Warhol (*Rainforest*, 1968), but inviting a fashion designer was a first. Rei Kawakubo (b. 1942) originally turned him down. "Merce had asked me long ago if I was interested in doing the costumes, but not knowing anything about dance, I felt I couldn't do it."[35] Then Kawakubo began to design her now-famous Spring/Summer 1997 collection, titled "Body Meets Dress—Dress Meets Body." Due to the unique silhouettes, it has been nicknamed the "Quasimodo" collection by unamused critics; *New Yorker* writer Judith Thurman described it as "bulbous tumors of down."[36] Writer John Waters, a Kawakubo disciple, noted that the dresses featured "built-in pads" placed over "the very parts of the body most fashionable women go to the gym to eliminate."[37] This Kawakubo collection, more so than others, caused an earthquake and made fashion history. In Merce Cunningham's hands, it then made dance history.

Rei Kawakubo recalls, "While I was designing the [Spring/Summer 1997] collection, I suddenly had this intuitive feeling that it could become dancers' clothes as well."[38] Kawakubo did consider the necessities of the dancers when reinterpreting her designs for Cunningham's company, by

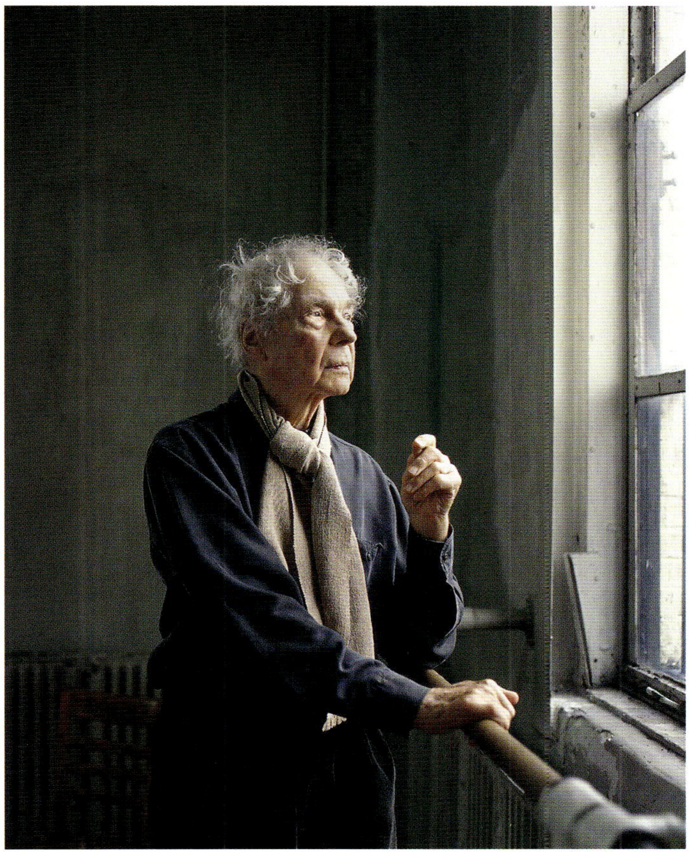

MERCE CUNNINGHAM

reinforcing the seams and re-commissioning the Orimono Kenkyu Sha Fabric Company to give the garments more stretch. Kawakubo's hesitancy faded: "I was excited about the prospect of the shapes being broken down by movement and new forms being created. When I saw the rehearsal for the first time, I was fascinated by how the shapes changed and came alive."[39]

The costumes challenged the dancers, used to navigating space with their own bodies, not those crafted by Rei Kawakubo. Dancer Jennifer Goggans, who performed in the 2006 *Scenario minEvent*, a condensed version of the original 1997 show, discussed performing in the costumes: "There was a section of choreography where I had to lay down and then roll onto my stomach. The pillows made this movement quite challenging. I flopped, more than rolled, and it was difficult for me to do so without laughing."[40] Despite the trials, original *Scenario* dancer Matthew Mohr appreciated how Kawakubo elevated the piece, adding sculptural elements to the body that Cunningham has been messing with for fifty years. As for its lasting impact, the success can be attributed to both Kawakubo's and Cunningham's willingness to welcome "accident, experiment, and risk" into the creative process.[41]

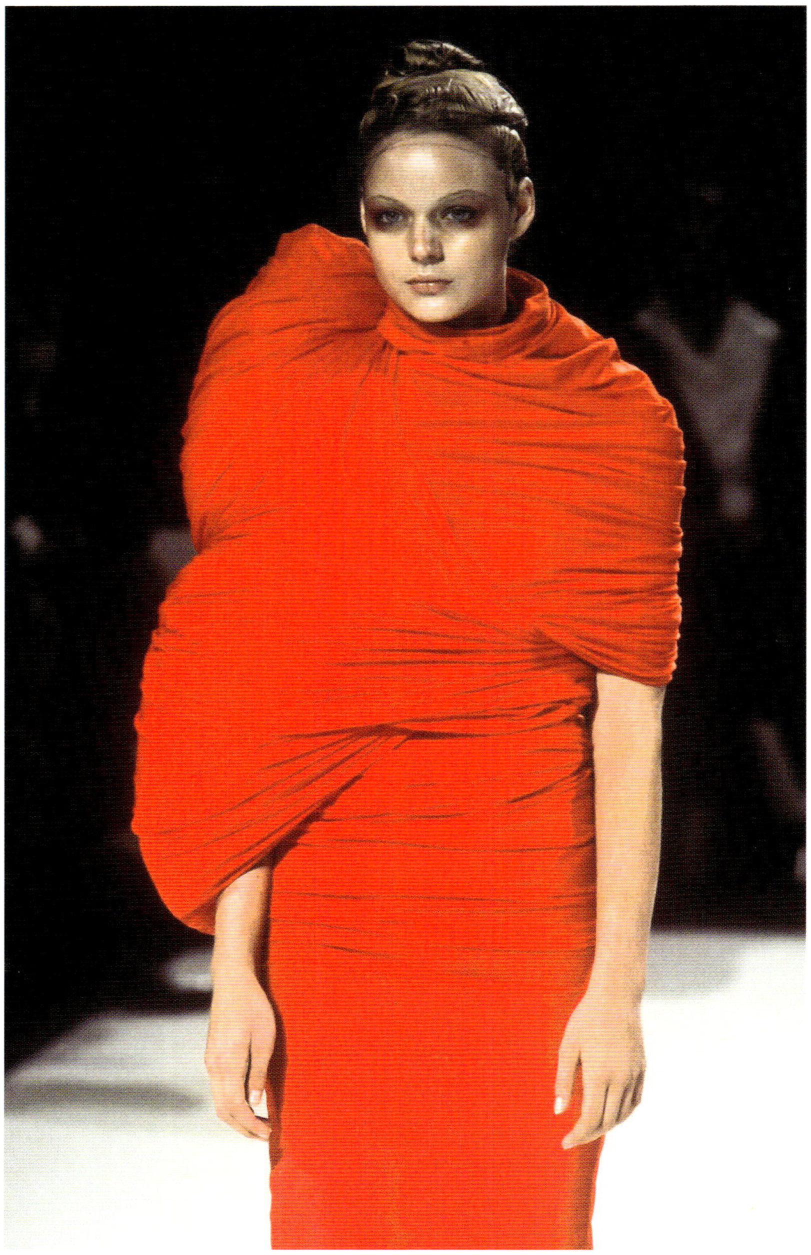

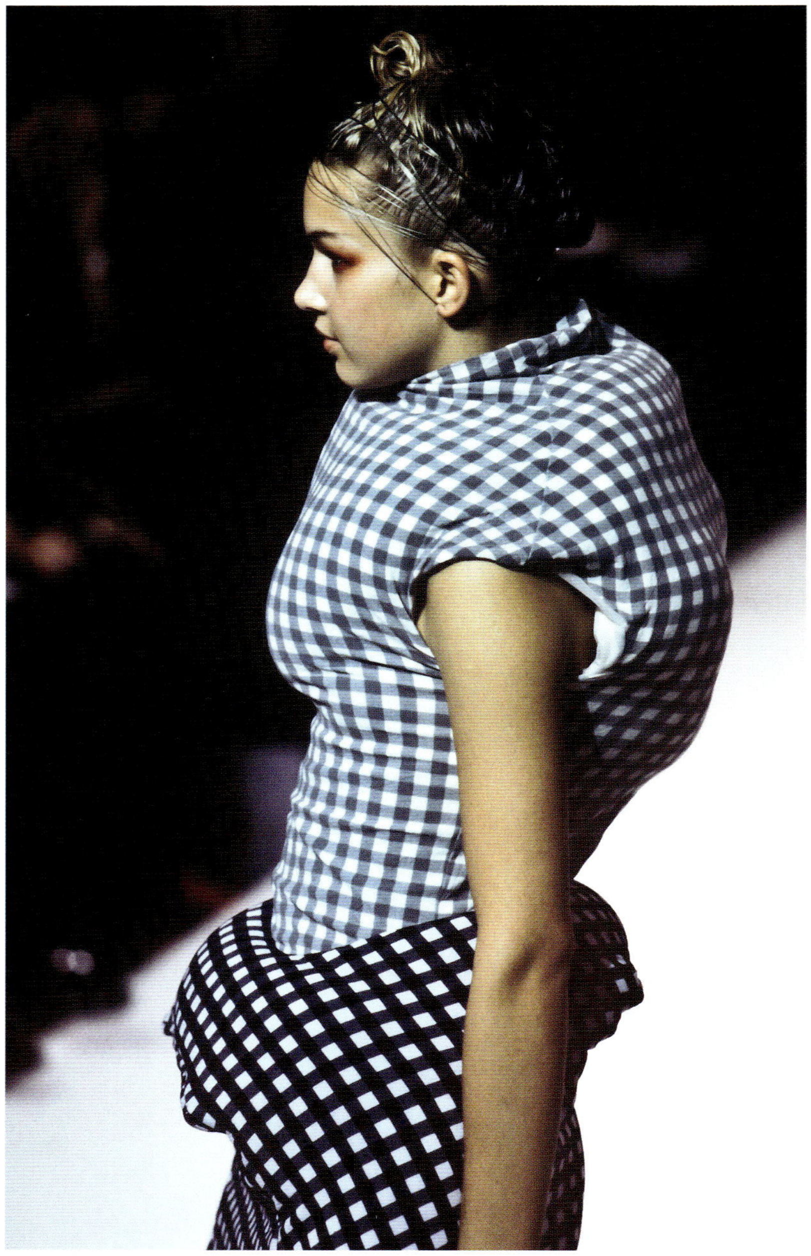

BODY MEETS DRESS, DRESS MEETS BODY DRESS | REI KAWAKUBO FOR COMME DES GARÇONS, 1997

BODY MEETS DRESS, DRESS MEETS BODY ENSEMBLE | REI KAWAKUBO FOR COMME DES GARÇONS, 1997

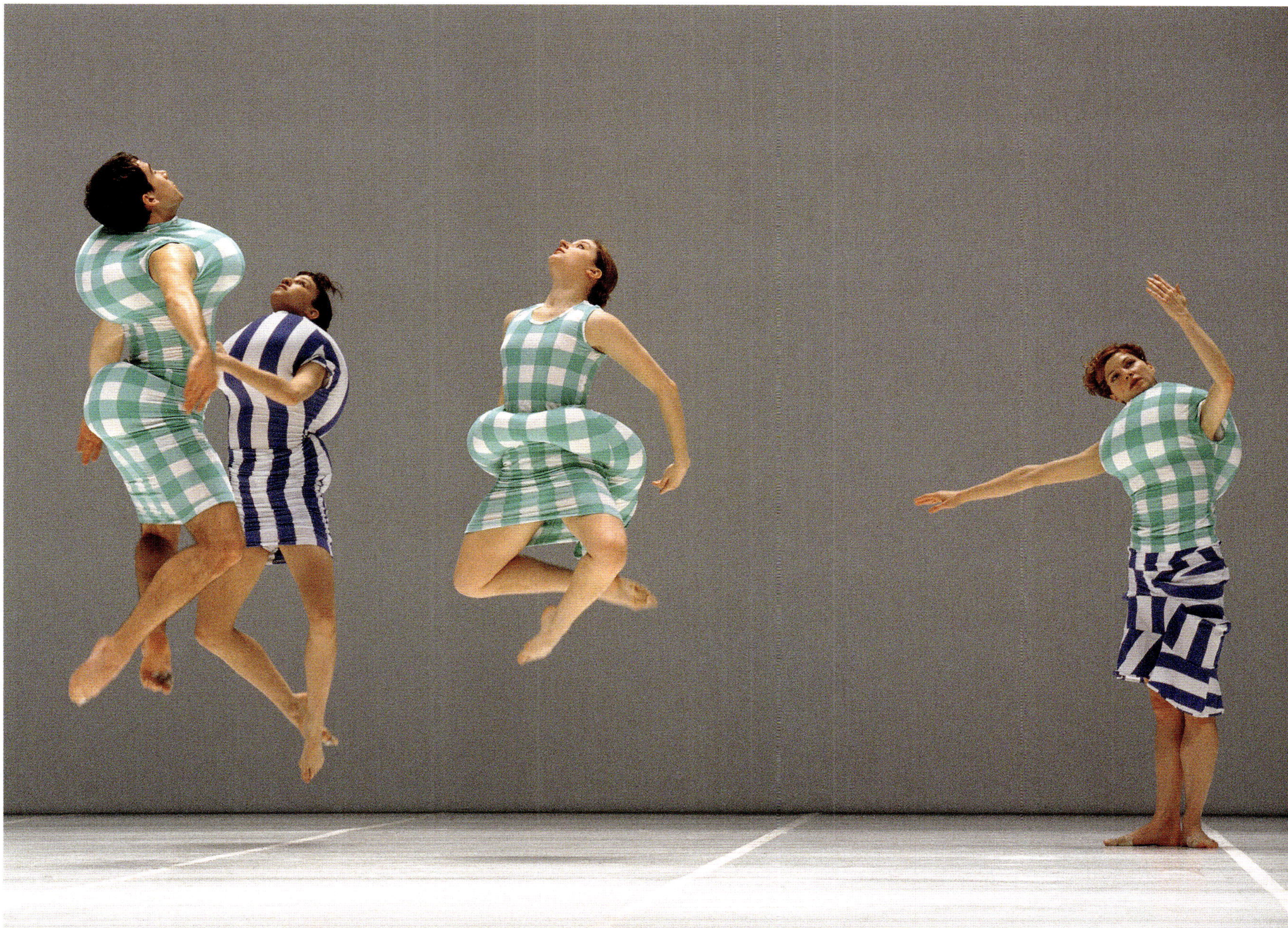

SCENARIO, PERFORMED BY THE MERCE CUNNINGHAM DANCE COMPANY IN COSTUMES BY REI KAWAKUEO | MERCE CUNNINGHAM, 1998

SCENARIO, PERFORMED BY THE MERCE CUNNINGHAM DANCE COMPANY IN COSTUMES BY REI KAWAKUEO | MERCE CUNNINGHAM, 1997

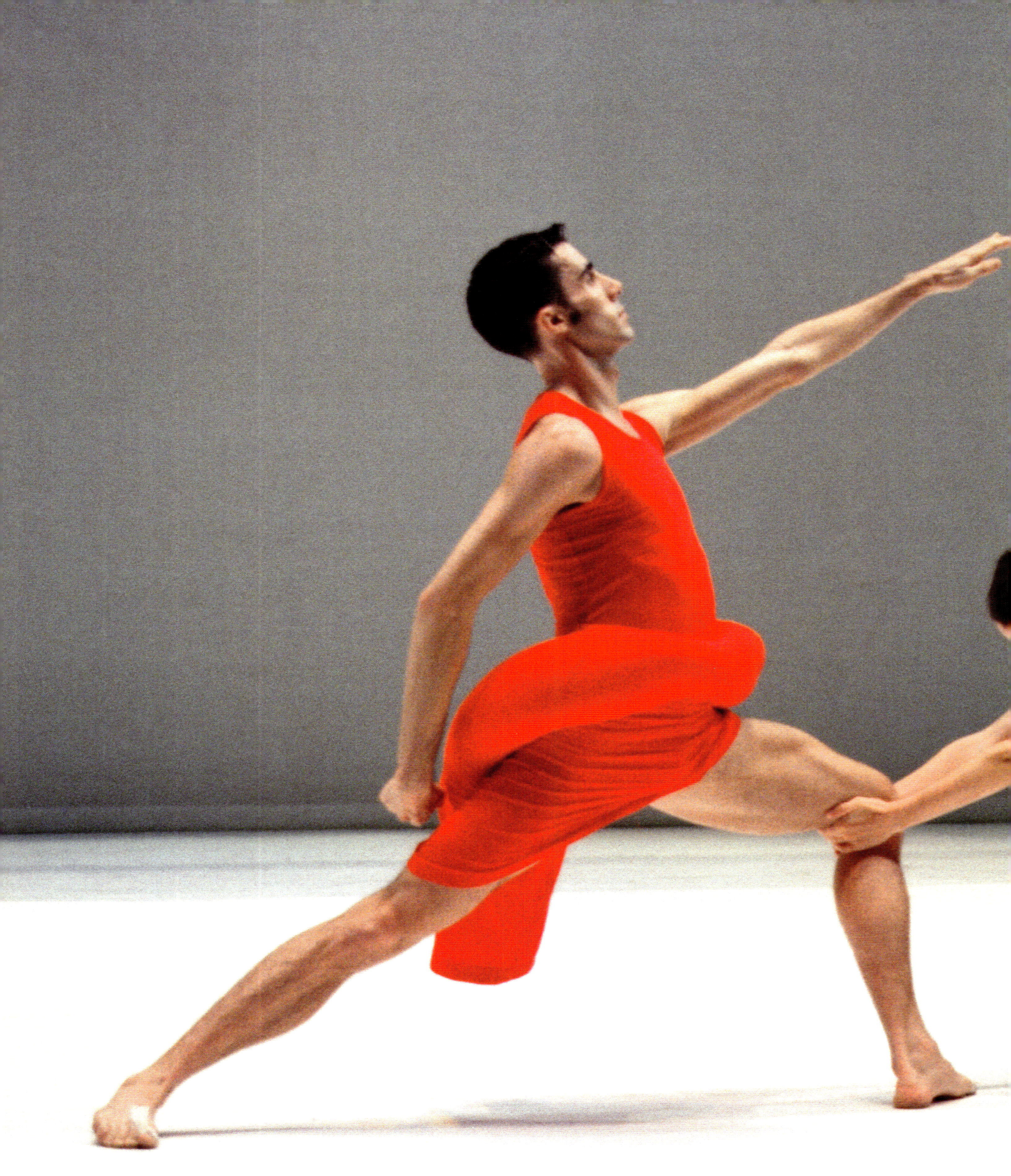

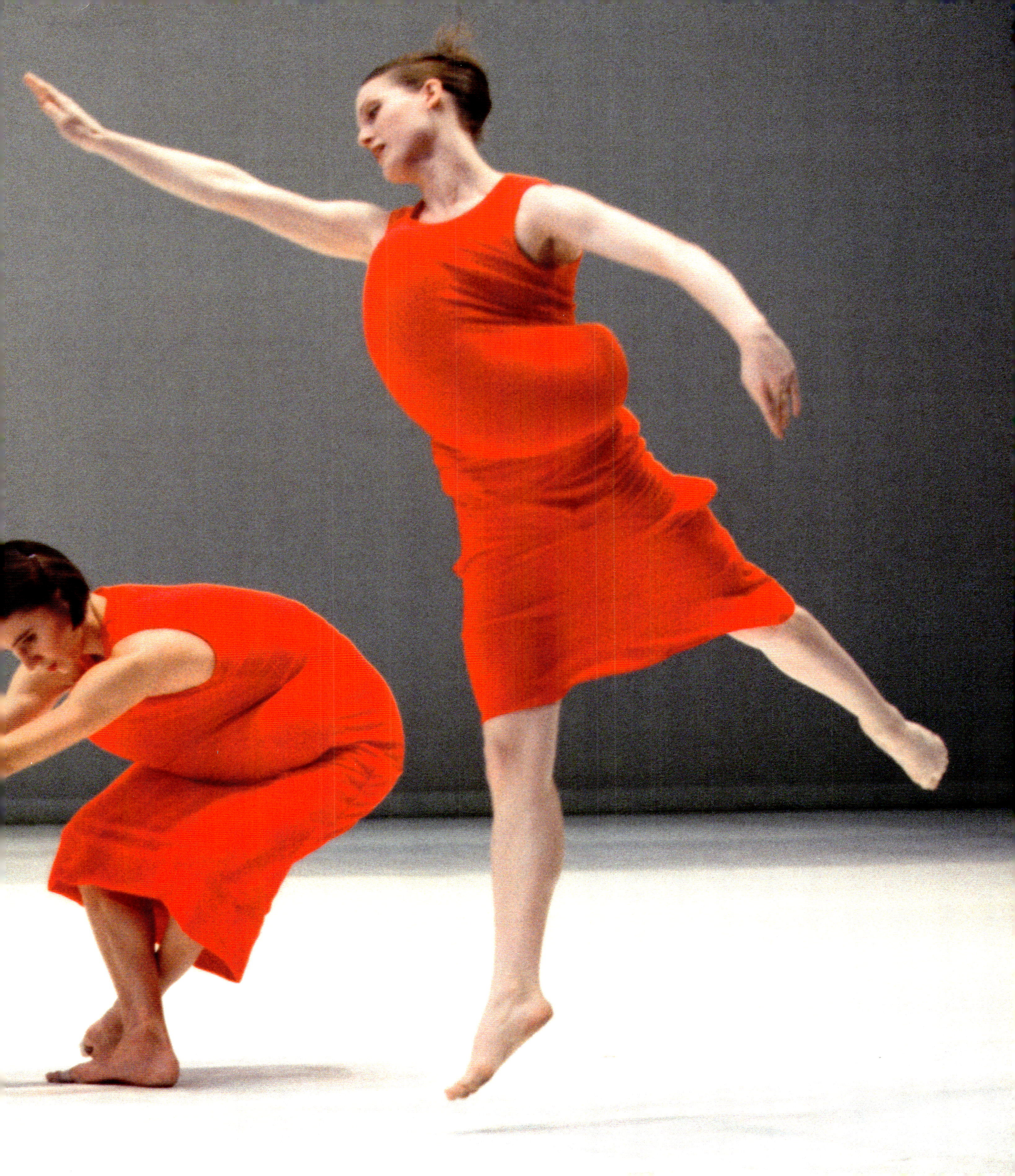

NAN GOLDIN

JAMES KING

FASHION MIRRORS SOCIETY.

While the whims of the industry and its penchant toward extremes of what is "in" and what is "out" may seem arbitrary at best or, at worst, tyrannical, they are in fact merely responding to the culture at large. Trends exist in garments but also in models—their looks, their body types. Even drugs have their heyday before becoming passé. Nowhere is this more clearly illustrated than in "James Is a Girl," the *New York Times* story by Jennifer Egan with accompanying photographs by Nan Goldin (b. 1953). Published on February 4, 1996, under the editorship of Joseph Lelyveld, Egan's article is not a glamorous portrait of sixteen-year-old female model James King (b. 1979) or the fashion industry. Egan shadows King as she makes her debut in Paris and then struts down catwalks in New York. Egan notes that King is a pierced and tattooed teen who chain-smokes, avidly imbibes alcohol, and continues working despite first a hacking cough, then shingles, and later pinkeye. While the story never mentions heroin, King was an active addict at the time, sobering up after the death of her boyfriend, Davide Sorrenti, a year to the day after the *New York Times* story ran. While Egan's text is powerful and poignant, Goldin's images showed James King's reality to devastating effect in ways words simply could not capture.

Nan Goldin came to prominence with *The Ballad of Sexual Dependency* (1986), a 700-plus-picture series taken between 1979 and 1986. Intimate and raw, Goldin's pictures displayed gender fluidity, partying, lust, love, and loss—primarily from the AIDS epidemic. By chronicling her own life and the lives of her friends, Goldin captured society at a turning point, becoming its mirror.

This same truth-telling is evident in Goldin's work with James King. As a model, King unabashedly confronts Goldin's lens, but her gaze is often the hazy one of a drug user. Her eyes are puffy, when not dilated or red. There is no innocence in the pictures of King, and the only time she looks happy and alive is next to Carolyn Murphy, backstage before the Spring/Summer 1996 Ghost show put on by London designer Tanya Sarne during New York Fashion Week. Goldin highlights the manufactured beauty of the fashion industry, and its ability to swallow people whole. Fashion reporter Patrick McCarthy put it bluntly: "Fashion eats people up and you know what? It attracts people that are willing to be eaten up. It is a very self-destructive

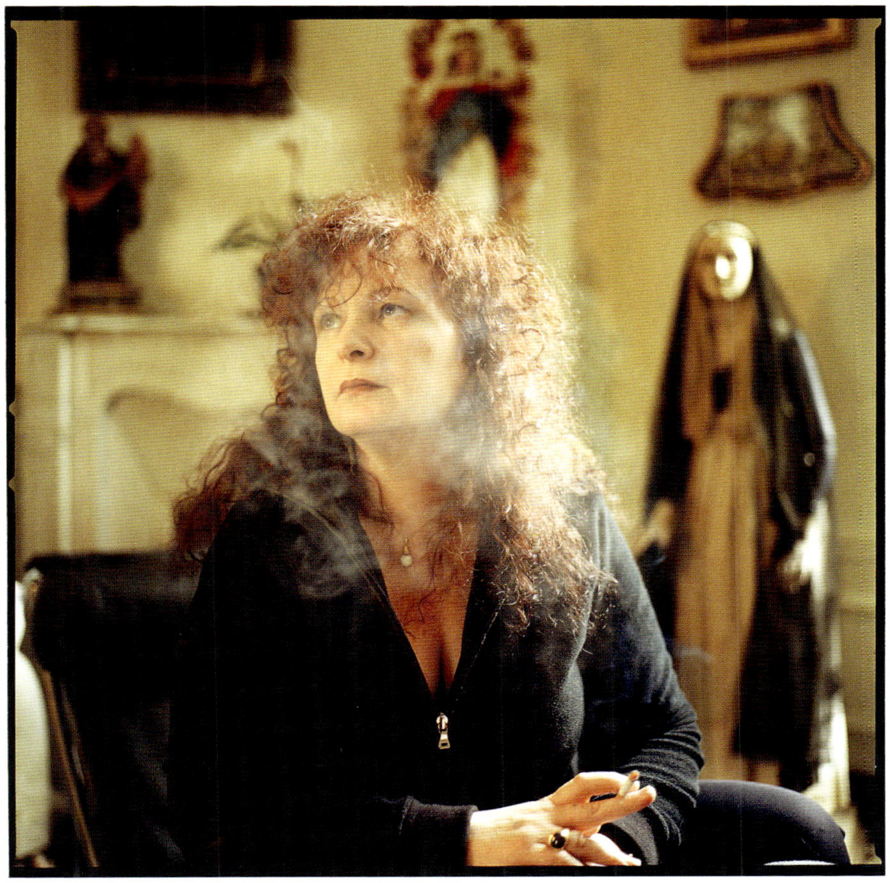

NAN GOLDIN

industry, which is probably what keeps it alive. It eats its young."[42] King later reflected, "At sixteen years old, you think you know everything . . . you don't know anything at all. I had grand illusions of what I though modeling would be. . . . I didn't realize the weight of responsibility that I would carry. I became very successful, and I didn't know how to handle that. . . . I experimented with drugs . . . [but] quickly realized this wasn't the path for me."[43]

Yet, "James Is a Girl" sparked a national controversy, as if Goldin alone were personally responsible for inventing "heroin chic." Rather than having her work seen as art or photojournalism, Goldin, because of her momentary association with the fashion industry, was accused of and berated for glamorizing a deadly lifestyle. Even President Bill Clinton chimed in, bellowing, "The glorification of heroin is not creative, it is destructive,"[44] wrongly blaming "Dan [*sic*] Goldin."[45]

Later that year, Nan Goldin was the subject of a major retrospective at the Whitney Museum (October 3, 1996–January 5, 1997). Her enduring, memorable work has since been given a retrospective at the Centre Pompidou in Paris. Appreciated there, Goldin was admitted to the French Legion of Honor in 2006.

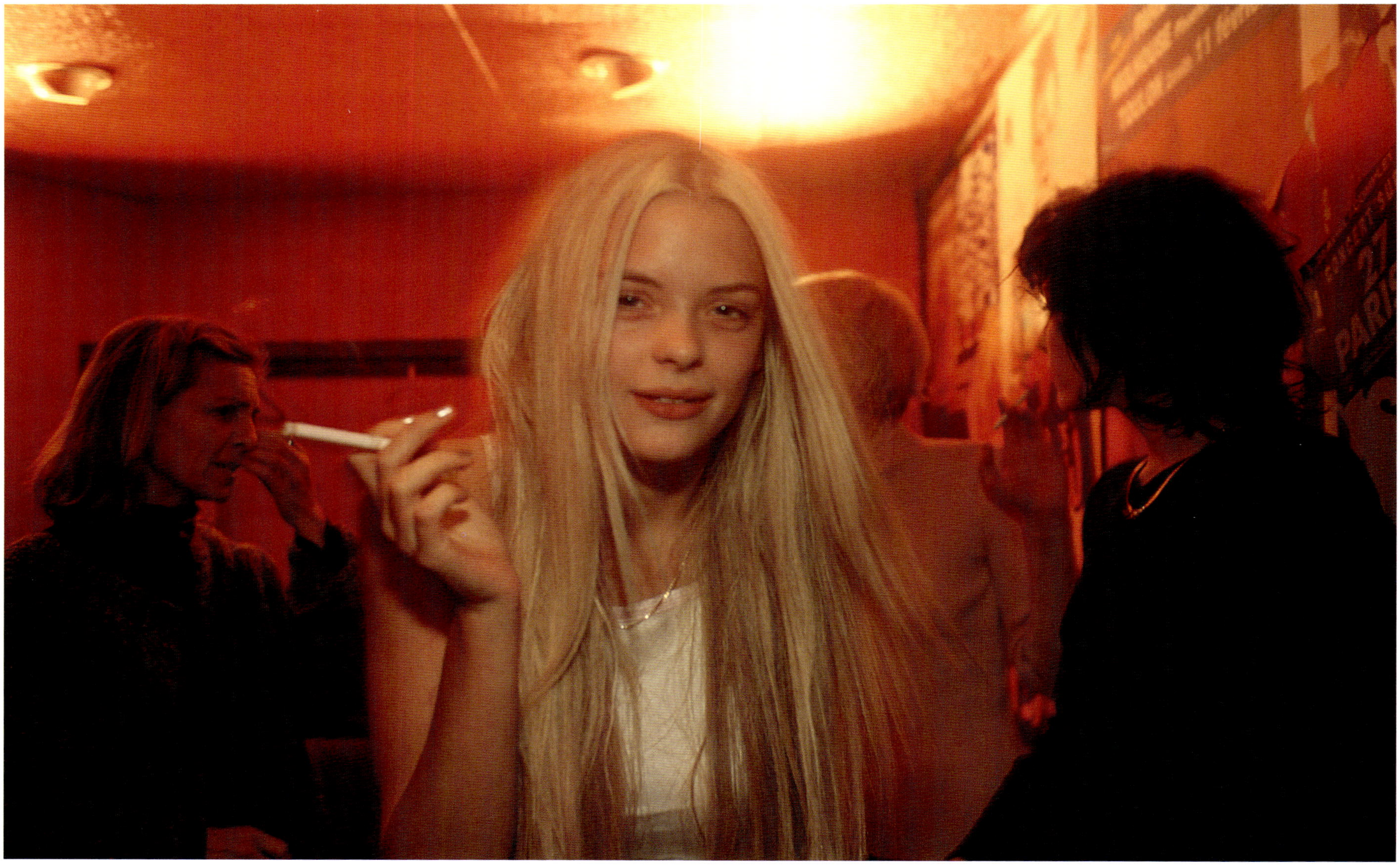

JAMES BACKSTAGE AT JEAN COLONNA, PARIS | C-PRINT | NAN GOLDIN, 1995

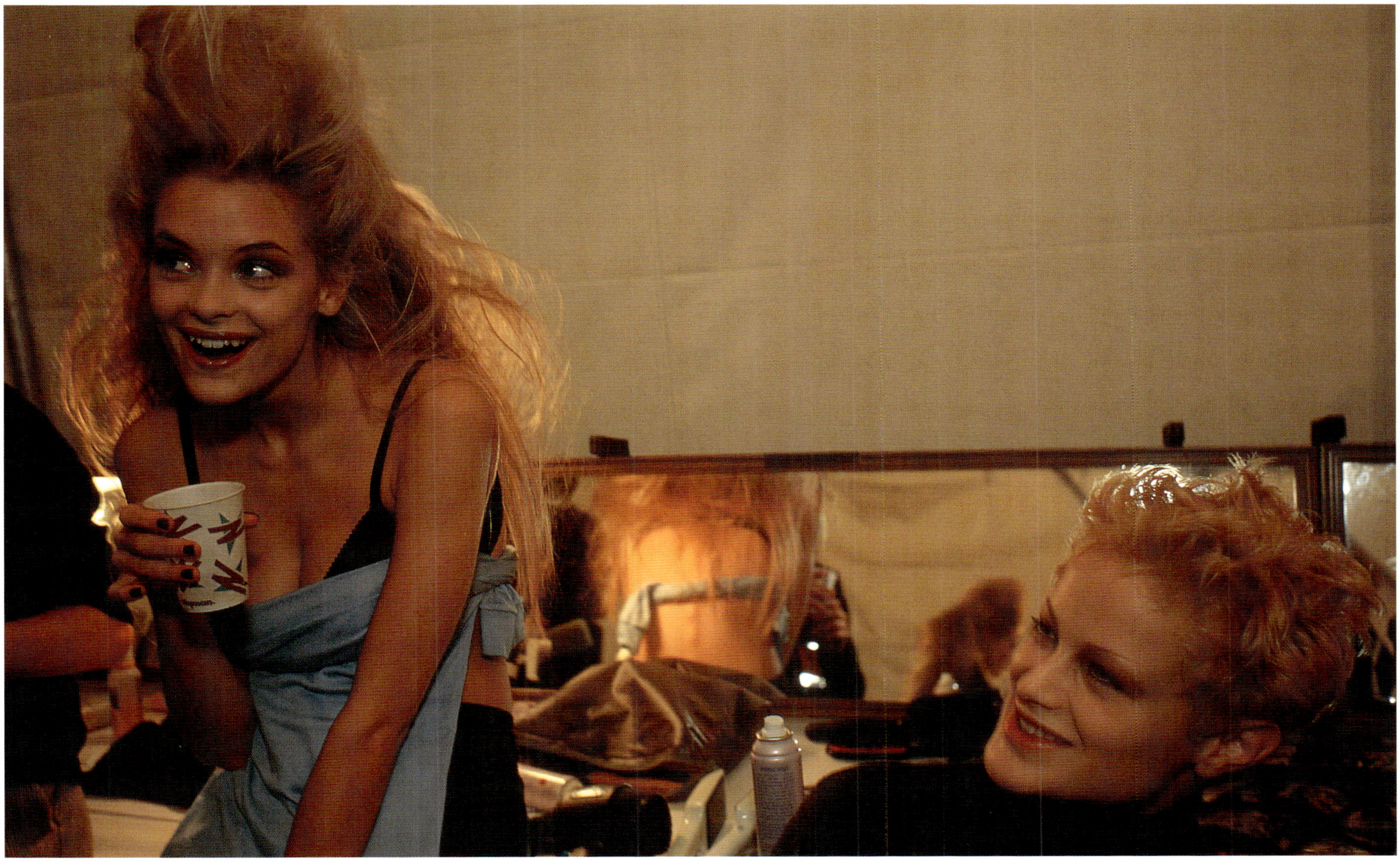

JAMES BACKSTAGE AT THE GHOST SHOW WITH CAROLYN MURPHY, NEW YORK | C-PRINT | NAN GOLDIN, 1995

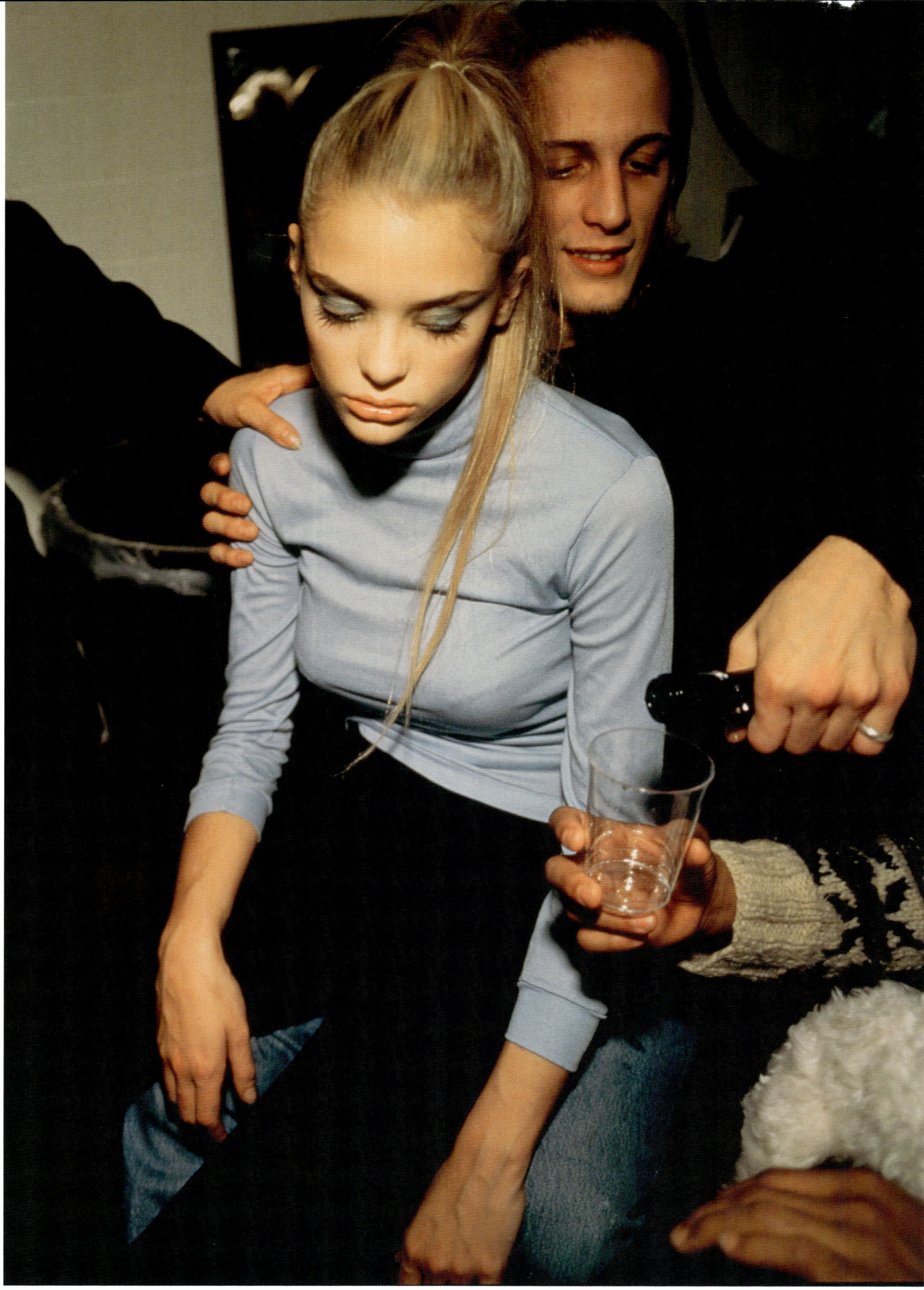

< *JAMES ON KYLE'S LAP BACKSTAGE AT THE MAGSHONI SHOW, NEW YORK* | C-PRINT | NAN GOLDIN, 1995

PETER SAVILL

.E + LACOSTE

DESIGN WORTHY TO

be called such resonates through time. Thirty-five years after Peter Saville (b. 1955) placed the CP 1919 pulsar wave on the cover of Joy Division's 1979 debut album, *Unknown Pleasures*, it has become a popular tattoo—thus, permanent design. And while Lacoste tattoos are not as prevalent, they do exist. While this is a testament to the brand's power, it is also a cultural indicator of identity today, as self and logo merge.

The Lacoste brand was born from a need, and further cemented by a myth. Tennis star Jean René Lacoste (1904–1996) dispensed of the impractical long-sleeved, starched shirts normally worn on the tennis court, adopting instead a cotton petit piqué polo, which he then began manufacturing in 1933. As for the infamous reptile logo, a decade earlier French Davis Cup captain Allan Muhr bet Lacoste an alligator suitcase if he won a key match. Today most assume the crocodile emblem grew from Lacoste's animalistic aggressiveness on the tennis court.

For the French brand's eightieth birthday, design director Christophe Pillet and creative director Felipe Oliveira Baptista, who became enamored with British design, pop culture, and Peter Saville's work during his years at Kingston University, invited Saville to help Lacoste celebrate. While Saville is a regular collaborator with a long history of working with fashion houses (like Yohji Yamamoto and Givenchy), he has made damning comments about the ephemeral industry, flippantly referring to its tendency toward "existentialism one season, and polka dots the next."[46]

Despite Saville's condescending quip, the London Design Award winner was given nearly free rein by the brand, as were past Lacoste collaborators. In 2009, the Campana Brothers featured the Lacoste logo multiplying like an illegal Florida breeding ground, and a year later, Li Xiaofeng made a shirt of porcelain shards—the design later digitally printed on cotton. The only consistent edict from above? Leave the logo alone.

Having never shed the idealistic post-punk ideology of his youth, Saville could hardly have been expected not to rebel; he presented a "completely fucked crocodile" that "digitally

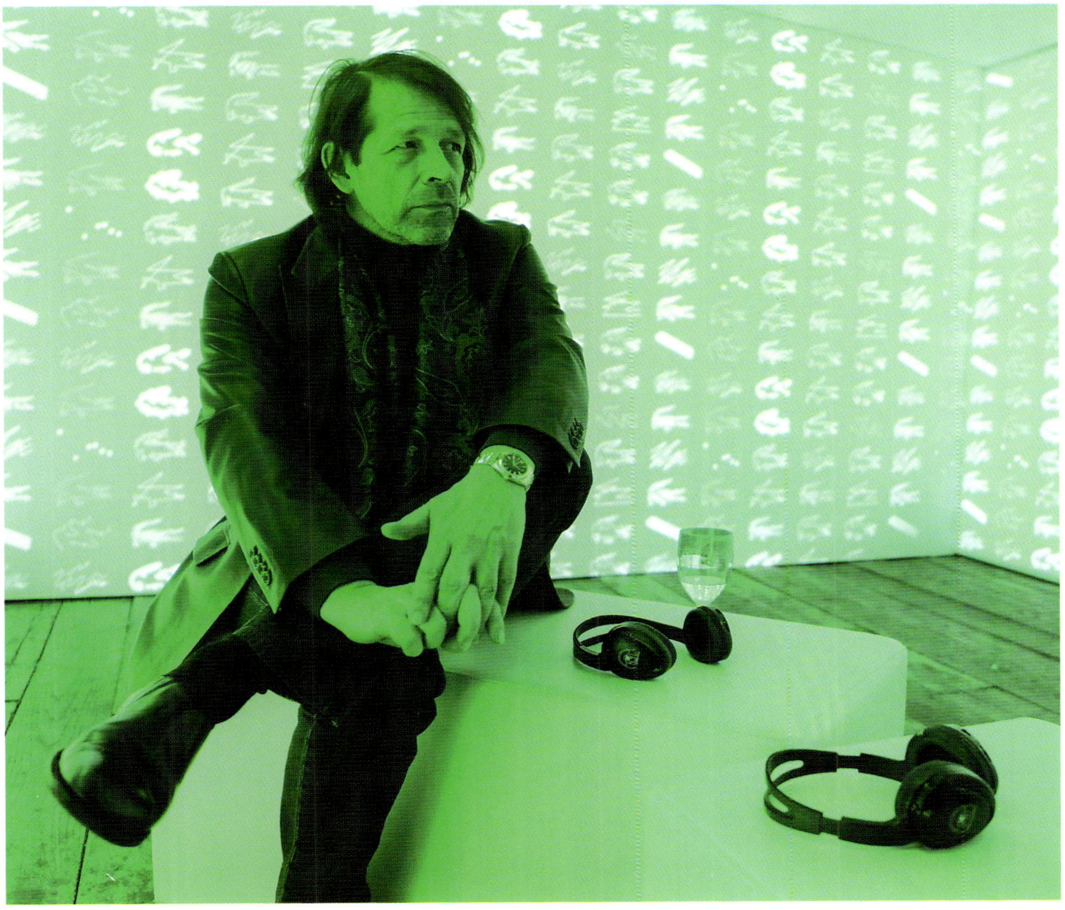

PETER SAVILLE

shattered" the sacred reptile in eighty different ways (his ode to the brand's anniversary).[47] Explaining the reaction to his work, Saville recalls: "Of course, there were gasps, 'What has he done?!' But the images were funny. They had a wit to them. So, after this sharp intake of breath, eventually some smiles followed. A sense of 'Why not?' went around the table. It's a crocodile. It's not the Red Cross, it's not the church, the military; it was someone's nickname woven in for fun."[48]

Saville's disfigured reptile, now comprised of dots, squiggles, and jagged lines, was available as a true limited edition. (A total of eighty women's and eighty men's shirts, each given one of Saville's eighty croc logos, were made.) The brand also released a limited production run of Saville × Lacoste shirts—with eight logos to choose from—that was more readily available to consumers.

Peter Saville's collaboration with Lacoste brilliantly illustrated that its logo is so ingrained in today's society that nothing can strip away its consumer power. While that might be a CEO's dream, it has damning societal implications, giving Saville's critique a crocodile bite.

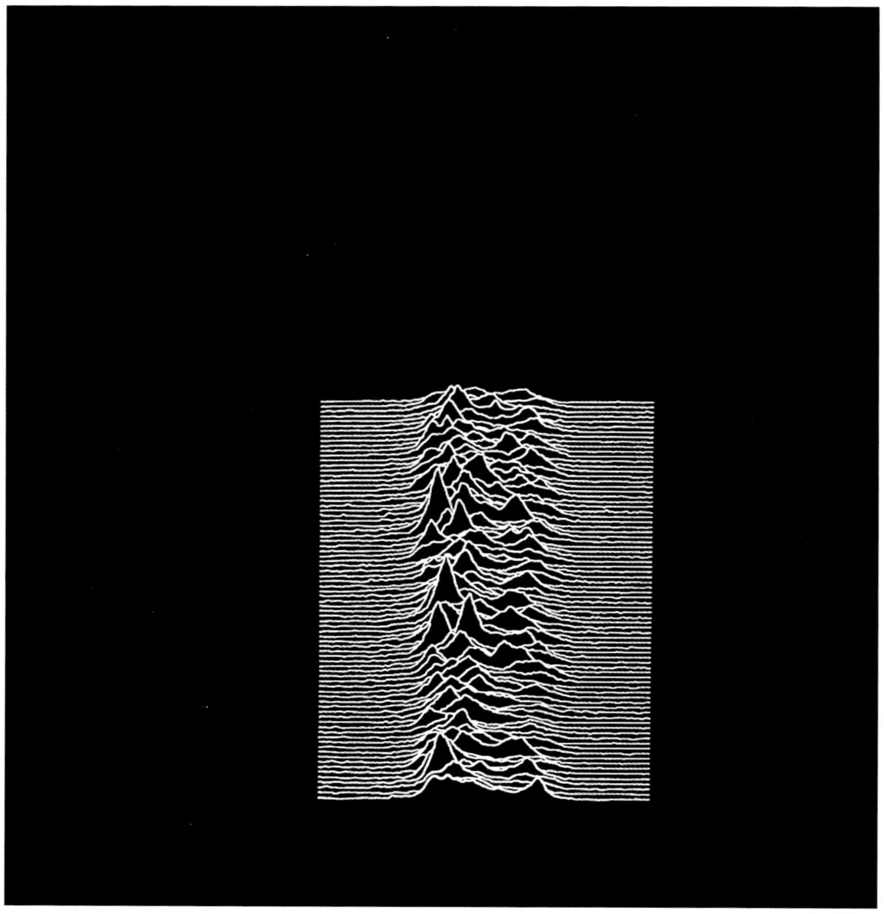

ALBUM COVER ART FOR *UNKNOWN PLEASURES* | JOY DIVISION AND PETER SAVILLE FOR FACTORY RECORDS, 1979

EIGHTY REINTERPRETED LACOSTE LOGOS | PETER SAVILLE, 2013

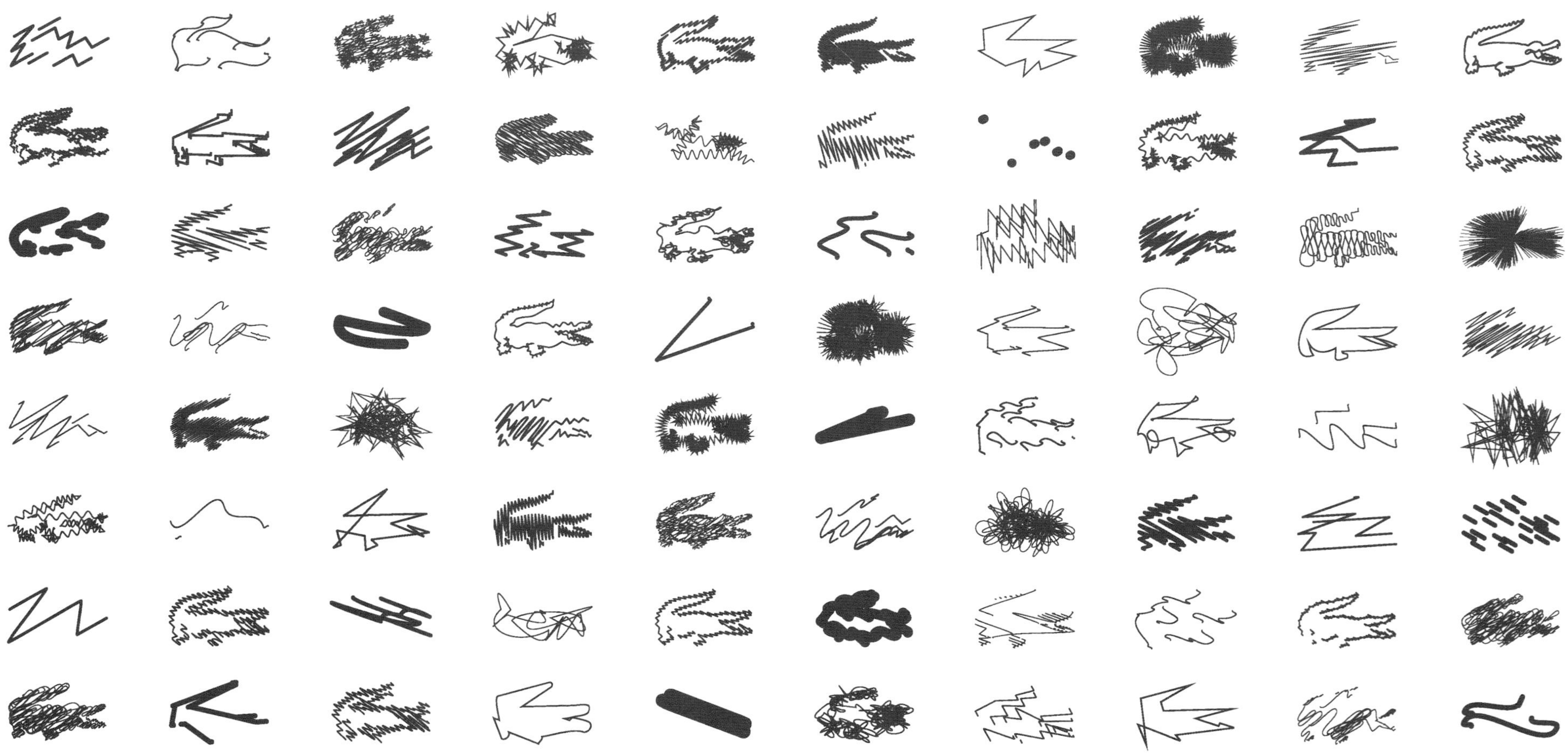

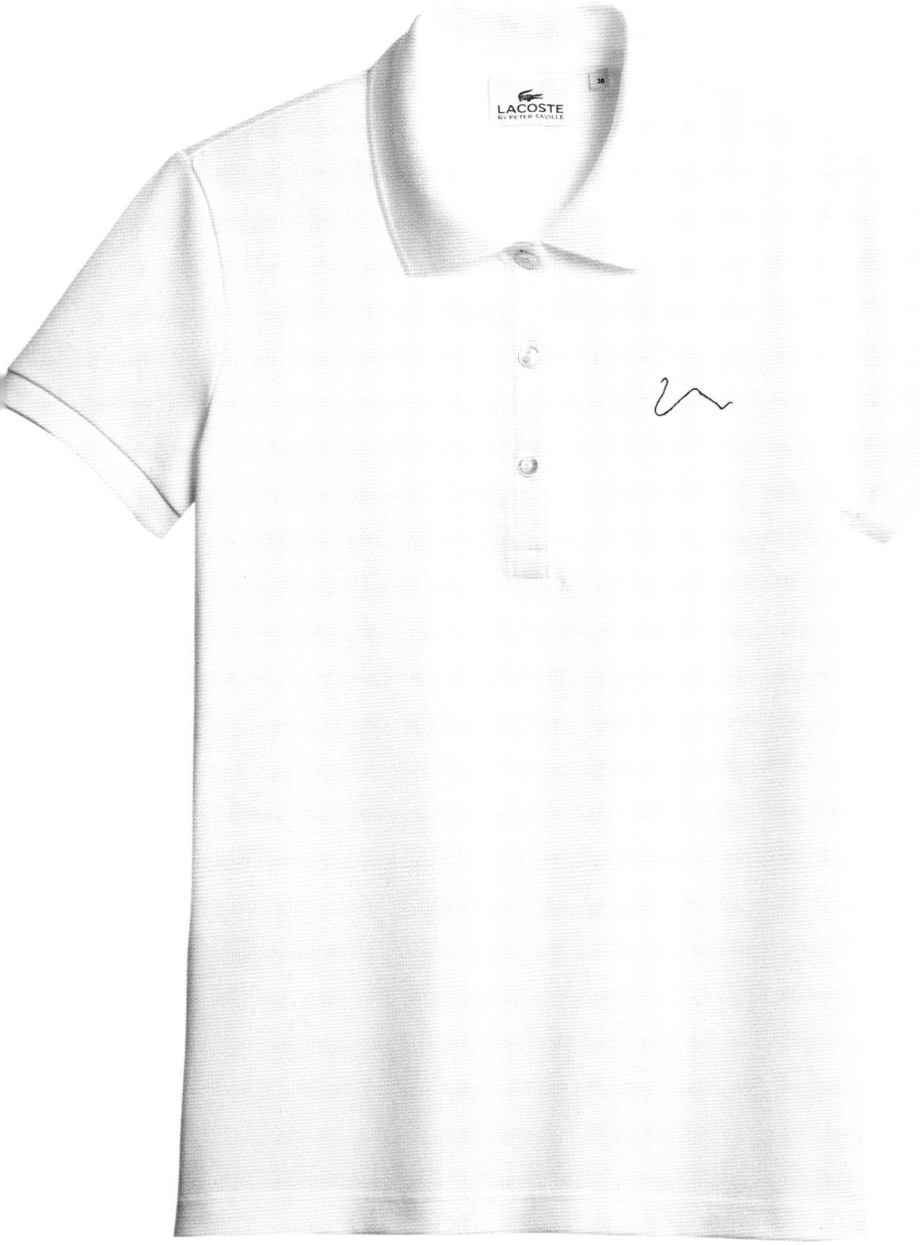

POLO SHIRT WITH PETER SAVILLE–REINTERPRETED LOGO | LACOSTE, 2013

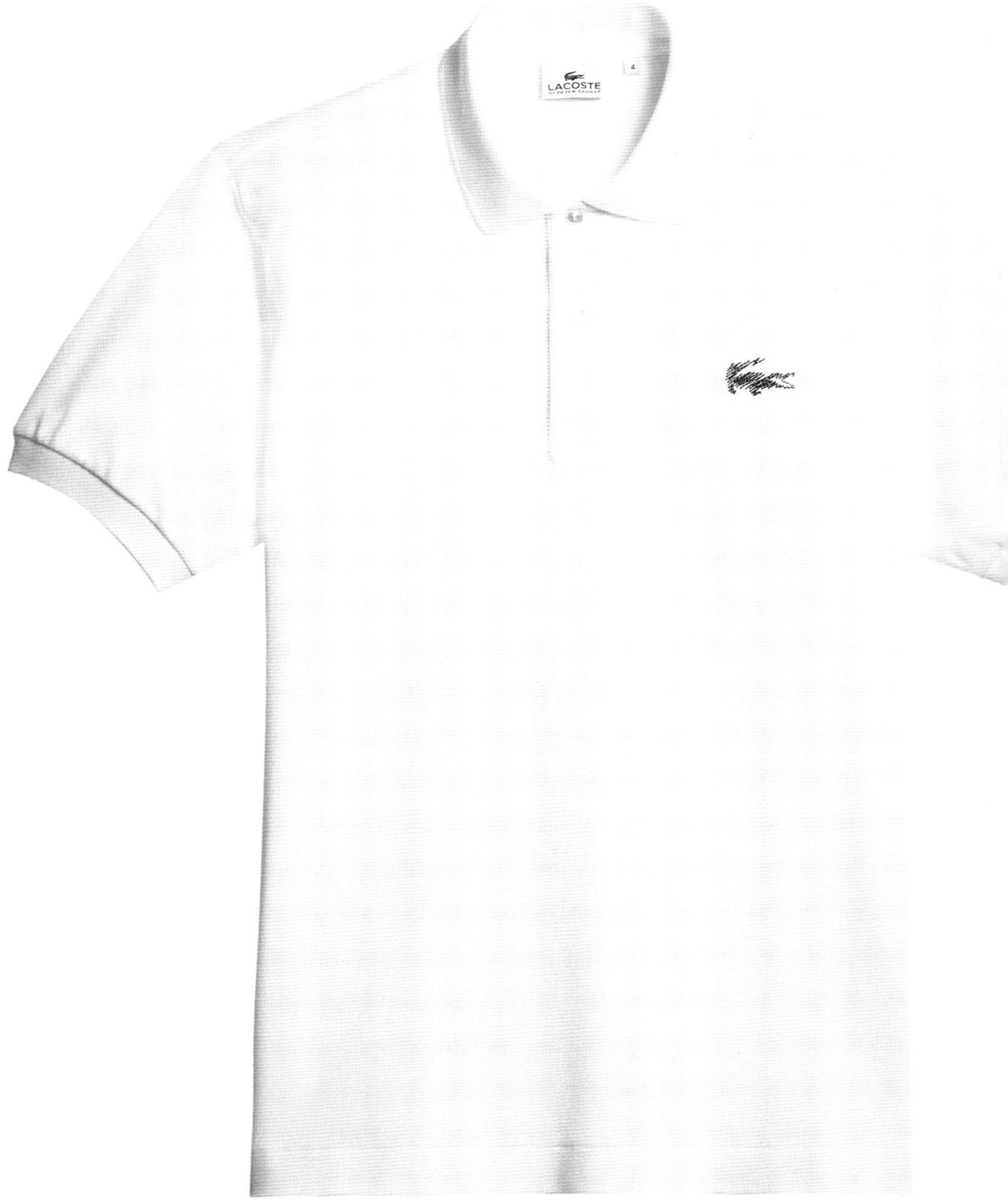

POLO SHIRT WITH PETER SAVILLE–REINTERPRETED LOGO | LACOSTE, 2013

JEFF KOONS + ST

ELLA McCARTNEY

AMERICAN ARTIST JEFF Koons (b. 1955) first called an inflatable bunny "art" in 1979. The readymade work was reminiscent of Marcel Duchamp, with a major wink toward postmodern appropriation. Author Gregor Muir, now the executive director of the Institute of Contemporary Art in London, excitedly explained that Koons's stainless steel cast of an inflatable toy rabbit took a common object, rescued it from the detritus of everyday life, and raised its status to museum-worthy.

Throughout his career, Jeff Koons has continued to revisit this work, exploring it in different forms. In 1986, Koons made the rabbit statuary, casting it in stainless steel. Twenty years later, collaborating with British designer Stella McCartney (b. 1971), Koons miniaturized the rabbit, making a 3-D version in resin and realizing it as a pendant in a more precious metal: platinum. Fifty were made for lovers of fashion and art. McCartney used the *Rabbit Necklace* in her Spring/Summer 2006 advertising campaign—legendary model Kate Moss nibbled seductively on it, making the already must-have accessory even more desirable.

When Stella McCartney was first introduced to Jeff Koons's work, she fawned: "It was love at first sight."[49] McCartney, a Central Saint Martins grad, gathered acclaim for her clean, wearable high-fashion designs during her time as creative director at Chloé. She started her own label in 2001. McCartney possessed no shyness when it came to inviting artists to collaborate, having welcomed painter Gary Hume, illustrator David Remfry, and cartoonist Robert Crumb to contribute to her eponymous label in differing capacities.

McCartney approached Jeff Koons to use his collage-based paintings on her garments, in addition to crafting "cottontail" jewelry together. Koons enthusiastically said yes, and Spring/Summer 2006 London Fashion Week got an injection of art. For the show's finale, Stella McCartney presented five gowns printed with Koonsian paintings, including *Lips* (2000). Worn on models Natasha Poly, Eugenia Volodina, Mariacarla Boscono, Kim Noorda, and Anja Rubik, Jeff Koons's other featured pieces from the mid- to late-1990s became nearly unrecognizable. In the hands of Stella McCartney, Koon's work appears ambiguous, morphed on her dresses and floor-length gowns. Koons, who attended the show, was characteristically over

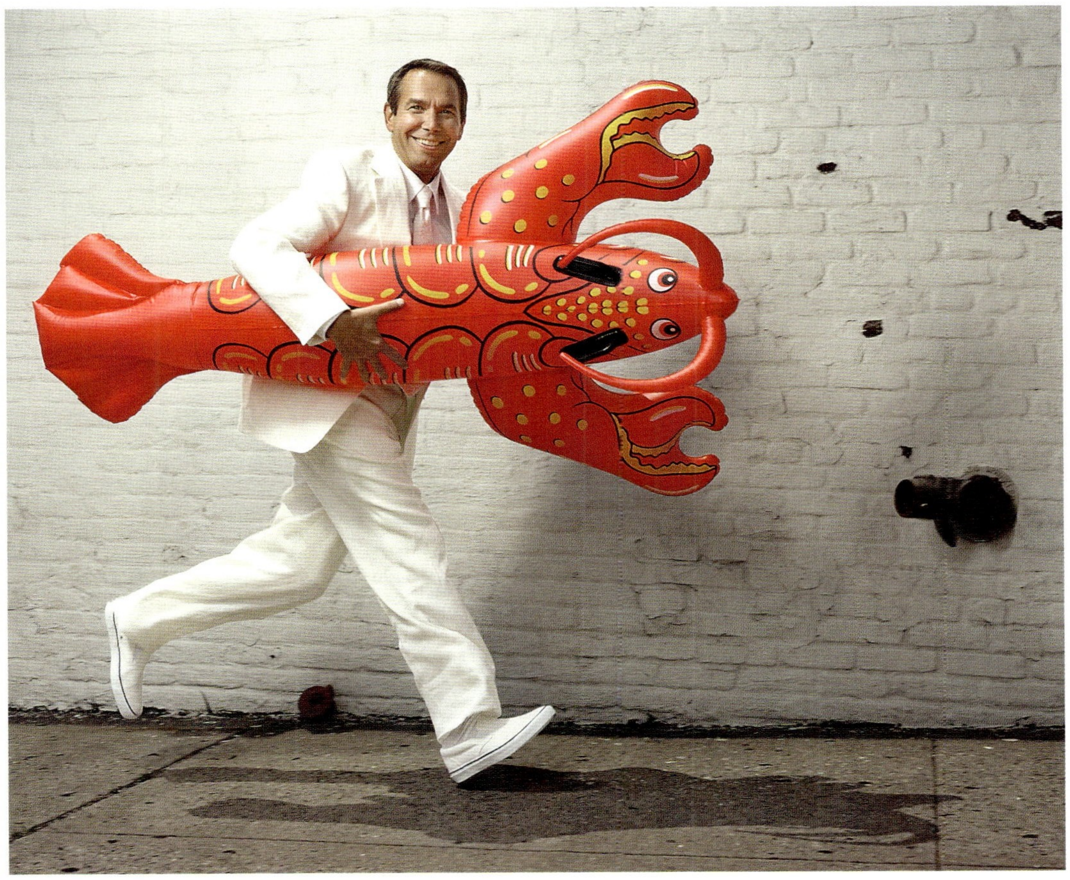

JEFF KOONS

the moon: "I was terribly excited about having some of my pictures printed on her clothes."[50]

Where Koons's thirty-five year interest in mirror-like mediums and, more specifically, bunnies comes from is a bit bizarre. He attributes it to the overlooked beauty of bucolic suburbia, where garden gazing balls are pervasive. Koons considers the ubiquitous lawn ornament to be a type of "generosity," allowing neighbors perspective-shifting fish-eye views in passing. Focusing on generic glee is something of a theme for Koons. Artist Chuck Close suggests that part of the key to understanding Koons is to appreciate that "all of Koons's work hinges on pleasure in some way."[51] So, perhaps Koons paired up with McCartney simply for the fun of it.

The collaborative jaunt into jewelry Koons took with McCartney was originally intended for the fashion world, not the art one. Yet, as if Koons has a type of artistic Midas touch, his fashionable *Rabbit Necklace* ended up at the Museum of Arts and Design at Columbus Circle in their 2011 exhibition *Picasso to Koons: Artist as Jeweler*. With so few pieces made, perhaps placing one on display was a way to spread the joy.

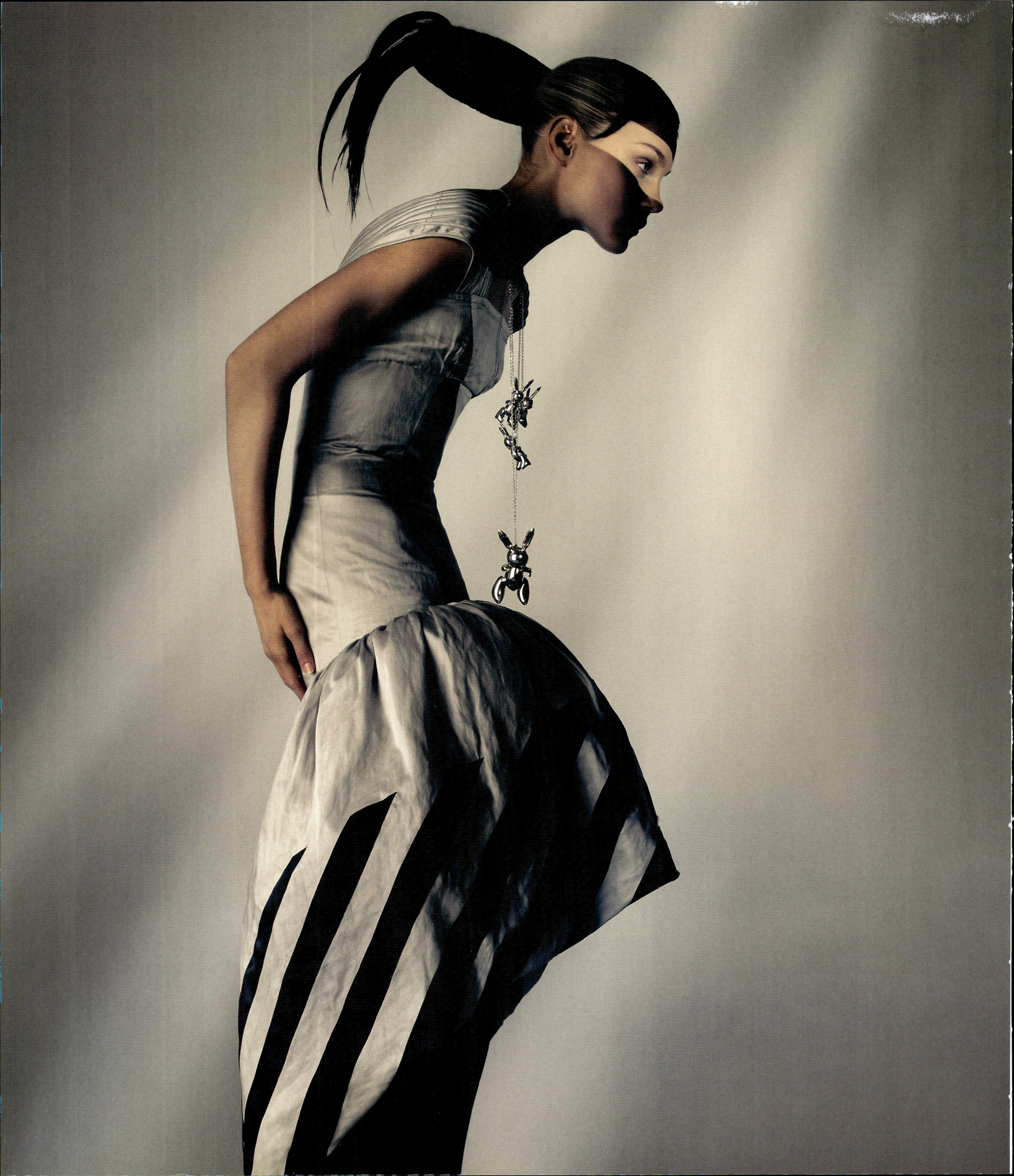

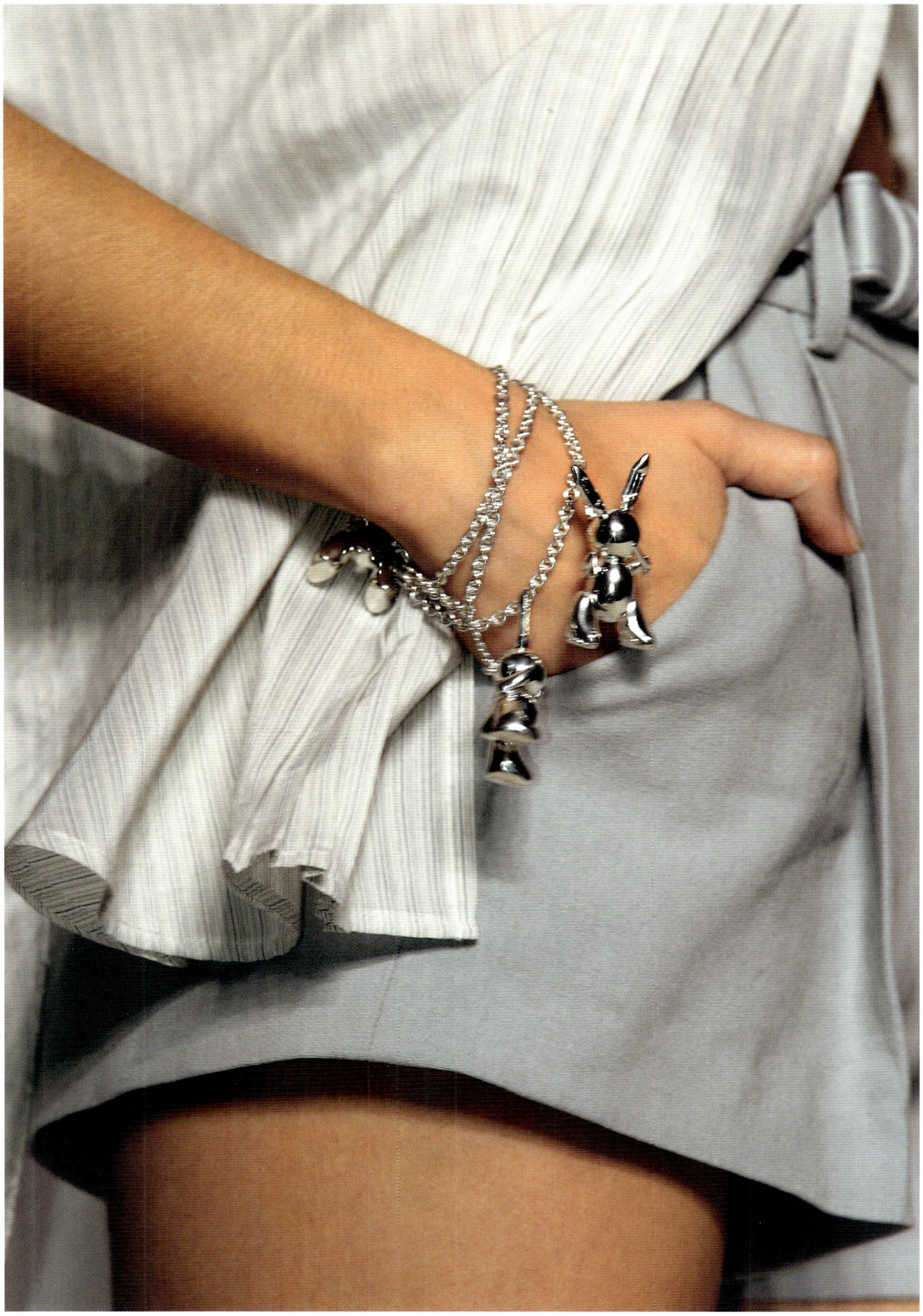

JEFF KOONS–INSPIRED GOWN AND NECKLACES | STELLA McCARTNEY, 2006

BRACELET WITH JEFF KOONS–INSPIRED CHARMS | STELLA McCARTNEY, 2006

DRESS WITH JEFF KOONS-INSPIRED PRINT | STELLA McCARTNEY, 2006

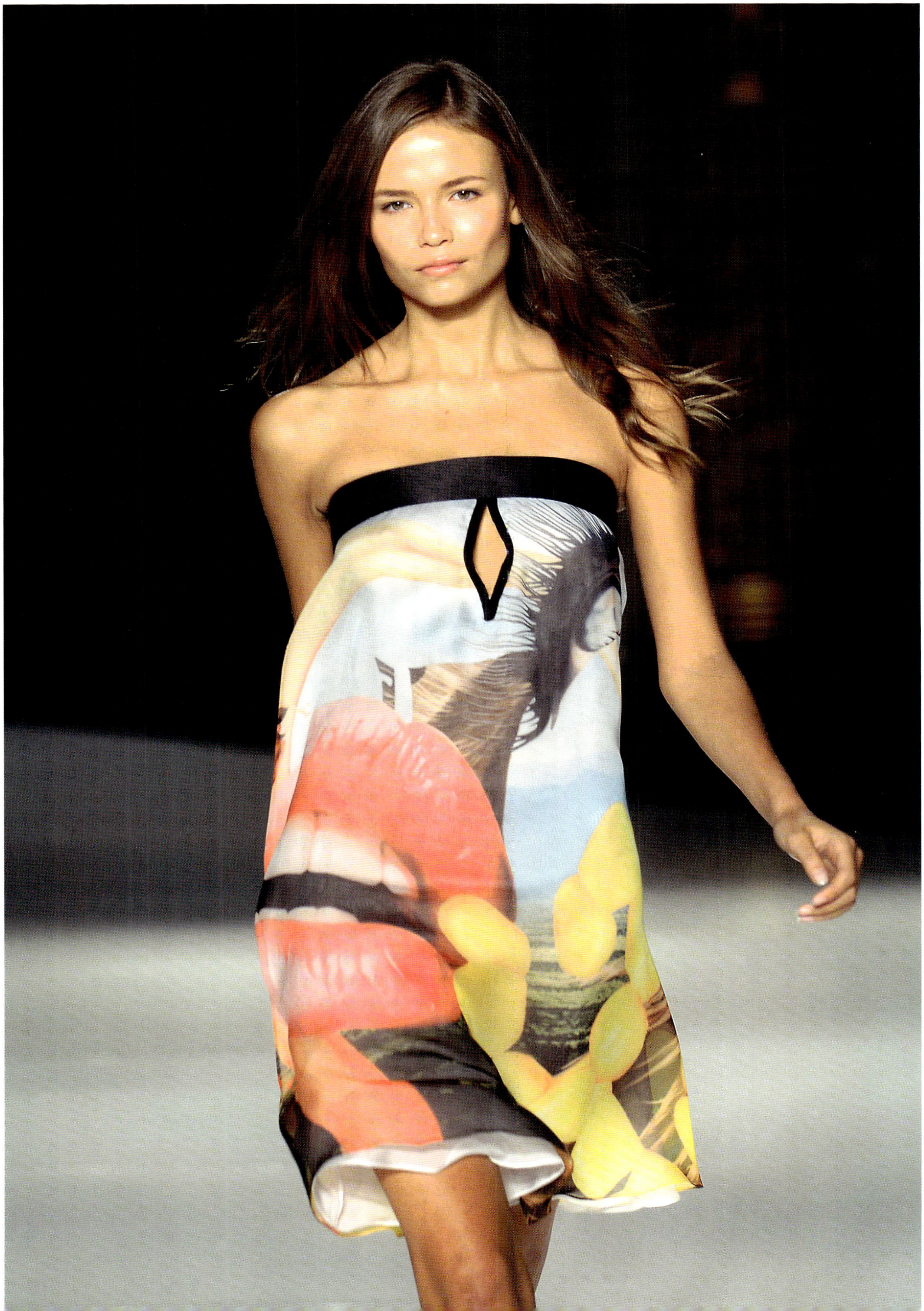

DAMIEN HIRST + AL

EXANDER McQUEEN

DEATH, WHILE IT MIGHT be a physical impossibility in the mind of someone living, is intertwined with existence: the two faces of Janus, *thanatos* and *eros*. The late fashion designer Lee Alexander McQueen (1969–2010) and aging Young British Artist Damien Hirst (b. 1965) shared a macabre obsession with inevitable fatality, so much so that McQueen was called the "Damien Hirst of fashion."[52] Hirst's fly-breeding-and-zapping *A Thousand Years* (1990), infamous pickled tiger shark (1991), and chainsaw-bisected cow with calf—*Mother and Child (Divided)*—from 1993 all place expiry on display. For Alexander McQueen's gothic Fall/Winter 1996–97 collection, the designer placed a skeleton in one of the coveted front row seats. McQueen's Spring/Summer 2001 "Voss" collection was spurred by his interest in photographer Joel-Peter Witkin, who primarily used deceased subjects as models. McQueen's ode to the afterlife was realized by placing robust fetish writer Michelle Olley in a glass box full of rare moths of various species, both alive and not, to replicate an image of Witkin's. McQueen continued this unnerving theme in 2003 with skull scarves, which turned cadaver craniums into a wardrobe-essential, now-ubiquitous accessory. The skull came to further characterize Alexander McQueen in part because the last images taken of him alive (by fashion photographer Tim Walker) featured McQueen and a skeletal head, both smoking.

Damien Hirst started "getting a reputation for being the death guy" as a teenager, when he began visiting the Leeds Anatomy School's morgue to practice drawing.[53] The Goldsmith College graduate, whose 1988 *Freeze* exhibition kicked off the YBA movement, grew butterflies in his bedroom to make money during his starving-artist years. This monetary endeavor inspired his *In and Out of Love* piece of 1991. The work featured metamorphosis on display, as chrysalises hatched into butterflies on the ground floor, while on the second, paintings in blindingly bright hues featured butterflies that appeared to have rested on wet canvas and died, caught.

Recognizing his talent, London contemporary art magazine *Frieze* prophetically featured a lone Damien Hirst butterfly on the cover of its first issue. Hirst continued to work with the winged creatures, first in 2007 with *Doorways to the Kingdom of Heaven*, where they, when arranged

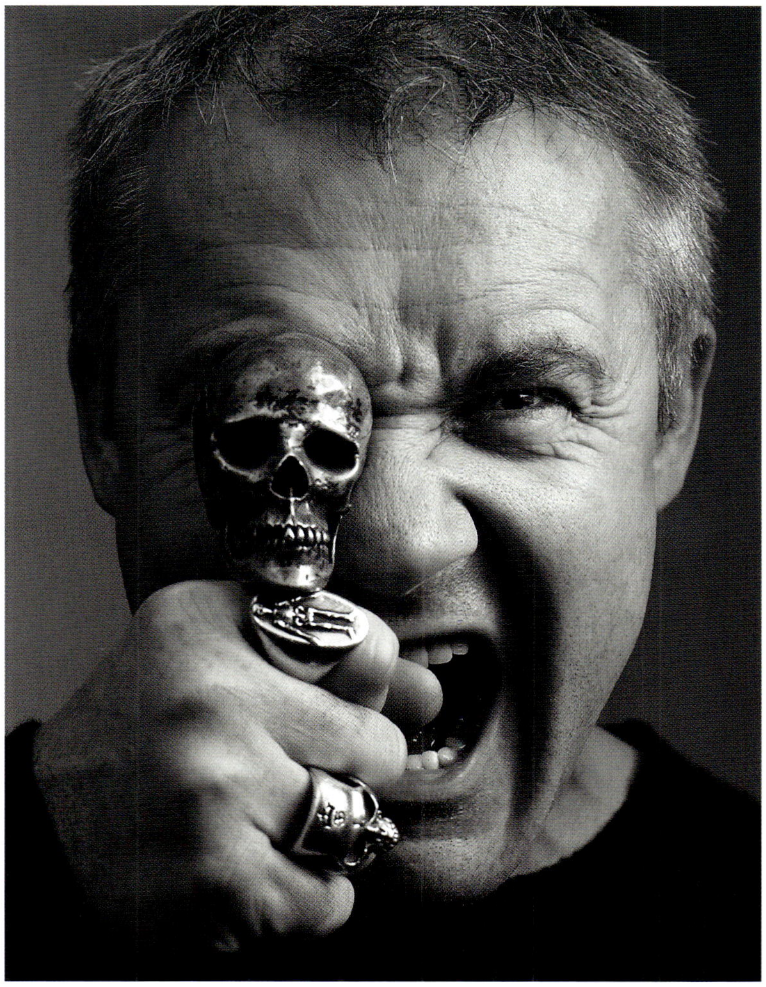

DAMIEN HIRST

en masse, created the appearance of stained-glass windows, and then again in his 2009–12 Entomology series. Ruminating on his work, Hirst quips, "Butterflies are strange, aren't they? They give us hope, because they look alive when they are dead. They aren't rotting corpses."[54] As for corpses, Hirst's 2007 piece *For the Love of God* is a platinum skull with human teeth, encrusted with 8,601 diamonds. It cost £14 million ($23.8 million) to make.

For Damien Hirst's 2013 celebratory limited-edition collaboration with Alexander McQueen (under the creative direction of Sarah Burton), marking the tenth anniversary of the brand's skull scarves, Hirst configured thirty unique designs of butterflies and insects, some in the form of skulls, others in geometric images akin to a kaleidoscope pattern. Hirst's designs stay true to his aesthetic and artistic themes, and seamlessly merge those with the ones present throughout McQueen's oeuvre.

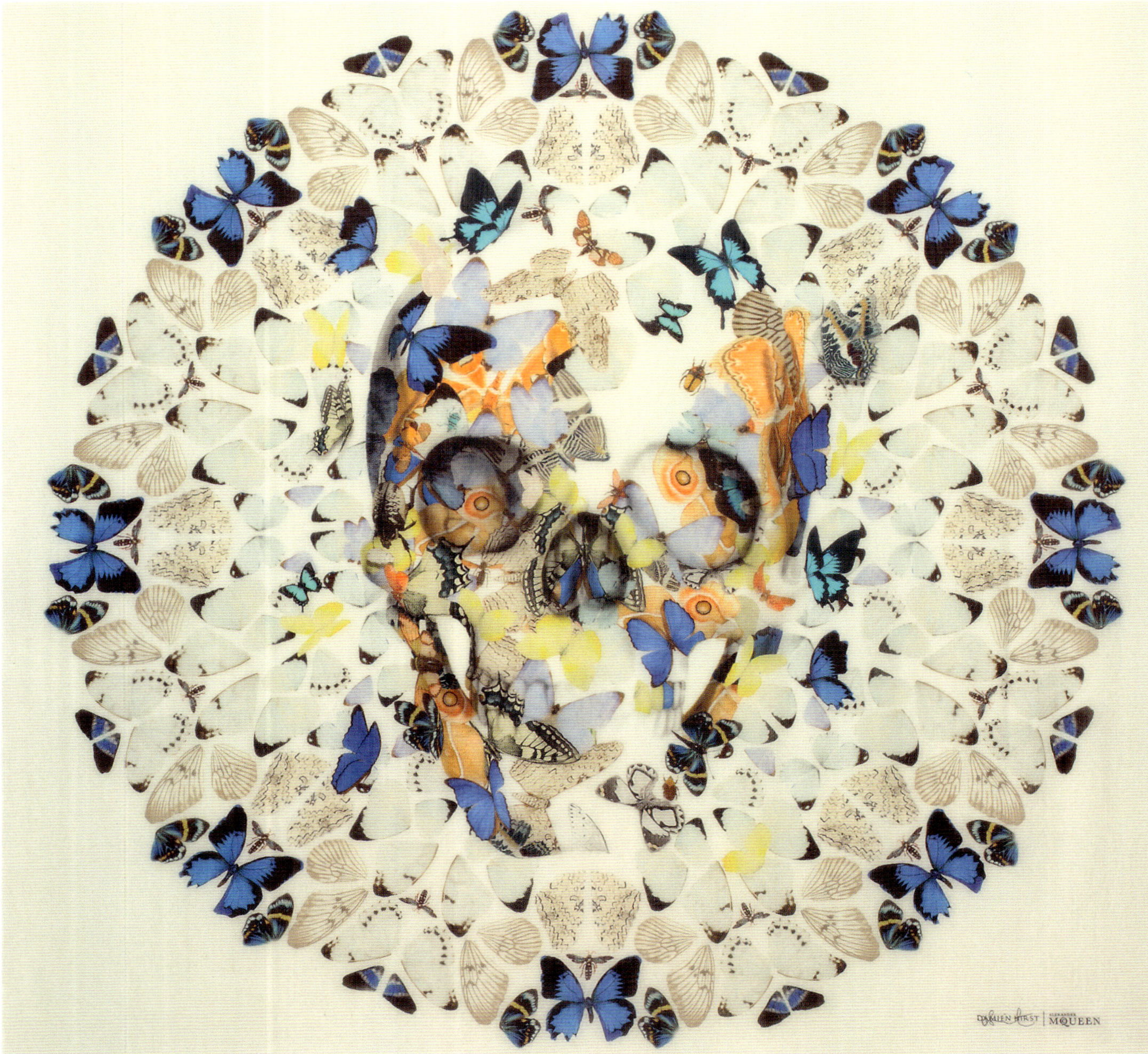

ALEXANDER McQUEEN *FORGIVENESS* CIRCULAR SKULL SCARF | DAMIEN HIRST, 2013

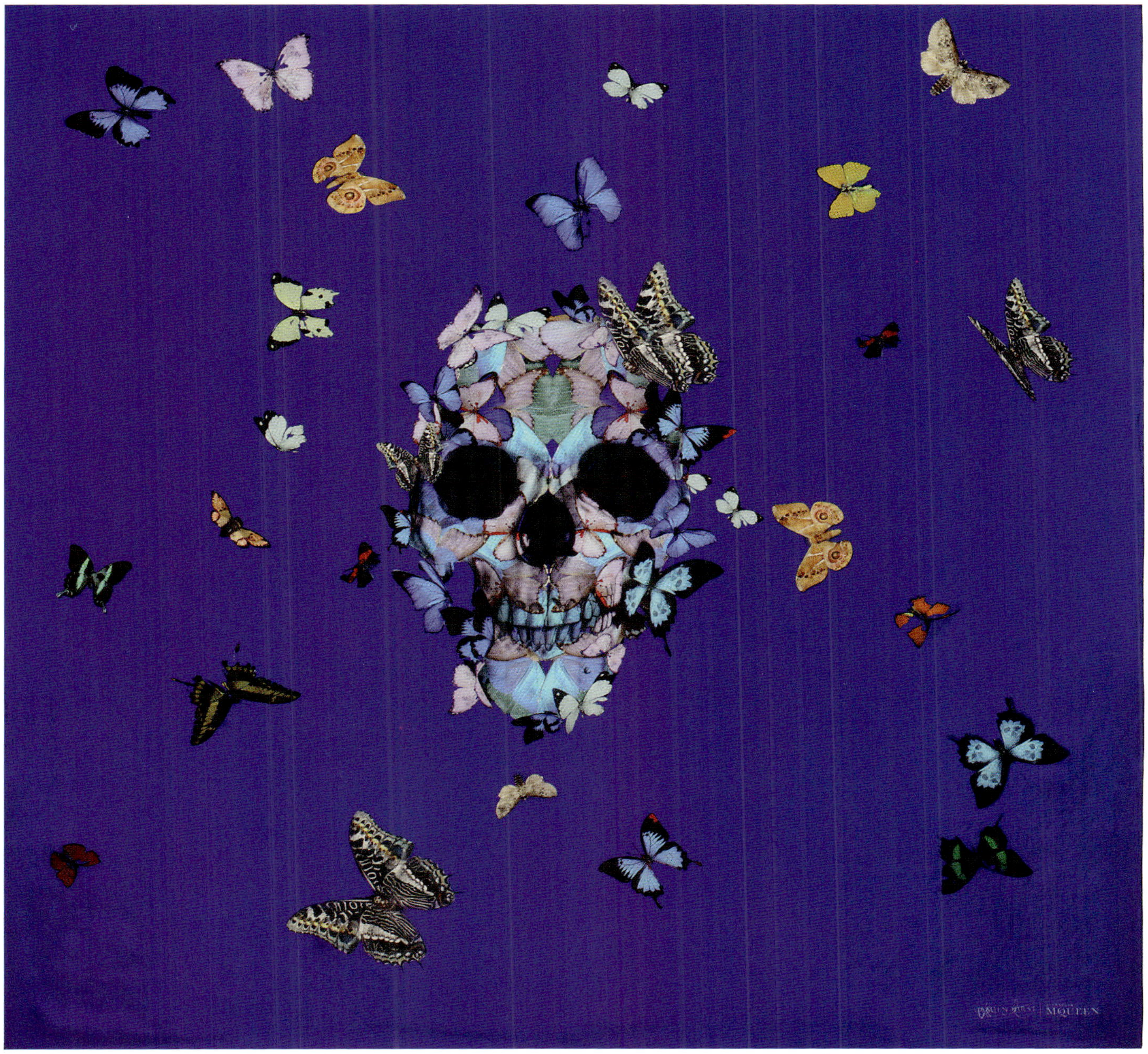

ALEXANDER McQUEEN *PERFECT MOMENT* SKULL SCARF | DAMIEN HIRST, 2013

ALEXANDER McQUEEN *FORGIVENESS* CIRCULAR SKULL SCARVES | DAMIEN HIRST, 2013

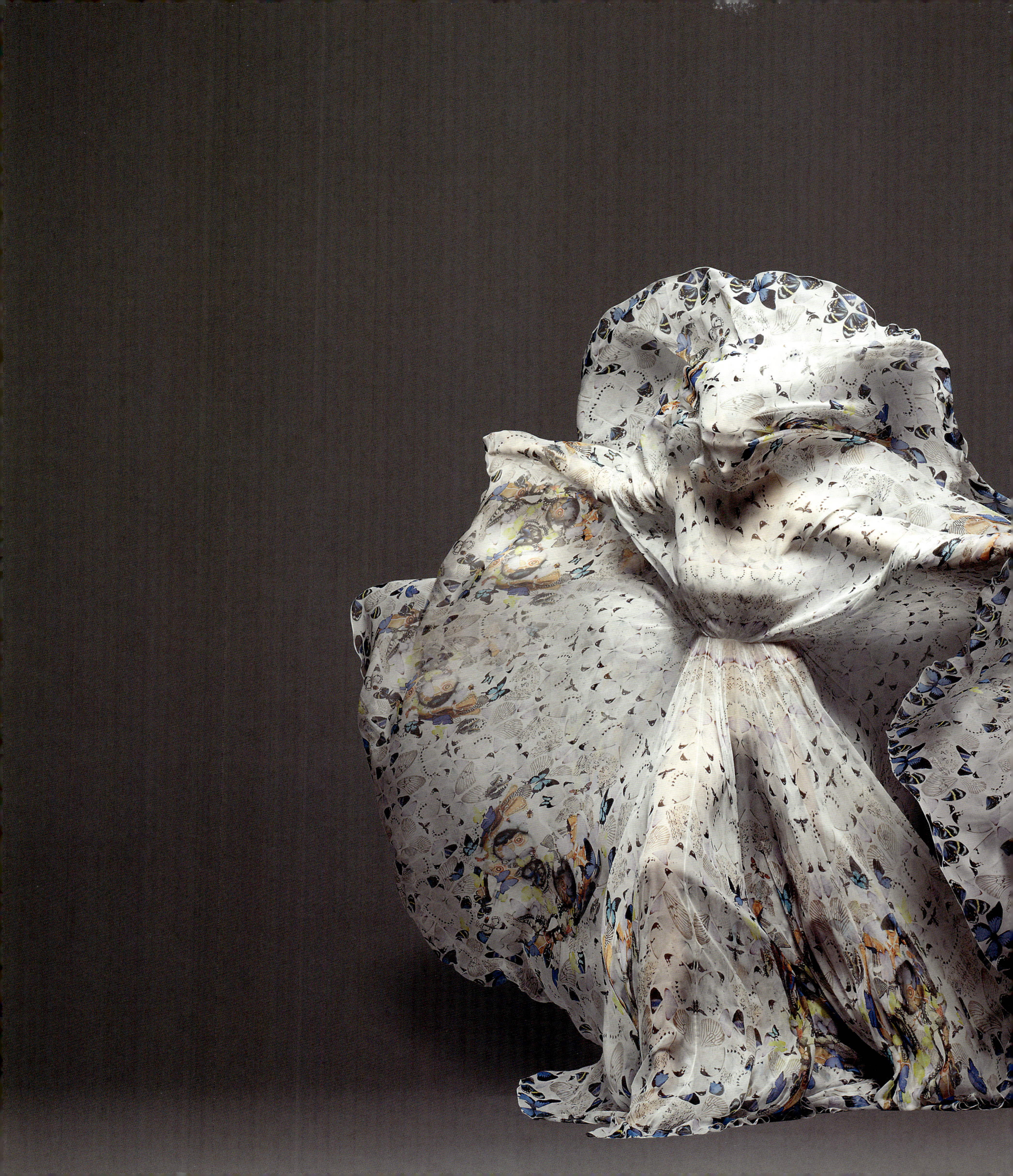

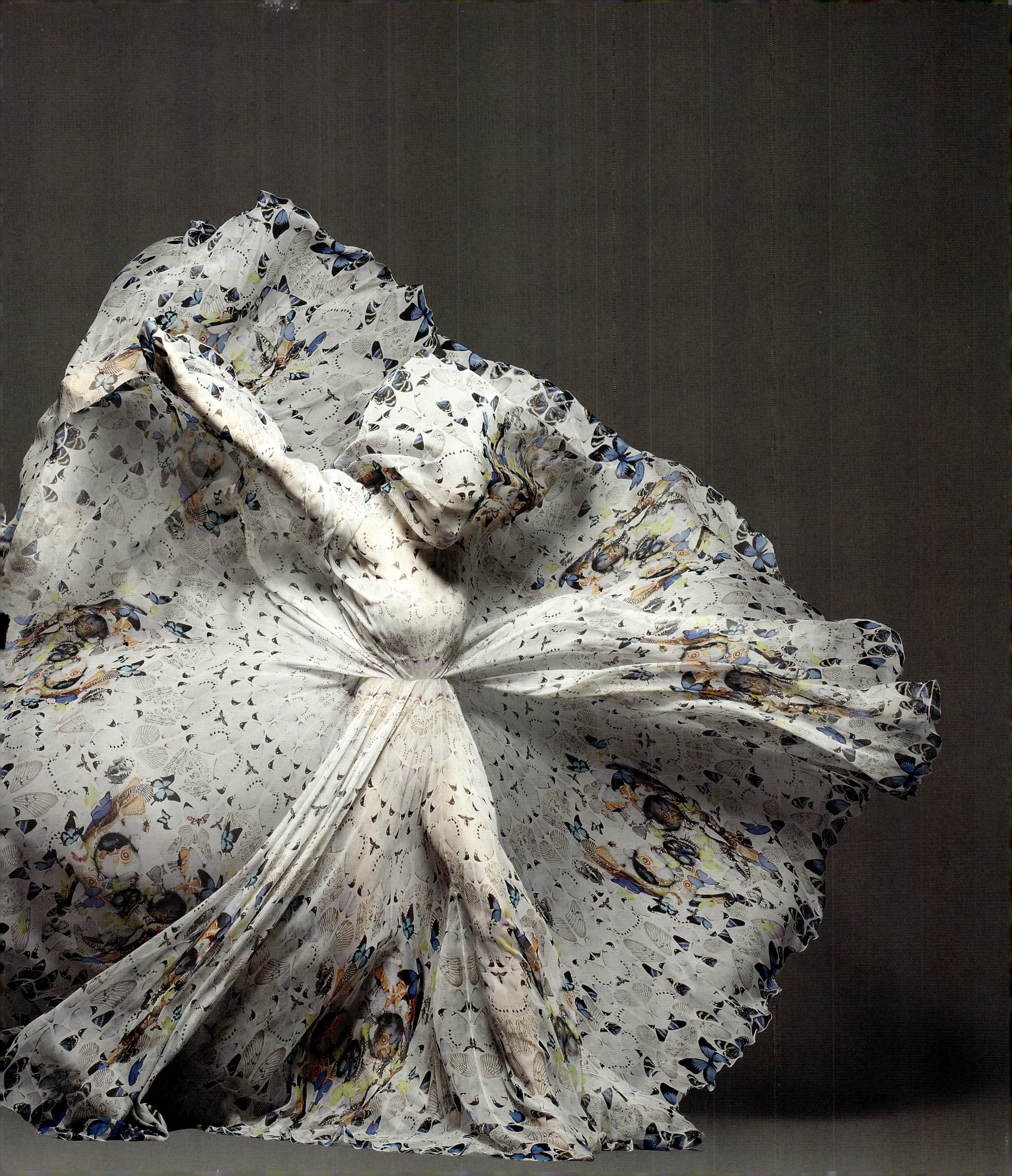

NICK CAVE + RA

AYMOND MEIER

NICK CAVE + RAYMOND MEIER

"MY WORK IS AN amalgamation of both fashion and art, and I exist within their fluid interface." —Nick Cave[55]

It took some time for *Vogue*, and the general public no less, to embrace performance art. But in 1980, *Vogue*'s editor in chief Grace Mirabella (b. 1930) got the ball rolling with a write-up on German Fluxus artist Joseph Beuys and his performative "actions," following a Guggenheim retrospective of his work.

When Anna Wintour (b. 1949) became editor in chief of *Vogue* in 1988, she continued the magazine's legacy of incorporating the arts. *Vogue* devoted two spreads to shape-shifter Matthew Barney in 1994 and 1996, and subsequently dedicated pages to sexually provocative Karen Finley, emotionally charged Marina Abramović, esoterically childlike Yoko Ono, and publically engaging Francis Alÿs, in turn.

Yet, even though it increased their visibility, the manner in which *Vogue* introduced performance artists remained relatively stagnant throughout the decades. Formulaically, all were placed in either profile pieces or the magazine's "People Are Talking About" pages. The hallowed fashion bible once again outdid itself, however, with its eight-page spread of Nick Cave (b. 1959) in costume for the September 2010 issue.

Swiss photographer Raymond Meier (b. 1957) came across Nick Cave's traveling exhibit during its stop at the Fowler Museum in Los Angeles and pitched it as an editorial idea to *Vogue*. When Meier received the green light, he reached out to Cave, who was simultaneously honored and dismayed—his new work had just been shipped and his studio was empty. But, saying "no" to *Vogue* is impossible, and the Nick Cave Studio went into overdrive to produce new works for the shoot.

Meier photographed Cave in eight fresh Soundsuits for the Fun Fall Accessories shoot, titled "Monsters, Inc." Fashion editor Elissa Santisi matched the creations with the season's furry goodies, like shoes by Guiseppe Zanotti and a blue-fox bag by Proenza Schouler. The exuberant visual story is joyously fantastical, with playful captions like "Party Animal" and

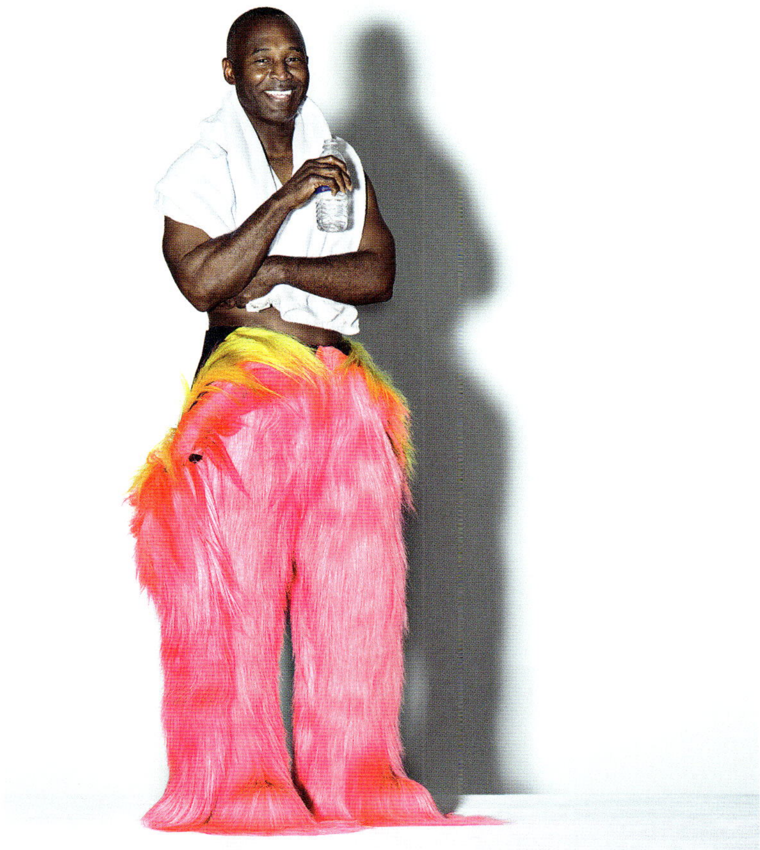

NICK CAVE

"Where the Wild Things Are." Cave recollects fondly, "The *Vogue* experience was like a dream. The actual shoot was surreal. There is a lot to think about and to coordinate when creating a relationship with an accessory. It took about six hours, but the experience was beautiful and very professional."[56]

However, the history of Nick Cave's Soundsuits is far from gleeful. Cave, who titled one of his former exhibitions "Reparations," made his looming Soundsuits, nearly ten feet tall, as a response to the 1991 police beating of Rodney King. Cave, who received an MFA from the Cranbook Academy of Art and studied modern dance at the Alvin Ailey American Dance Theater in New York, wanted to make a type of protective armor, part reaction and part necessity. Those unfamiliar with the political nature of Cave's work see something more like adult Muppets than an indictment of the ugly nature of race relations in America. Cave considers being featured in the "prestigious" magazine an honor and is proud that it is part of the legacy of his work.[57] In the future, perhaps other fashion magazines will increasingly address difficult and uncomfortable topics with the same regularity as the art world.

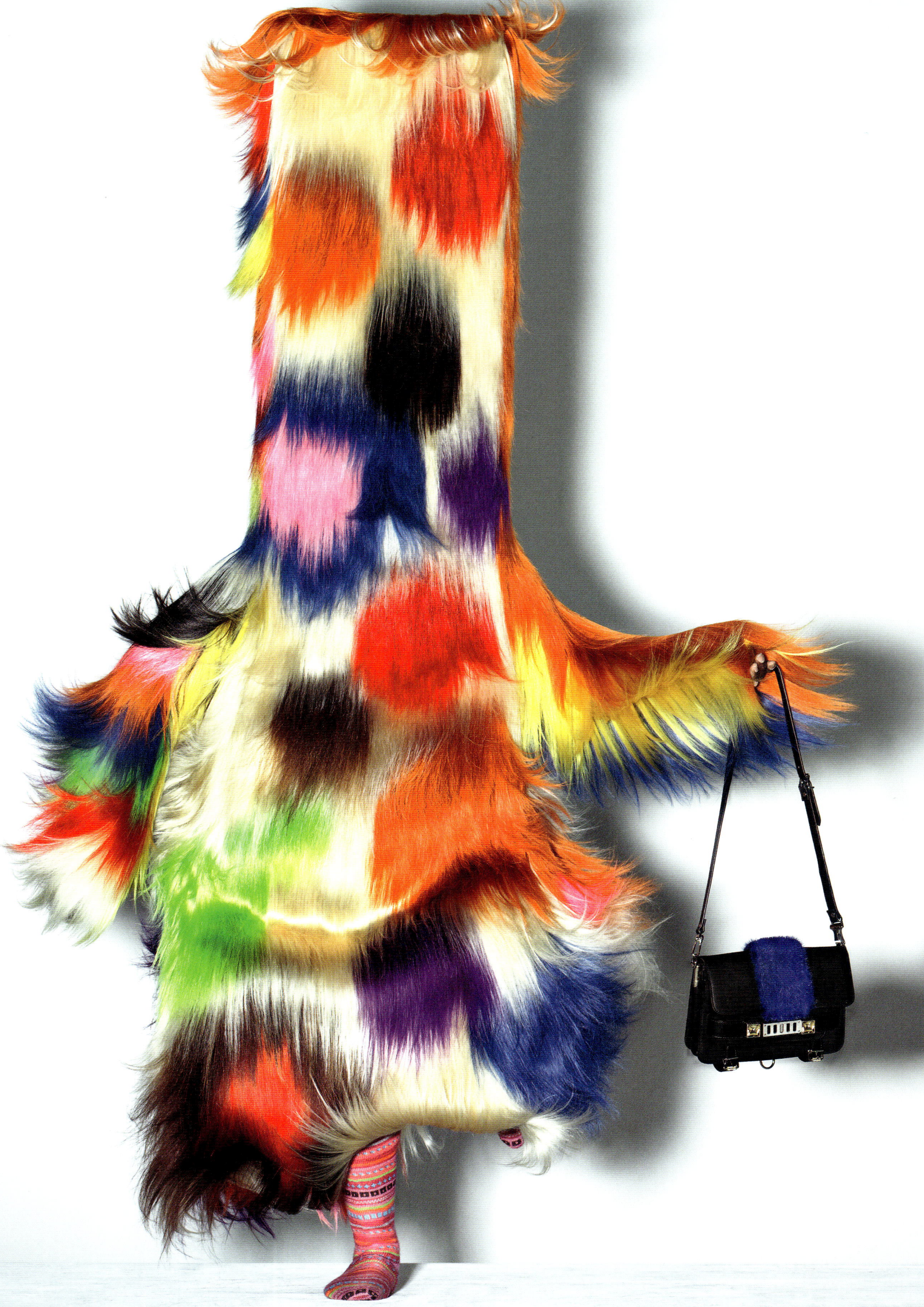

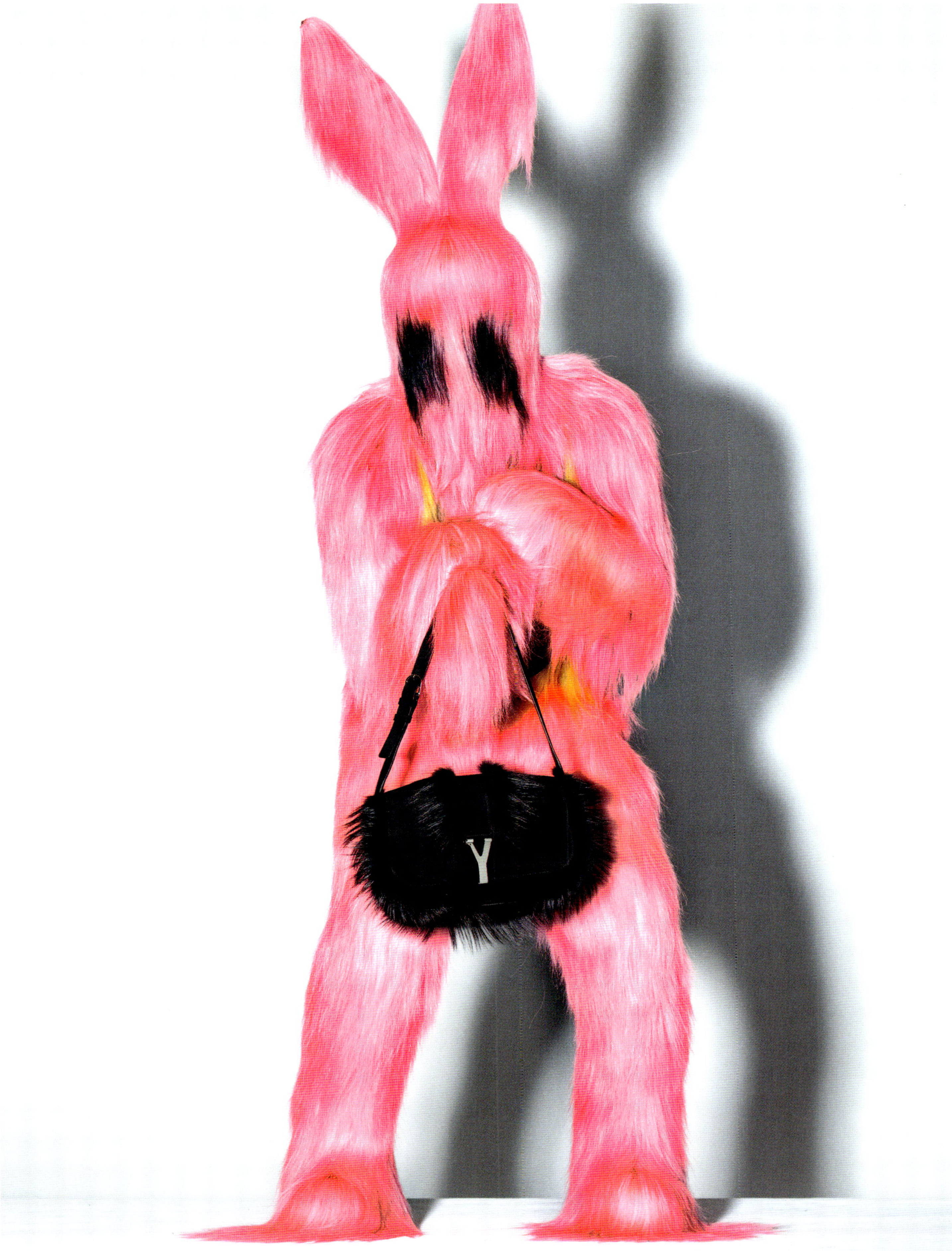

NICK CAVE IN HIS *SOUNDSUIT* WITH PROENZA SCHOULER BAG | RAYMOND MEIER FOR *VOGUE*, 2010

NICK CAVE IN HIS *SOUNDSUIT* WITH YVES SAINT LAURENT SHOULDER BAG | RAYMOND MEIER FOR *VOGUE*, 2010

NICK CAVE IN HIS *SOUNDSUIT* WITH DOLCE & GABBANA AND TOD'S HANDBAGS | RAYMOND MEIER FOR *VOGUE*, 2010

NICK CAVE IN HIS *SOUNDSUIT* WITH J. MENDEL MITTENS AND A PIERRE HARDY BOOT | RAYMOND MEIER FOR *VOGUE*, 2010

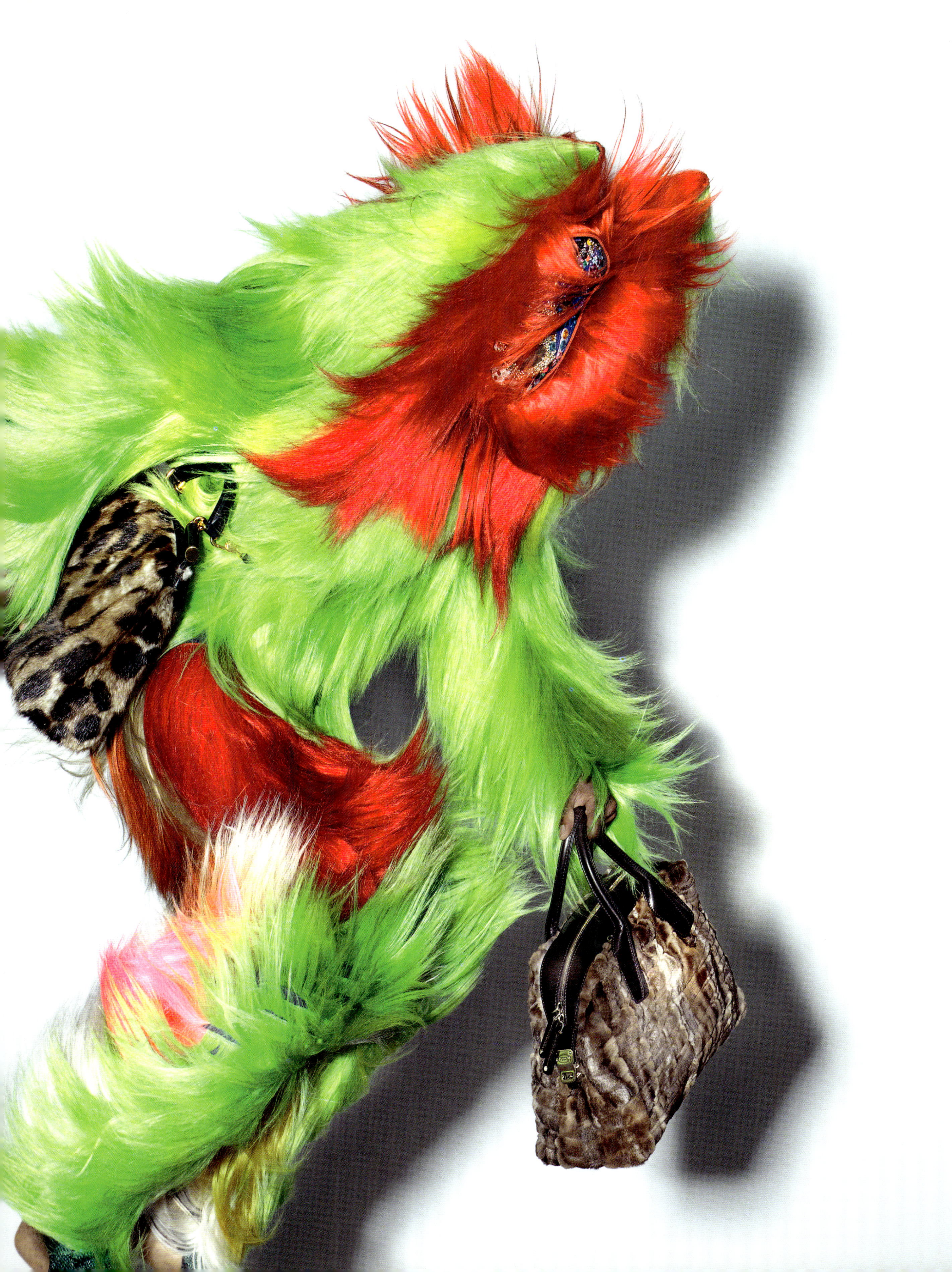

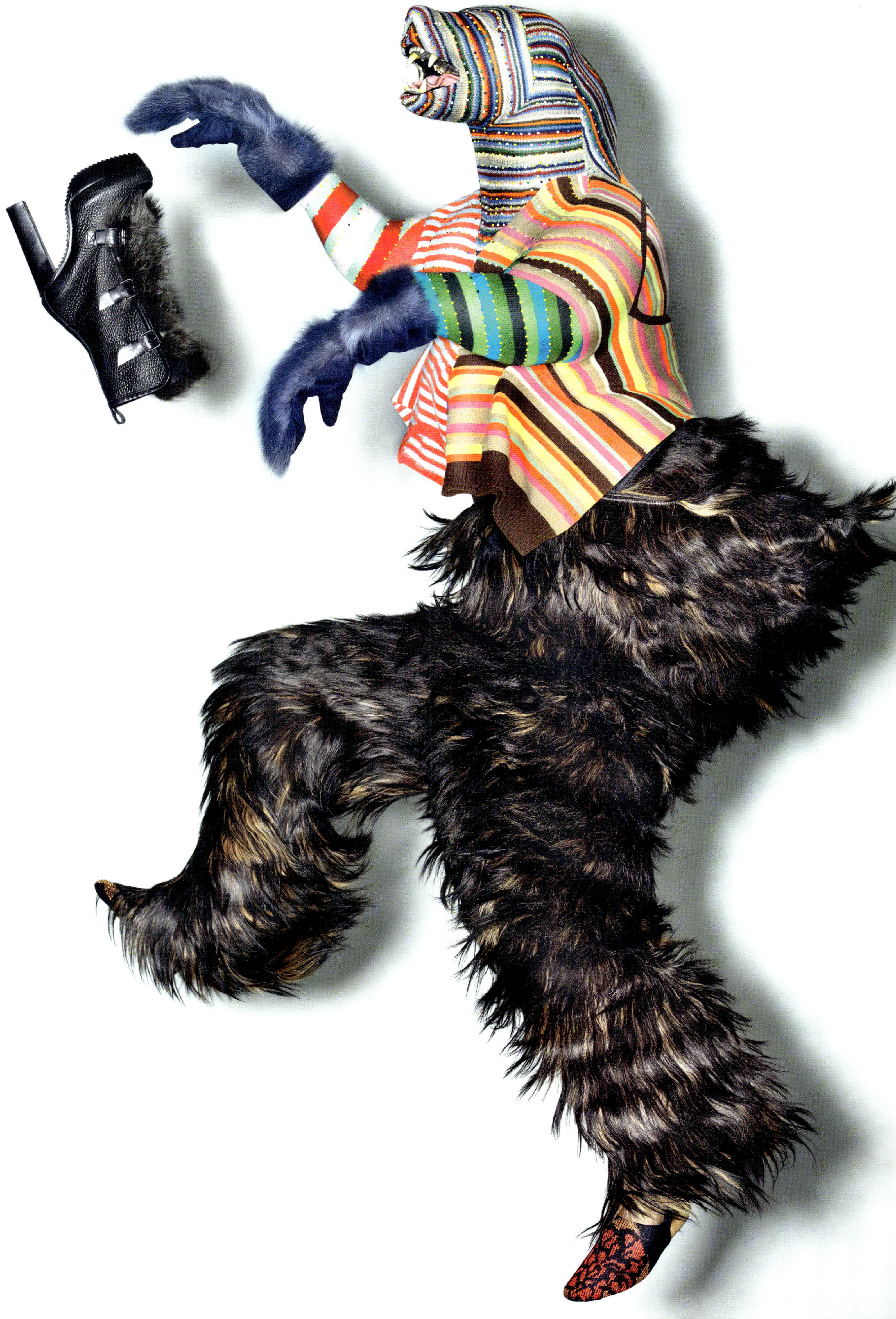

YASUMASA MORIMU

URA + ISSEY MIYAKE

THE POLITICALLY charged Paris riots of the late 1960s inspired designers Yves Saint Laurent and Issey Miyake to flip fashion's trickle-down pyramid and make clothes for the people. To do that, Miyake set up his own Tokyo-based label in 1970, after studying at L'Ecole de la Chambre Syndicale de la Couture Parisienne and working with fashion legends Guy Laroche, Hubert de Givenchy, and Geoffrey Beene.

Innovative Issey Miyake (b. 1938) began playing with pleating in 1988, inspired by the "rhythm pleats" in Henri "Le Douanier" Rousseau's painting *The Dream* (1910). Three years later, he collaborated with William Forsythe to design permanently pleated costumes for the Frankfurt Ballet. This collaboration furthered Miyake's ongoing experimentation as he continued to work on perfecting his new intricate pleating technique. The pleats themselves are a technically impressive feat. To achieve the desired effect, the garment is made two-and-a-half to three times larger than the end result. It is folded, ironed, sewn-over, and then placed between *washi* paper before being heat-pressed, which shrinks it down to size. In 1993, Issey Miyake debuted his user-friendly Pleats Please line, which flatters a range of body types.

In 1996, Miyake undertook a new challenge with his Guest Artist series. Working with various artists, Miyake printed their art on oversized garments, which were then pleated with precision so as to not distort their work. The first artist to collaborate with Miyake was Osaka native Yasumasa Morimura (b. 1951), whose work has been collected by the Carnegie Institute Museum and the Contemporary Museum of Art in Chicago. Considered an appropriation artist, Morimura uses himself to re-create historical, iconic works of art, like his 1985 self-portrait as ear-amputee Vincent van Gogh, the piece that first put Morimura on the international art world's radar. For his collaboration with Issey Miyake, Morimura intertwined his body with a female nude from Jean-Auguste-Dominique Ingres's *La Source* (1856). Fashion journalist extraordinaire Holly Brubach reflects upon Morimura's piece with Miyake, observing the effect of its juxtapositions: "This incongruity is exactly what Morimura is aiming for in his work; fascinated by 'gray areas' between east and west, male and female . . . art history and modern art, Morimura chooses to embrace these 'imbalances' in his work."[58] In

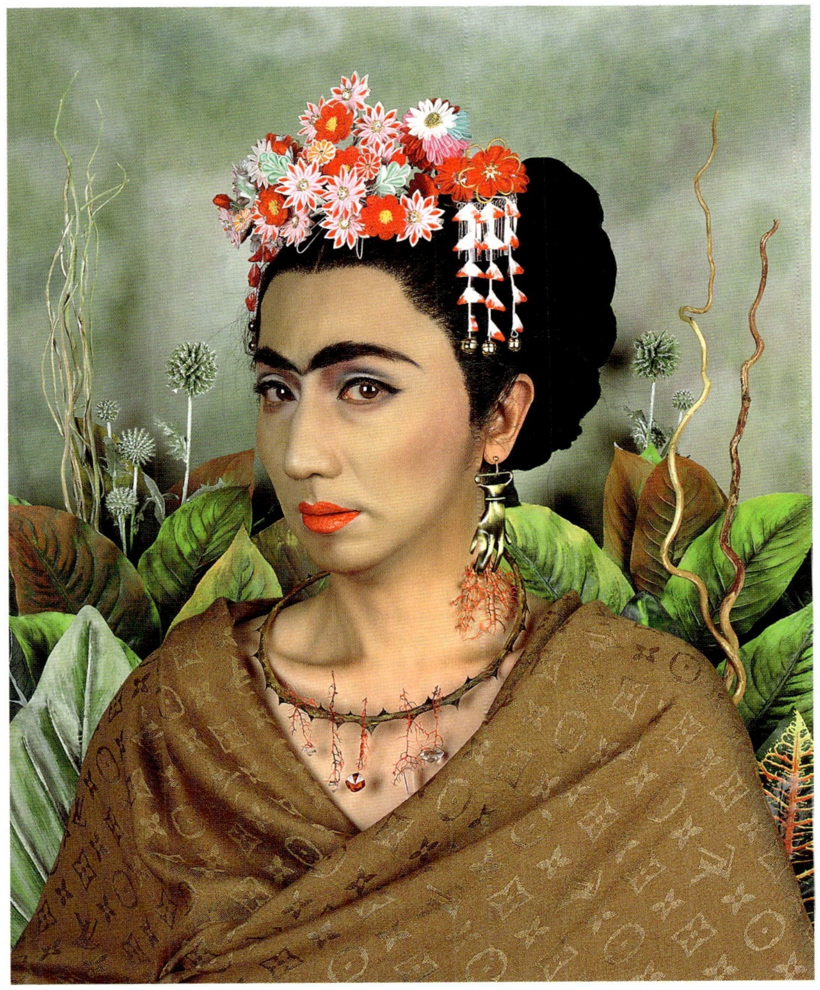

AN INNER DIALOGUE WITH FRIDA KAHLO (HAND SHAPED EARRING) | COLOR PHOTOGRAPH | YASUMASA MORIMURA, 2001

doing so, Morimura bridges constructs normally at odds and introduces a spectrum of inclusivity. This comprehensive confluence is seen in, and complements, Miyake's work.

Both Yasumasa Morimura and Issey Miyake consider the garment's owner to be the third collaborator; the two-dimensional, painting-like work becomes three-dimensional when worn, and the design changes with the wearer's body and movements. Issey Miyake is vehement about the purpose of his designs: "To me, design must get into real life. Otherwise, it's just couture, it's just extravaganza."[59] While Issey Miyake has pieces in the Museum of Modern Art's permanent collection, and was the first fashion designer featured on the cover of *Artforum*, he does not identify himself as an artist or consider his work art: "I may work with artists, but what I do is make things to be used, not looked at, like a picture or a sculpture. You can't use art."[60]

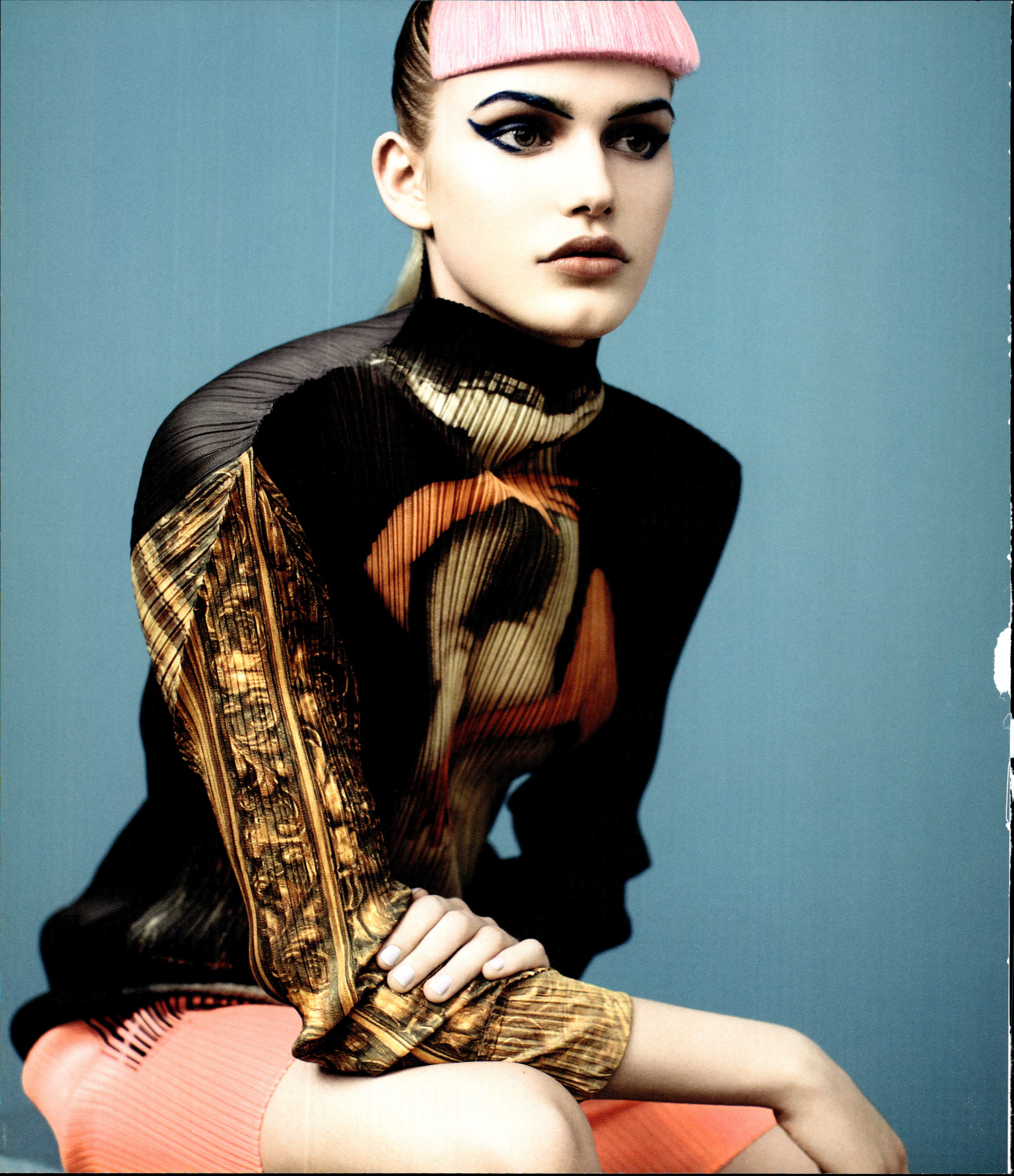

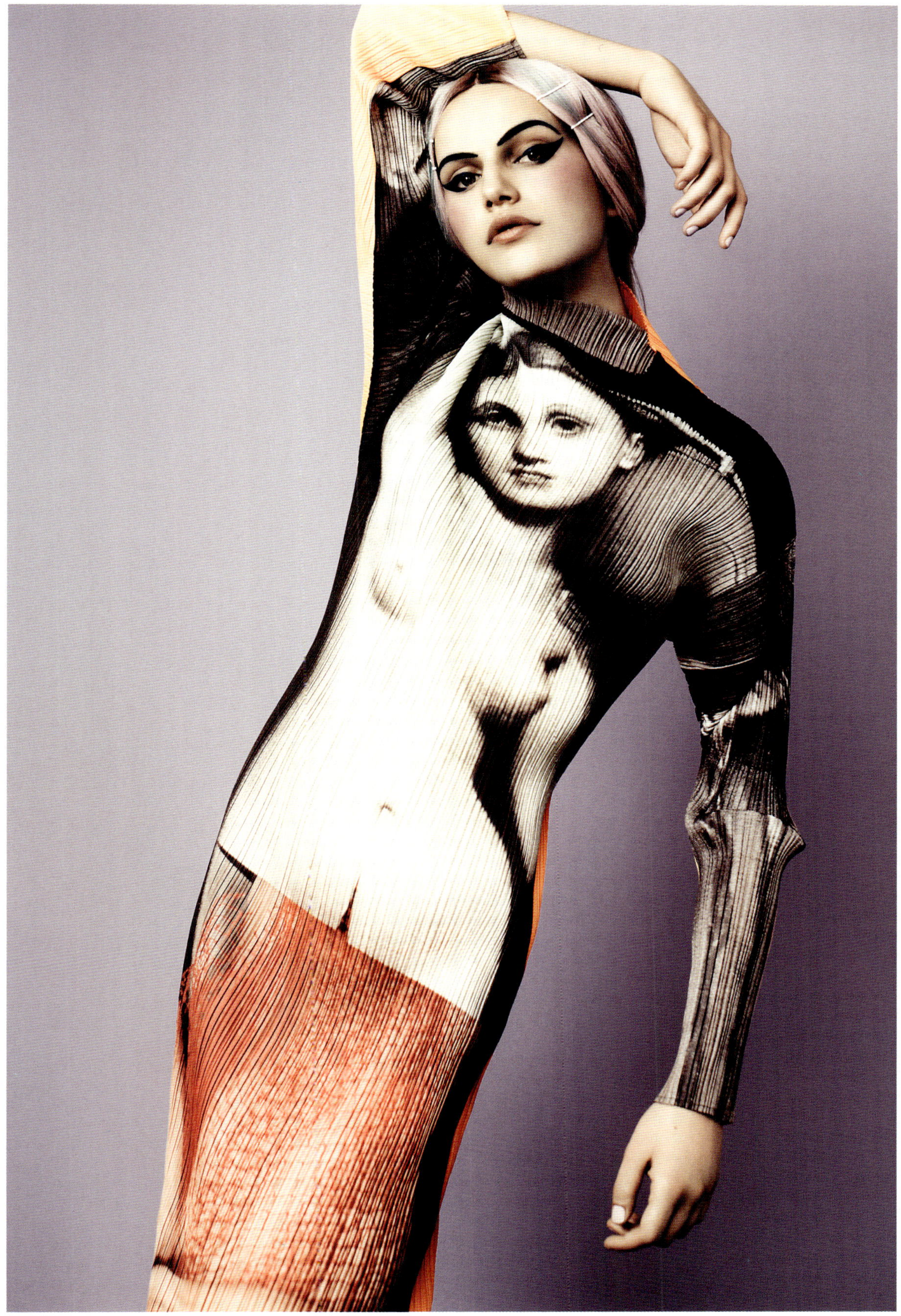

< ISSEY MIYAKE GUEST ARTIST SERIES NO 1 *PLEATS PLEASE* DRESS | YASUMASA MORIMURA, 1996

Λ ISSEY MIYAKE GUEST ARTIST SERIES NO 1 *PLEATS PLEASE* DRESS | YASUMASA MORIMURA, 1996

ELMGREEN & DR

AGSET + PRADA

ITALIAN DESIGNER

Miuccia Prada has definitively stated, "If I was only creative, I would become an artist. A designer can be very creative, but art is something that stands by itself, and fashion is something you sell."[61] Despite her aphorisms demarcating disciplines, Miuccia Prada fought a losing battle in her attempt to keep her passions divided. Throughout her tenure at Prada, the luxury leather business founded by her grandfather, Miuccia Prada has engaged with art. In 1995 she and her husband, Prada co-CEO Patrizio Bertelli, established Fondazione Prada, a nonprofit dedicated to contemporary art. The following year, for Florence's first Biennale di Firenze, Miuccia Prada joined other designers in pairing up with artists to craft unique creations for the event. She then courted some of the world's top architects, Rem Koolhaas and Herzog & de Meuron, who returned the affection by designing flagship Prada stores, the former for New York (2001) and Los Angeles (2004), the latter for Tokyo (2003).

The artist duo Danish Michael Elmgreen (b. 1961) and Norwegian Ingar Dragset (b. 1969) had been working together "like a two-headed monster" for a decade. In 2005, they inaugurated a sealed Prada store, coproduced by The Art Production Fund and Ballroom Marfa, full of that season's delectable Prada accessories. After being informed of Elmgreen & Dragset's work, Miuccia Prada selected and donated bags and shoes to be displayed in the project, as well as corporate branding rights. Affectionately referred to as *Prada Marfa*, the installation is actually roughly thirty-five miles away from Marfa, the rural city made famous by minimalist-artist-turned-resident Donald Judd in the 1970s. Elmgreen & Dragset originally intended the permanently closed shop to slowly disintegrate into the desert landscape, a testament to the power of time and nature over human attempts at beauty.[62] However, misguided and bizarre vandalism has required not only its sporadic upkeep but also the installation of stronger windows and alarms.

Elmgreen & Dragset still consider it a success, in part because of how it's been received by the public at large, vandals excluded. Michael Elmgreen admitted, "When we did the Prada Marfa store out in the desert, we didn't know how the public would react. And today, it's really great. The [truck] drivers are coming along Highway 90 and they pass the store. There is this Prada

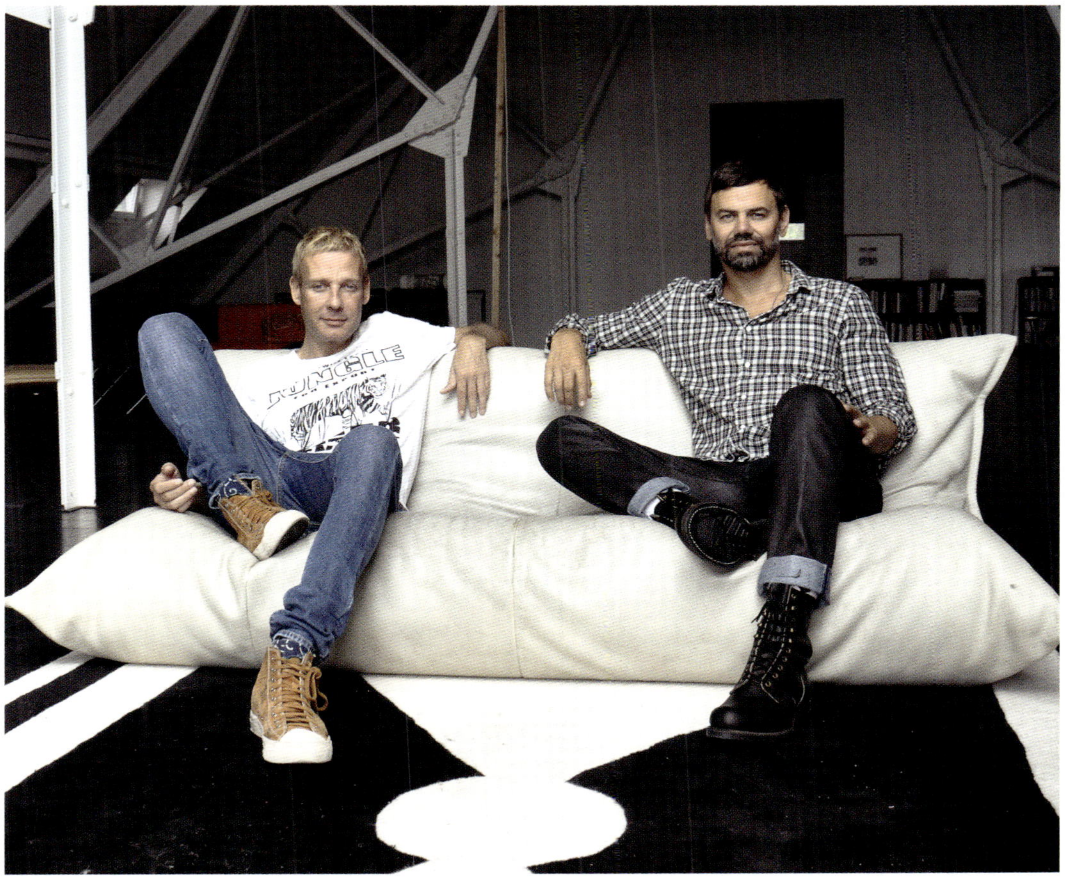

MICHAEL ELMGREEN AND INGAR DRAGSET

store in the middle of the desert. And they stop the [truck], walk out, look at it in disbelief, scratch their head: 'What the fuck is going on?!' And they don't care about it being 'art' or not. They just think it's really strange. And for public art, that's maybe the ideal situation, that people don't have to think 'art,' and be appreciating it in terms to 'art' so much, but they can just react on it, in a different way, in a more immediate way."[63]

Elmgreen & Dragset's Prada shop, and the publicity surrounding it, introduced the pair to a wider audience, and their artistic opportunities increased. Public works of theirs, including *It's Never Too Late to Say Sorry* (2011), *Powerless Structures, Fig. 101* (2012), and *A Space Called Public* (2013), have been displayed and/or performed in Rotterdam, London, and Munich. Elmgreen & Dragset's work has been exhibited at the Tate Modern, the Victoria & Albert Museum, and MUSAC (Museo de Arte Contemporáneo de Castilla y León). In 2009, the pair won a Special Mention at the Venice Biennale.

Of course, Prada Marfa also further cemented Prada's commitment to and relationship with art. In 2014, fashion critic Sarah Mower wearily remarked, "No Prada show proceeds without an art-slash-social commentary seeping through the walls."[64] Not the worst thing ever said about a fashion show!

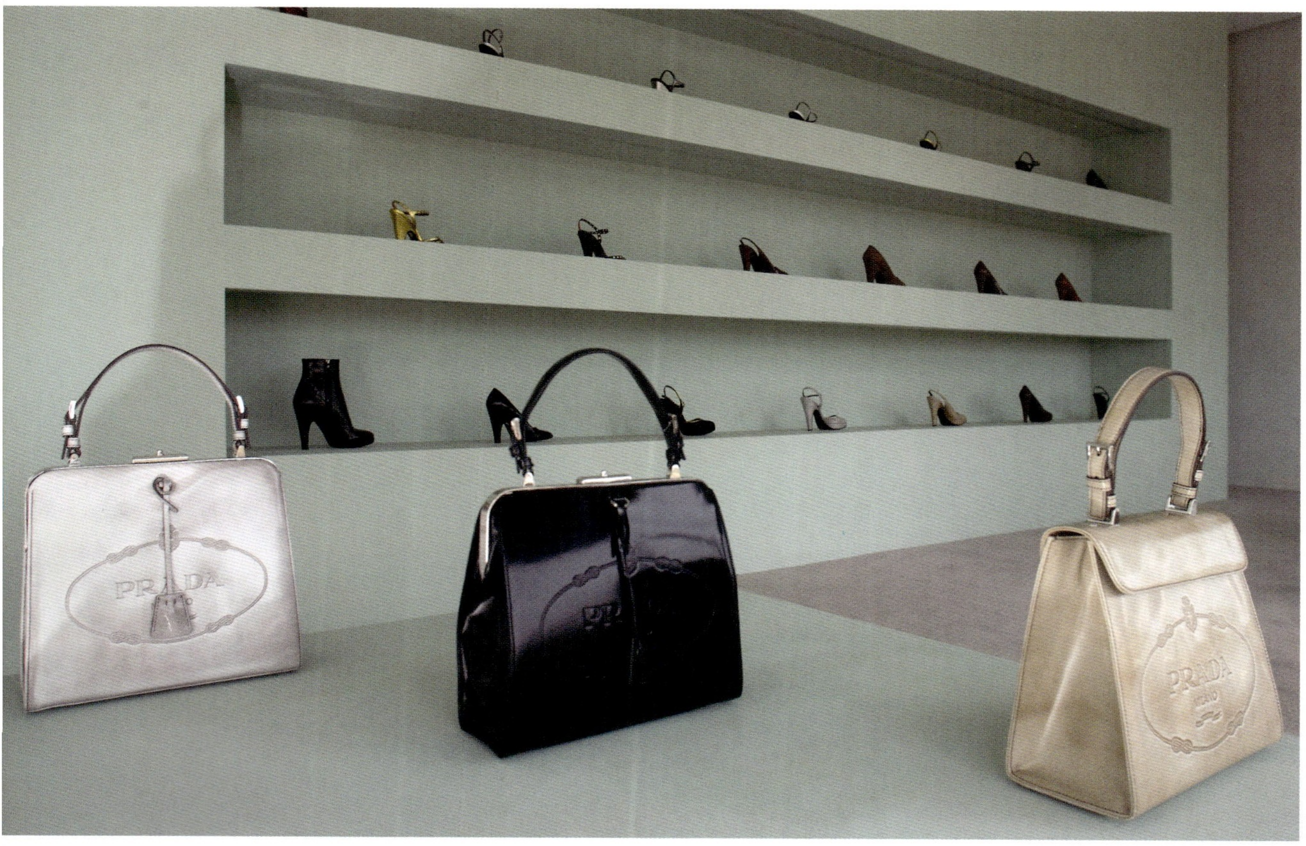
PRADA
PRADA

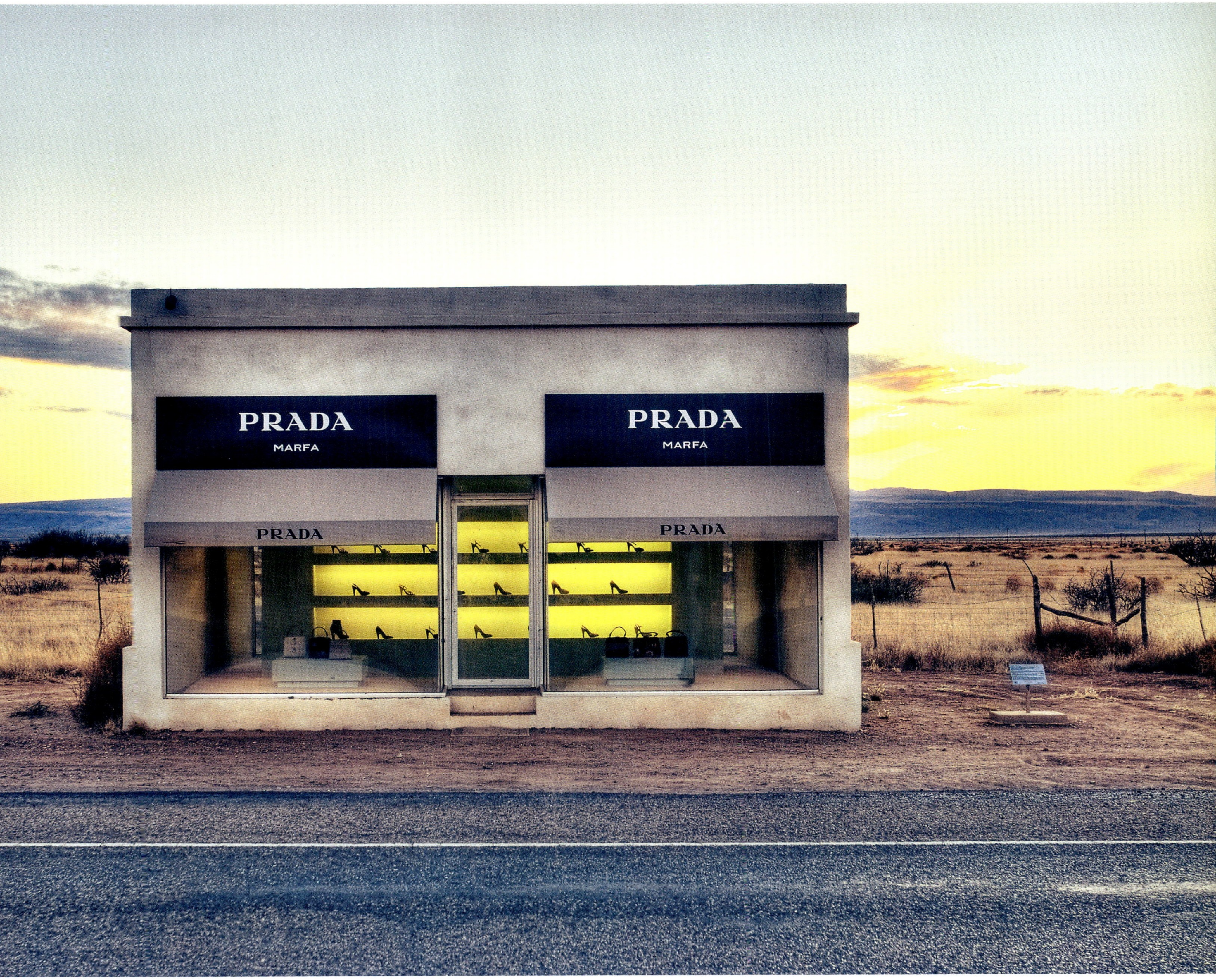

PRADA MARFA | ELMGREEN AND DRAGSET, 2005
PRADA MARFA | ELMGREEN AND DRAGSET, 2005

WING SHYA

RODARTE

THE ART WORLD

adores Rodarte with the same intensity as the fashion world, a nearly unheard of accomplishment. The ideology and working process of Rodarte, founded by sisters Kate (b. 1979) and Laura (b. 1980) Mulleavy in 2004, fit with the art world. The self-taught sisters' early designs were handmade, relying on pinking shears, and their first marketing scheme involved sending out personally fashioned paper dolls of their pieces. Kate and Laura Mulleavy work from their own inspiration, which springs more from their life experience and imagination than trend reports or studies of consumption practices. Fungi inspired one Rodarte collection; *Star Wars* another. Based in Los Angeles, Rodarte—named after the un–Ellis Island version of their mother's maiden name—is not in the heart of a fashion capital. And while Rodarte made limited-edition T-shirts for Gap and collaborated for an affordable collection with Target, the brand does not generally have easy, affordable entry points for aspirational high-fashion customers, like key fobs or perfume. To snare Rodarte for less than four figures, one needed to snap up the Gap or Target collaborations, or grab their sweatshirts for Opening Ceremony, which are printed with adorable phrases like "RADARTE," "Rohearte," or "J'aime Rodarte." Taken in totality, the notoriously fickle art world did not stand a chance against the whims of the Mulleavy sisters. The Museum of Contemporary Art, the Los Angeles County Museum of Art, and the Cooper-Hewitt have all curated Rodarte shows. The admiration goes both ways. Rodarte is also enamored with the art world, having invited Catherine Opie and Alec Soth to create new bodies of work for a collaborative book examining the brand and its creative process.

But first and foremost, Rodarte is a fashion brand, and the fashion world loves it dearly. The genius of Rodarte was immediately noticed by high-fashion specialty boutique Kirna Zabête in New York. Critic Mary Tannen was so besotted with Rodarte's Fall 2006 collection, she wrote in the *New York Times* that it was "exquisite to the point of pain."[65]

Rodarte's 2010 collaboration with filmmaker Wing Shya (b. 1964) was only one element of a multifaceted event. Ambitious, it required the cooperation of numerous creatives, a department store, and a multinational charity. Firstly, the sisters created four one-of-a-kind dresses inspired by the cinematic performances of award-winning actress Maggie Cheung in *Heroic*

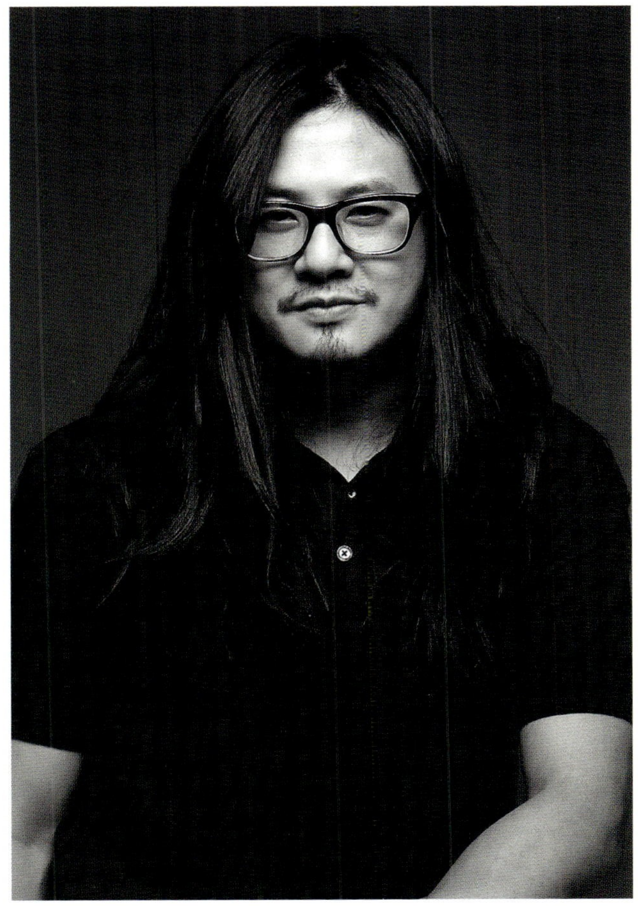

WING SHYA

Trio (1993), *In the Mood for Love* (2000), *Hero* (2002), and *Clean* (2004).

In turn, those dresses were featured on models Yu Xiao, August Zhang, and Jun Kim in a short video about the collection by Wing Shya, known for his fashion imagery in publications like *i-D*, *Visionaire*, and *Tank*. The video, made all the more haunting by Peter Kam's piano- and string-heavy soundtrack, took its time allowing the intricacy of the Rodarte dresses, and the Swarovski crystals adorning them, to be highlighted as they billow underwater in a beam of light, or as strands of fabric twirl against the backdrop of a desolate street.

The dresses were then displayed at Joyce, Hong Kong's version of Barneys, fulfilling Andy Warhol's prophesy: department stores will become museums. For each person who viewed Shya's film online, Joyce generously donated HK$1 to UNICEF, an organization dedicated to children's rights and emergency relief. The four Rodarte dresses were then auctioned off to benefit UNICEF. Maggie Cheung, the actress whose performances served as inspiration for the project and who is also an ambassador for UNICEF in China, attended the charitable event at Joyce with Rodarte's Kate and Laura Mulleavy. The event raised over a half-million HK dollars (roughly $65,000). Between their commitment to fashion, art, and charity, it's easy to RoHEARTe, no?

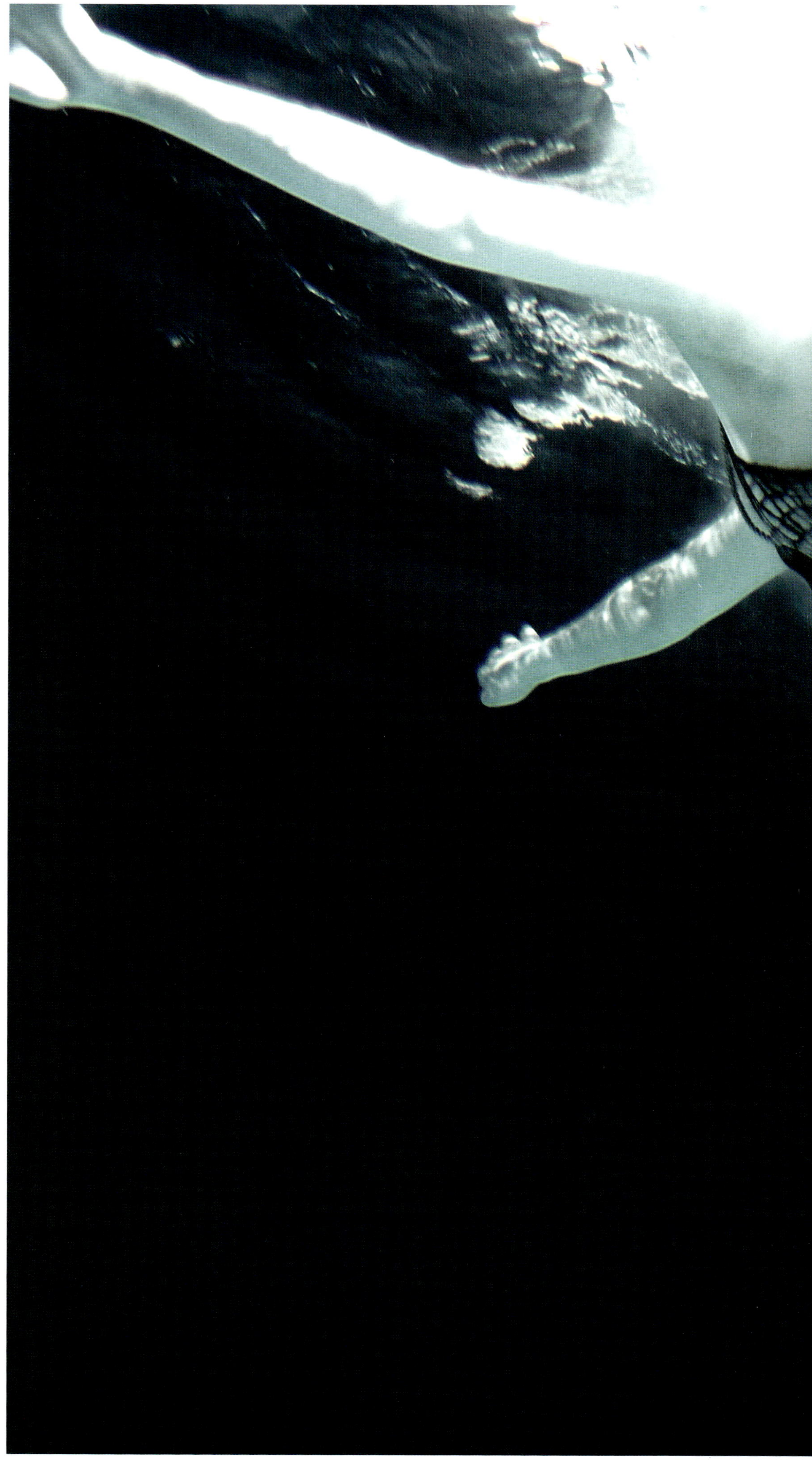

/\ **FILM STILL FROM** *RODARTE x MAGGIE CHEUNG COLLECTION*, **FEATURING A DRESS BY RODARTE** | WING SHYA, 2010

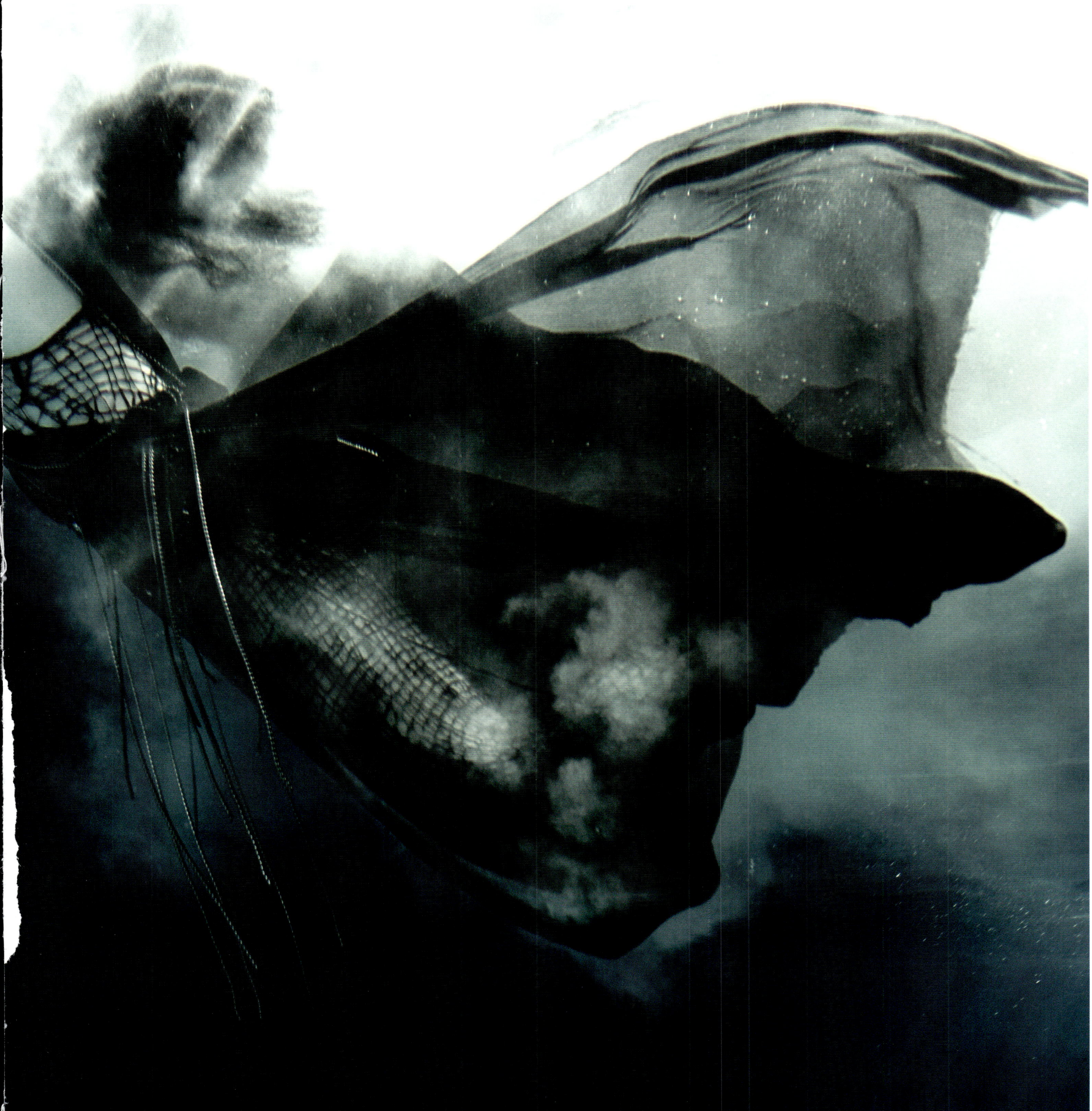

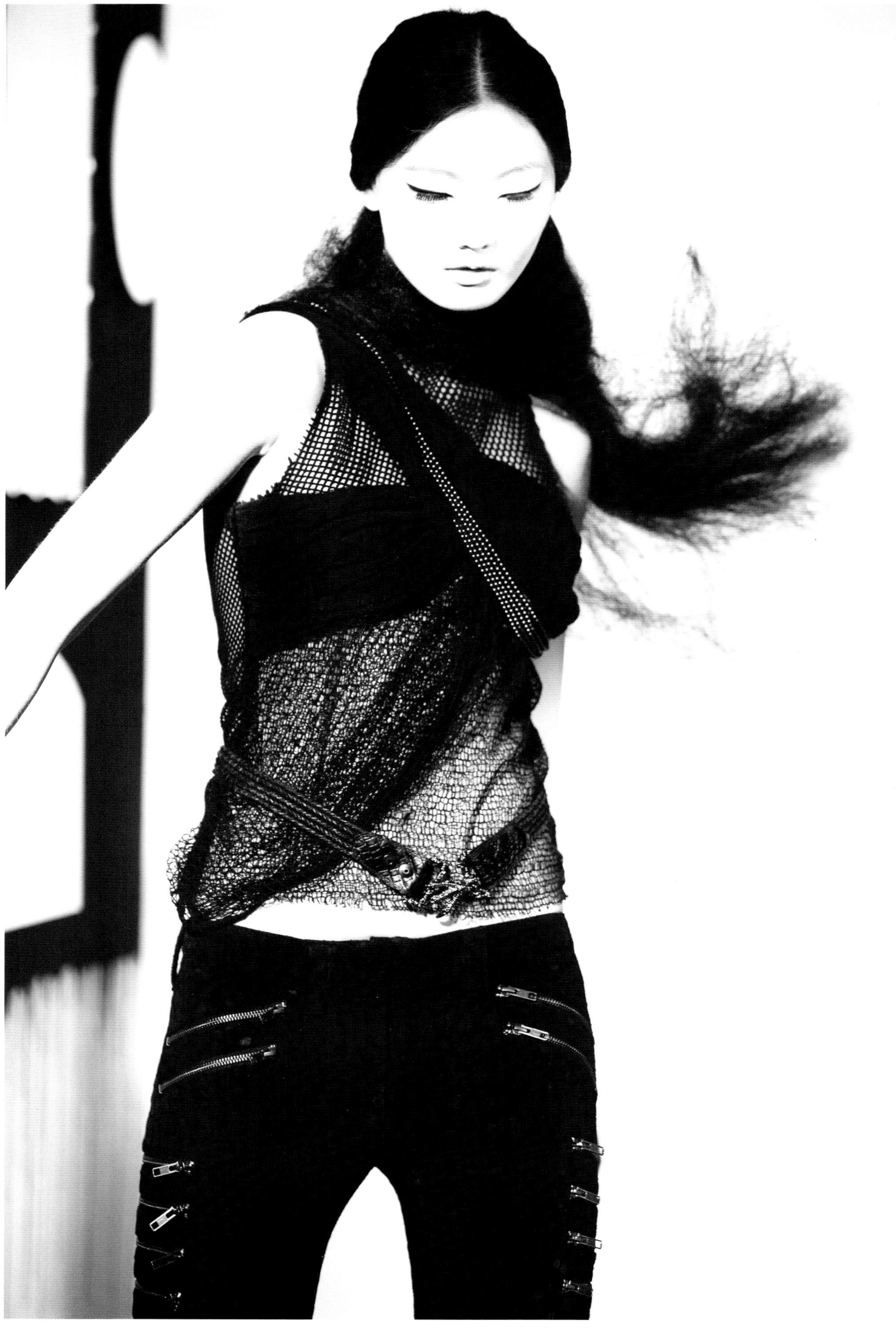

/\ FILM STILL FROM *RODARTE x MAGGIE CHEUNG COLLECTION*, FEATURING AN ENSEMBLE BY RODARTE | WING SHYA, 2010

> FILM STILL FROM *RODARTE x MAGGIE CHEUNG COLLECTION*, FEATURING AN ENSEMBLE BY RODARTE | WING SHYA, 2010

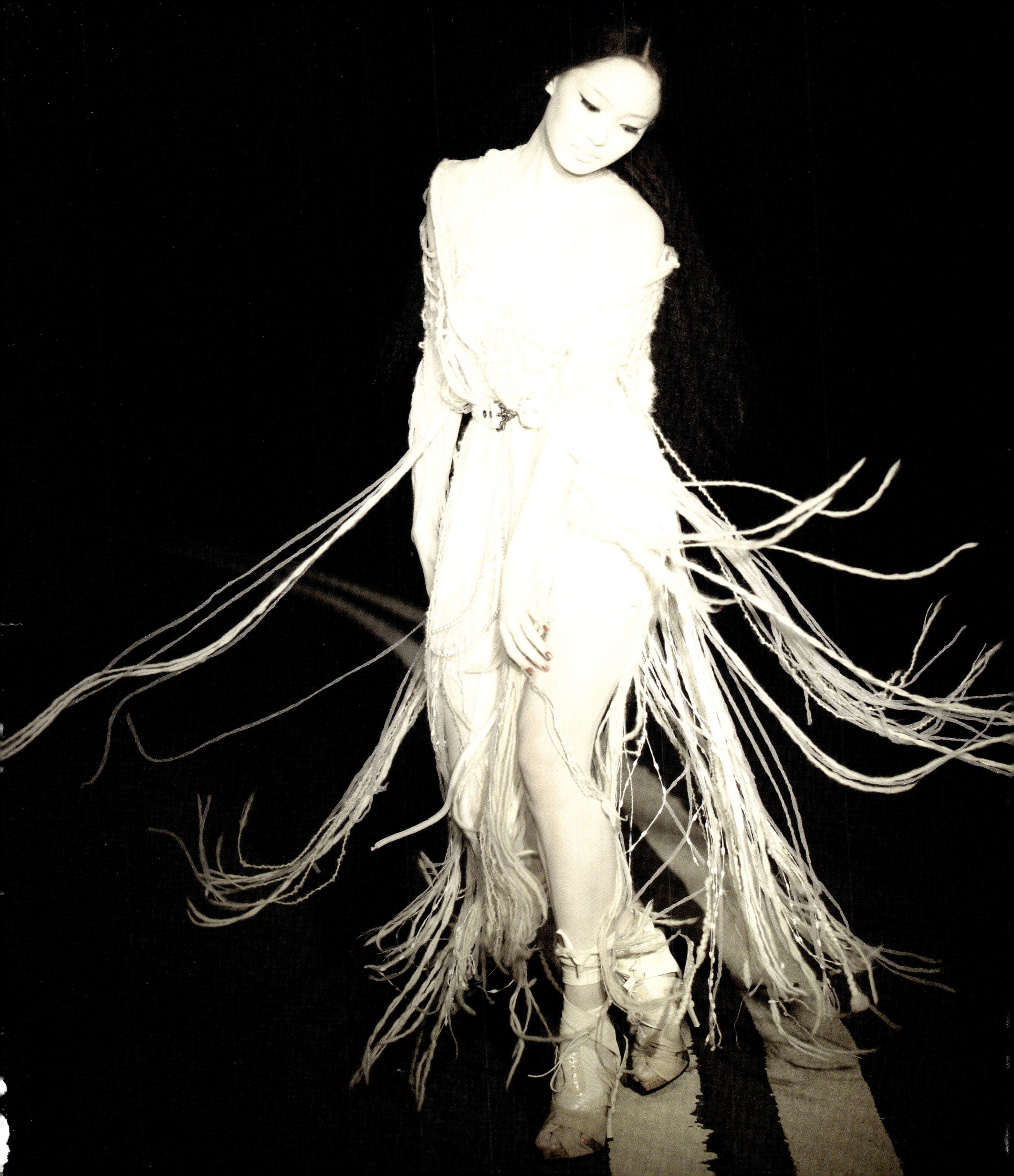

PIET MONDRIAN + Y

VES SAINT LAURENT

FRENCH DESIGNER YVES Saint Laurent (1936–2008) was not the first to turn the paintings of Dutch-born Piet Mondrian (1872–1944) into fashion. In 1961, New York designer Anne Klein made a slew of Mondrian-based dresses for her line Junior Sophisticates. American milliner Sally Victor made a Mondrian hat in 1962, and just prior to the debut of Yves Saint Laurent's Fall/Winter 1965 collection, the American magazine *Glamour* showed Mondrian-treated dresses.

It makes sense: Mondrian's neoplastic work easily complemented mod style. Mondrian's work was simple, yes, but also precise and modern—an idea in tune with the '60s, with the rise of simple *prêt-à-porter* (ready-to-wear) garments. Short shift dresses signified youth and devil-may-care rebellion, and they looked positively splendid on twig-like bodies, which were all the rage.

So, while Yves Saint Laurent did not do Mondrian first, he did it best, and to such an extent that its previous incarnations have been forgotten. In 1967, fashion journalist Marilyn Bender wrote in *The Beautiful People*, "A fashion ignoramus could detect . . . a Saint Laurent Mondrian dress."[66] What Saint Laurent brought to Mondrian-esque fashion that no one else did was the ability to solve an essential problem: how to make squares remain square on a female body. Even when thin, the female form is not two-dimensional, so translating a simple neoplastic work of two dimensions onto a woman's shape is nearly impossible. The straight lines perfect on a hanging garment easily become distorted, almost squiggly, on a woman's body. Oversizing the garments to rectify this issue makes them appear ill-fitting and clunky—certainly not the ideal style of the day. Saint Laurent's genius lay in his unique ability to translate Mondrian's straight lines onto female curves by imperceptibly hiding the shaping in the grid of seams. Such a marvel could only be produced by Yves Saint Laurent.

David Bailey photographed the multicolor Mondrian dress for the September 1965 cover of *Vogue Paris*. Diana Vreeland's stateside *Vogue* devoted a spread in mid-September to the dress, placing it in front of Irving Penn's lens on the unrivaled model Veruschka. Both magazines sold the patterns to women who wanted to try their hand at it at home.

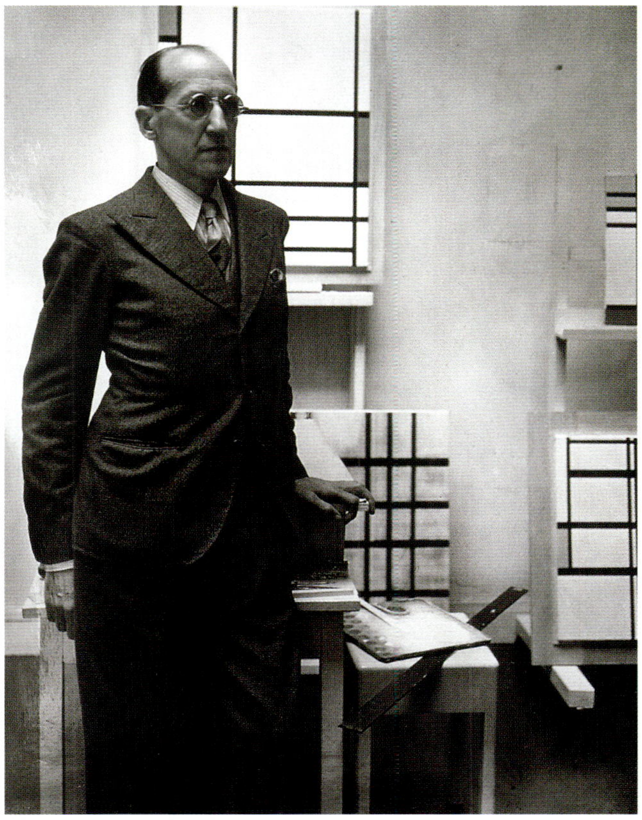

PORTRAIT OF PIET MONDRIAN IN HIS PARIS STUDIO | GELATIN SILVER PRINT | ANDRE ROGI, 1937

Yves Saint Laurent's Mondrian dress produced a Beatles-like fervor and copies abounded. Vinyl boots popped up with the design in 1966, the same year Burda Moden made Mondrian swimsuits.

Saint Laurent, who repeatedly revisited his best ideas, featured a fiercely square-shouldered Mondrian jacket in his Couture Spring/Summer 1980 collection, pieces of which Her Majesty Queen Noor of Jordan later wore to great applause. For his final show, Yves Saint Laurent sent three Mondrian dresses down the Spring 2002 Couture runway, a nostalgic ode to one of his greatest triumphs.

Using only black grid lines, primary colors, and white and gray, Mondrian pared down his palette to convey balance and universal harmony in abstract modernist terms. The continued resurfacing of Mondrian's influence in the late 20th and early 21st century work of artists, architects, and both fashion and industrial designers is due to its resonance, especially as society searches for simplicity in the digital age of endless imagery. Mondrian, and the work inspired by him, continues to provide a visual palate cleanser in an increasingly frenetic world.

Today, Yves Saint Laurent Mondrian dresses may be viewed in museum collections including those of New York's Metropolitan Museum of Art, the Victoria and Albert Museum, and the Los Angeles County Museum of Art. Or look toward the street; something similar is bound to pop up—it's in the air.

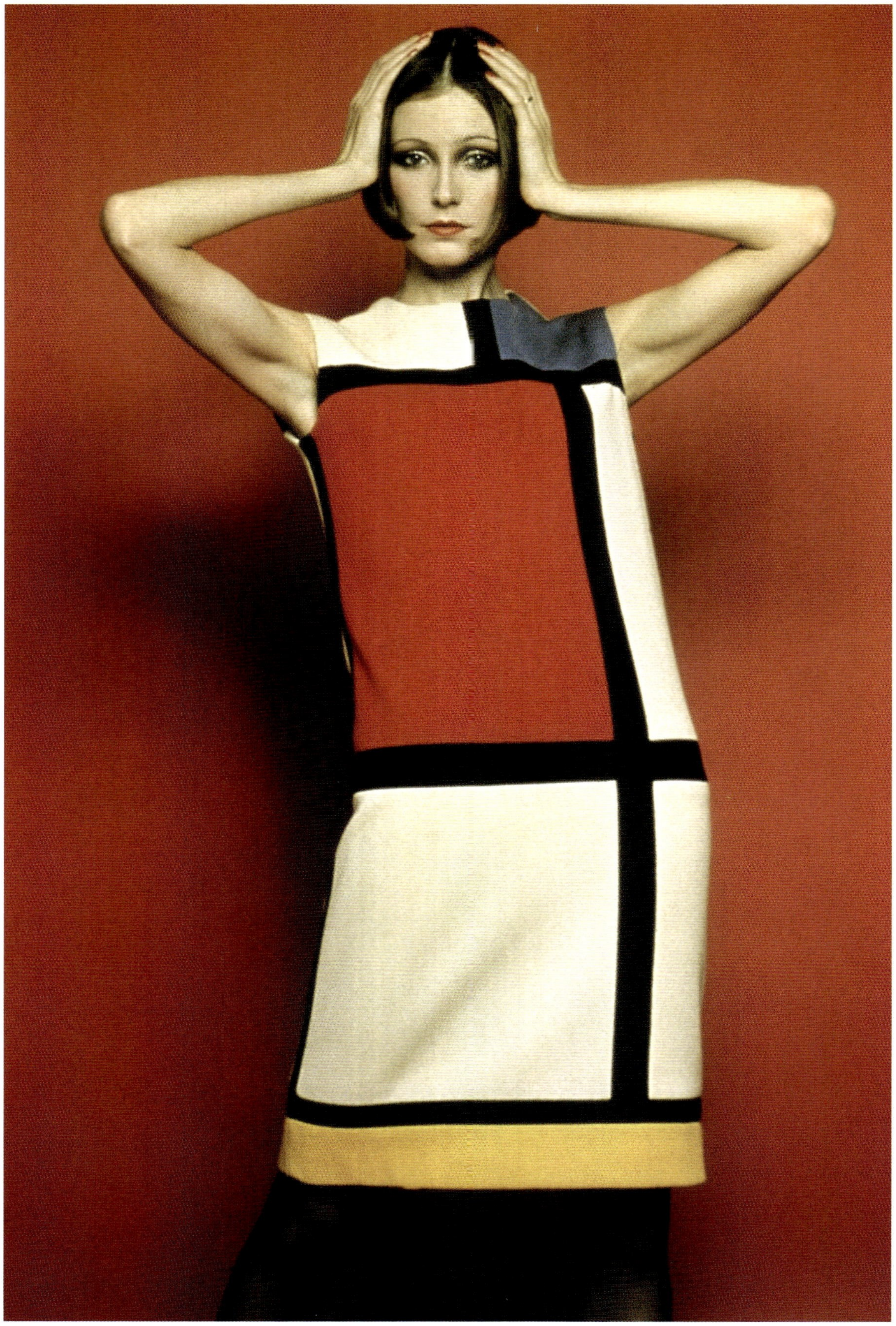

A MONDRIAN DRESS | YVES SAINT LAURENT, 1965

VERUSCHKA PHOTOGRAPHED BY IRVING PENN FOR *VOGUE* IN A MONDRIAN DRESS | YVES SAINT LAURENT, 1965

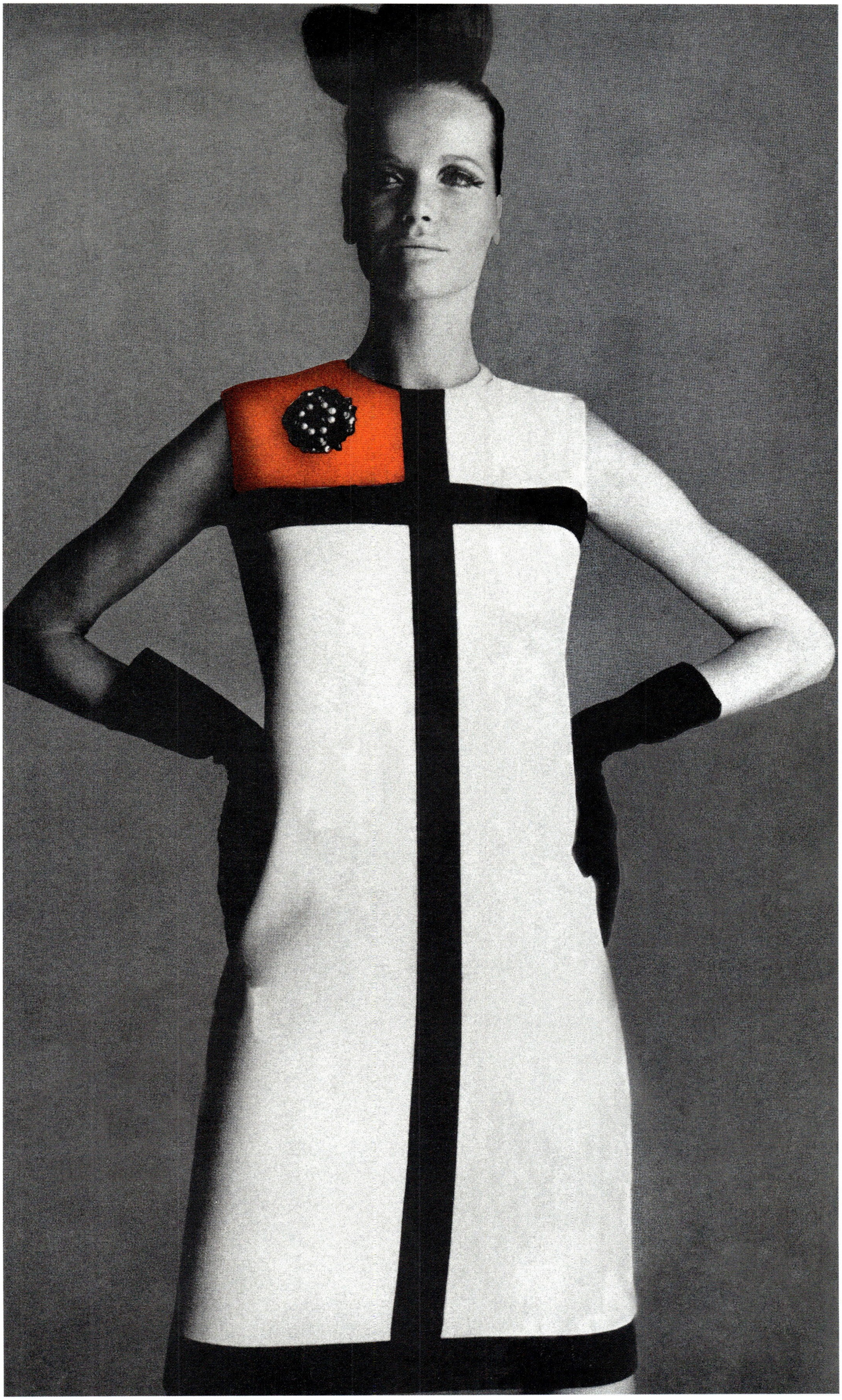

SALVADOR DALÍ + E

ELSA SCHIAPARELLI

WHILE NOT THE FIRST

collaboration between a couturier and an artist, the partnership between Elsa Schiaparelli (1890–1973) and Salvador Dalí (1904–1989) is often referred to as such—likely due to the extraordinary final products they birthed.

Italian-born Elsa Schiaparelli was something of an accidental designer. While living in New York, Schiaparelli made herself a sweater with a *trompe-l'oeil* bow. Her friends went mad for it, and she began selling them in 1927. Schiaparelli gathered steam quickly with her "hard chic" looks, becoming one of the most sought-after couturiers in 1930s Paris.

From 1935 until 1950, Schiaparelli and Dalí became creatively entangled, her fashions inspiring his art and vice versa. Salvador Dalí illustrated Elsa Schiaparelli's unusual zippers. She realized his 1934 idea of a "cabinet dress" with bureau drawers for pockets in Winter 1936–37, and his shoe hat for Winter 1937–38.

Elsa Schiaparelli and Salvador Dalí also collaborated on a rotary telephone dial compact (1935), gloves sporting painted fingernails (1936–37), a dress printed to look savagely ripped (1938), a skeleton dress (1938), and a ruby-lip brooch smiling with teeth made of pearls (1949), among others. (And while the two didn't work on the garment together, in Summer 1946, Schiaparelli made a rayon crepe dress that featured a playful caricature of Dalí.) Far from a sideline observer (or worse, a thief) of surrealism, Schiaparelli contributed to the artistic movement, inducing the citizens of New York and Paris to personify the bizarre waking-dream world of Dalí.

The most famous piece of their collaboration is the lobster dress. Lobsters feature heavily in Salvador Dalí's work. The story goes that during a boisterous and rowdy dinner party attended by Dalí, a lobster was knocked off a plate and landed atop the telephone—inspiring Dalí's 1936 lobster telephone. Having already played with elements of the telephone together, Dalí designed a lobster sketch with sprigs of parsley on it for Schiaparelli.

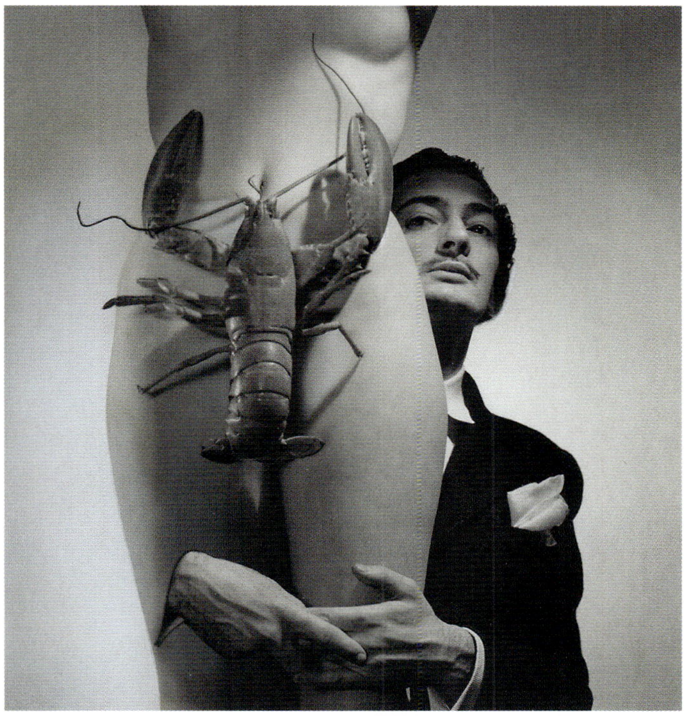

SALVADOR DALÍ WITH A MODEL IN HIS *LOBSTER THONG*

With the help of fabric expert Sache, Schiaparelli transferred the print onto casual cotton beach attire and a formal silk organdy summer evening gown in 1937. Dalí was annoyed, though—Schiaparelli would not let him put mayonnaise on the finished dress.

When Wallis Simpson wooed King Edward VIII away from the royal life, her extensive trousseau included eighteen Schiaparelli pieces. Simpson, known for her "*soignée*, not *dégagé*" (polished, but not relaxed) style, famously modeled the piece for photographer Cecil Beaton for *Vogue*.[67]

But, Schiaparelli and Dalí were far from "monogamous" in their collaborative endeavors. Schiaparelli also worked with other artists, including Jean Cocteau, Marcel Vertès, Kees van Dongen, Alberto Giacometti, Christian "Bébé" Bérard, Carl Erickson, Elsa Triolet, Leonor Fini, and Louis Aragon. Dalí imagined costumes for the Ballets Russes that Mademoiselle Chanel made, and he crafted textile prints of a "Desert Rock" and "Flower Ballet" for Hollywood designer Adrian. And Dalí's fashion-world jaunts were not relegated to just garments. He dressed windows for New York department store Bonwit Teller and designed covers for American and Parisian *Vogue* in December 1938, April 1944, December 1946, and December 1971—an issue he guest edited as well.

However, history has remembered the bond Schiaparelli and Dalí had—and the delectable lobster dress they made.

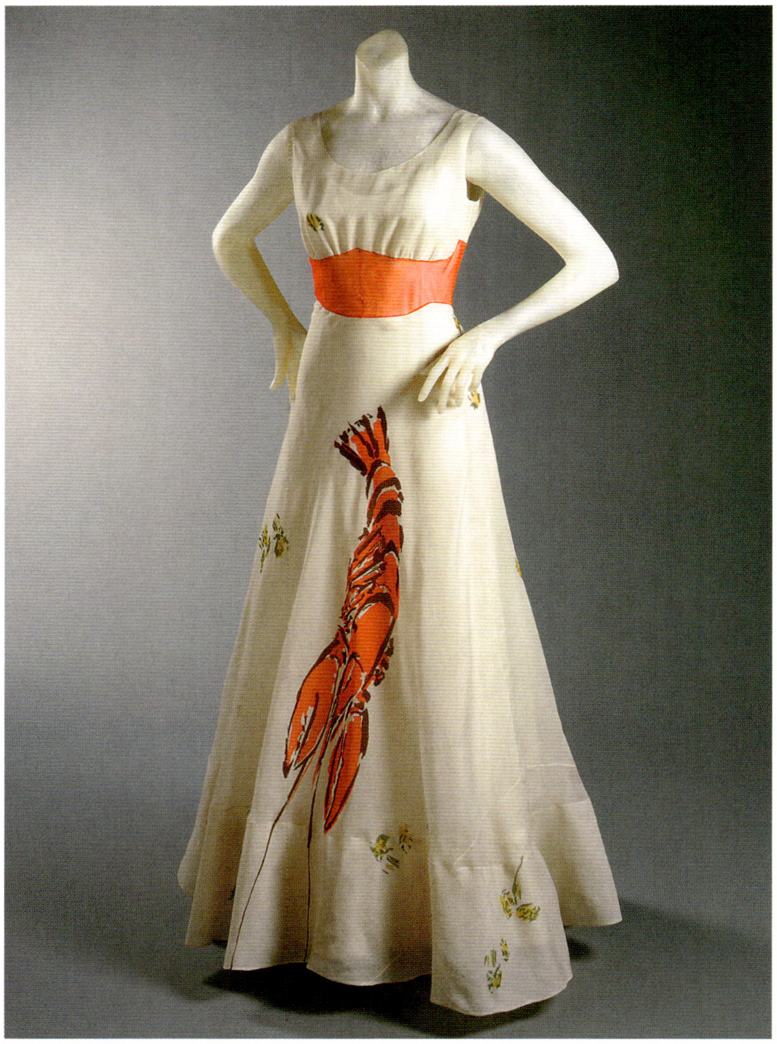

A LOBSTER DRESS | ELSA SCHIAPARELLI, 1937

DUCHESS OF WINDSOR WALLIS SIMPSON IN A LOBSTER DRESS | ELSA SCHIAPARELLI, 1937

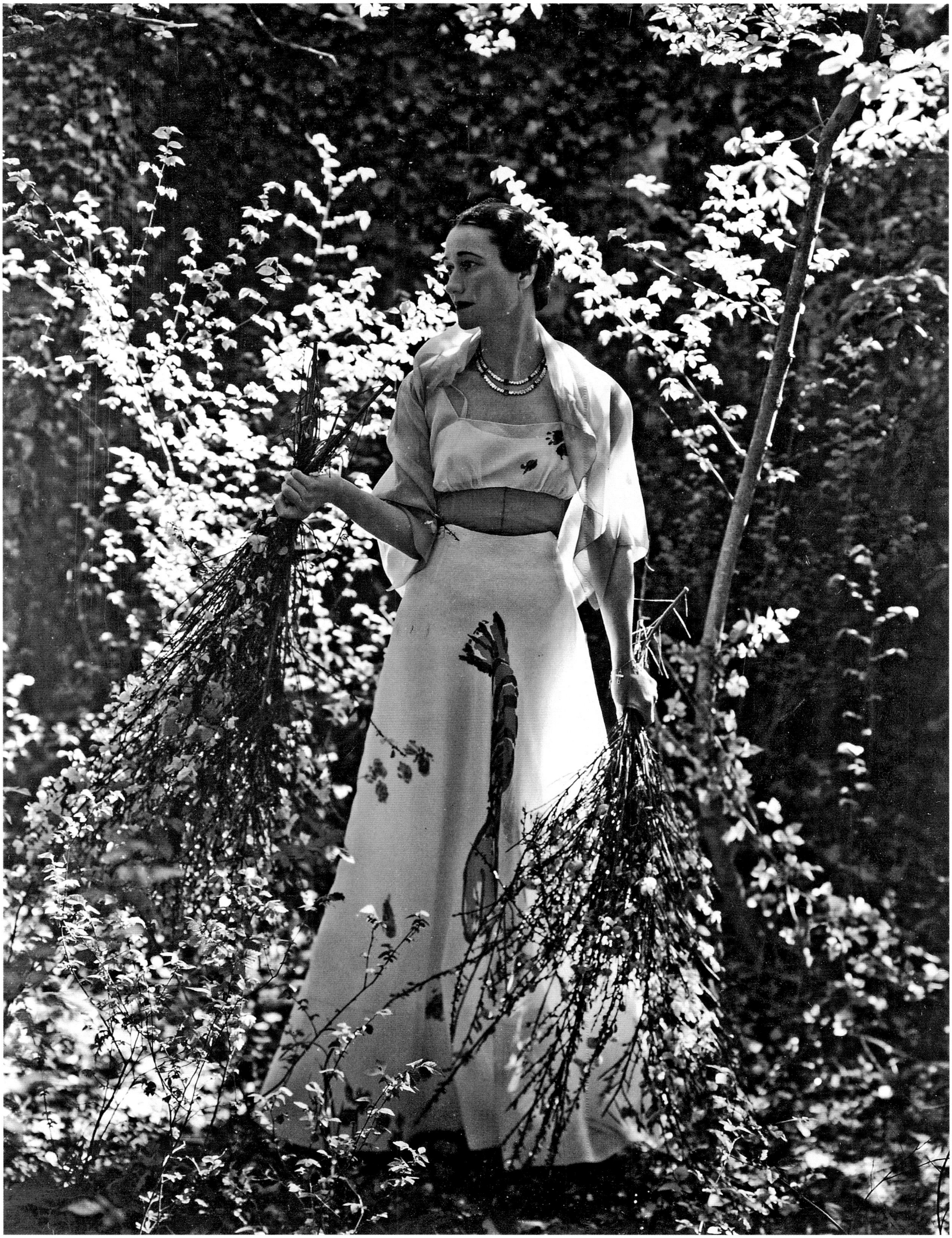

STERLING RUBY

RAF SIMONS

BELGIAN DESIGNER

Raf Simons (b. 1968) has crafted disillusionment into his eponymous menswear line since 1995, translating the aggression and alienation of urban youth into clothing through extreme cuts—very skinny or largely oversized—and distinctive imagery. In Los Angeles, German artist Sterling Ruby (b. 1972) channeled that same longing, anger, and hopelessness into an artistic form using multiple mediums.

Raf Simons considers art the lifeblood of his creativity: "There is no day that I am not looking at art. It's something that relaxes me, inspires me, and at the same time, it is also, I think, natural for me to connect it with what I do."[68] Simons met Sterling Ruby in 2005, and the two connected like long-lost brothers.

In 2008, Simons gave Ruby absolute autonomy to design his Tokyo flagship. The store appears violently ink-stained by Ruby's creation: wallpaper printed from photo negatives, from photographs of self-bleached denim. The following year, Simons and Ruby took the idea further with a capsule collection of artist-bleached jeans.

When Simons became creative director of Dior, his first collection for Autumn/Winter 2012–13 featured four Sterling Ruby prints on couture gowns, difficult to produce and challenging for the atelier. In order to accurately translate the rough quality of Ruby's brush strokes, Simons insisted upon using an original Christian Dior Couture technique: printing directly onto silk thread and using that thread to weave the fabric, rather than merely printing onto the fabric itself. Despite the astounding struggle to print Ruby's paintings onto thread and weave it into the shape of his work, it is precisely that type of outrageous craftsmanship that makes couture.

For Autumn/Winter 2014–15, Simons put his two-decades-old menswear label on hiatus, replacing it with the one-time-only label "Raf Simons/Sterling Ruby." Raf Simons shirts bleached by Sterling Ruby sport emblazoned buttons that read "RSSR: Raf Simons Studio Sterling Ruby Studio." Described as an "A to Z collaboration," every aspect of the collection was envisioned and designed by both men. Ruby echoed this, "There isn't one thing here that

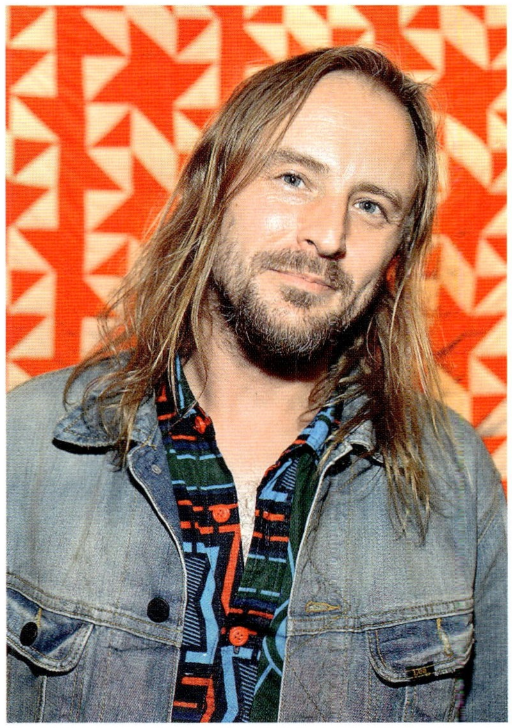

STERLING RUBY

isn't the result of collaboration."[69] By bleeding their work together and denying any division between what is touched by an artist and what is fashioned by a designer, Simons and Ruby have made fashion history. This intimate level of collaboration of this magnitude between a designer and an artist, which lasted for six months, has never since been attempted, let alone accomplished.

The collection consisted of coats hand-painted by Ruby and featuring "meta" embellishments that, rather than bearing actual curse words, proclaimed "abus lang," which translates to "abusive language." A theme throughout the collection is the word "fathers," which resurfaces on T-shirts and jackets. In the hands of Simons and Ruby, it comes across as an indictment, a type of psychological finger-pointing rather than an evocation of warm emotion.

Raf Simons/Sterling Ruby has a hierarchy within it. A coat labeled Limited Edition means it's one of five in existence. Limited Edition bleached shirts are one of fifty. Unique coats are more readily available, but each has randomly placed patches and badges, making them, well, unique.

The fervor of collectors to nab these pieces required a new approach to retail. An e-shop (inthenameof.be) launched on July 15, 2014, and up through September 1, 2014, it sold only two pieces at a time—making buying any of the pieces a mad electronic dash, a bit like trying to get tickets to a stadium show. Now the question may not be if Raf Simons is an artist or if Sterling Ruby is a designer but are they both rock stars?

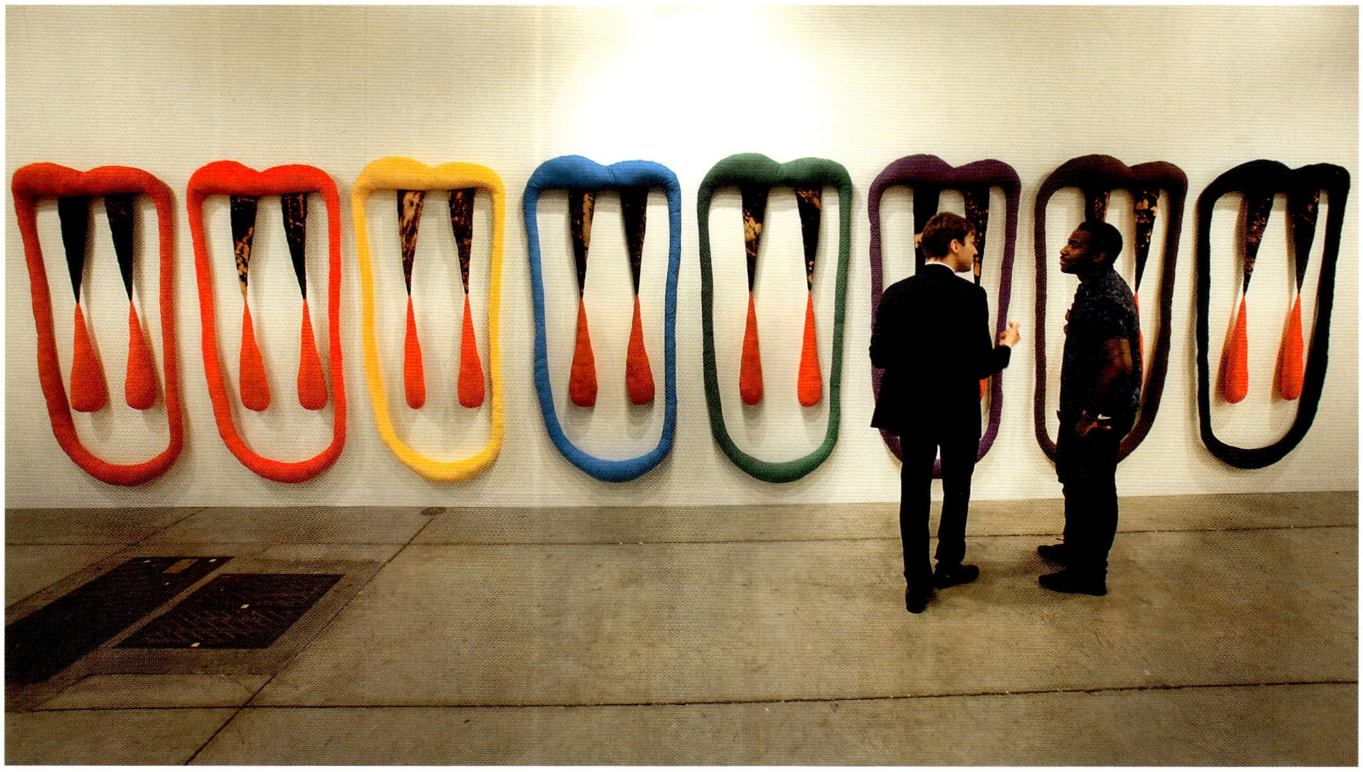

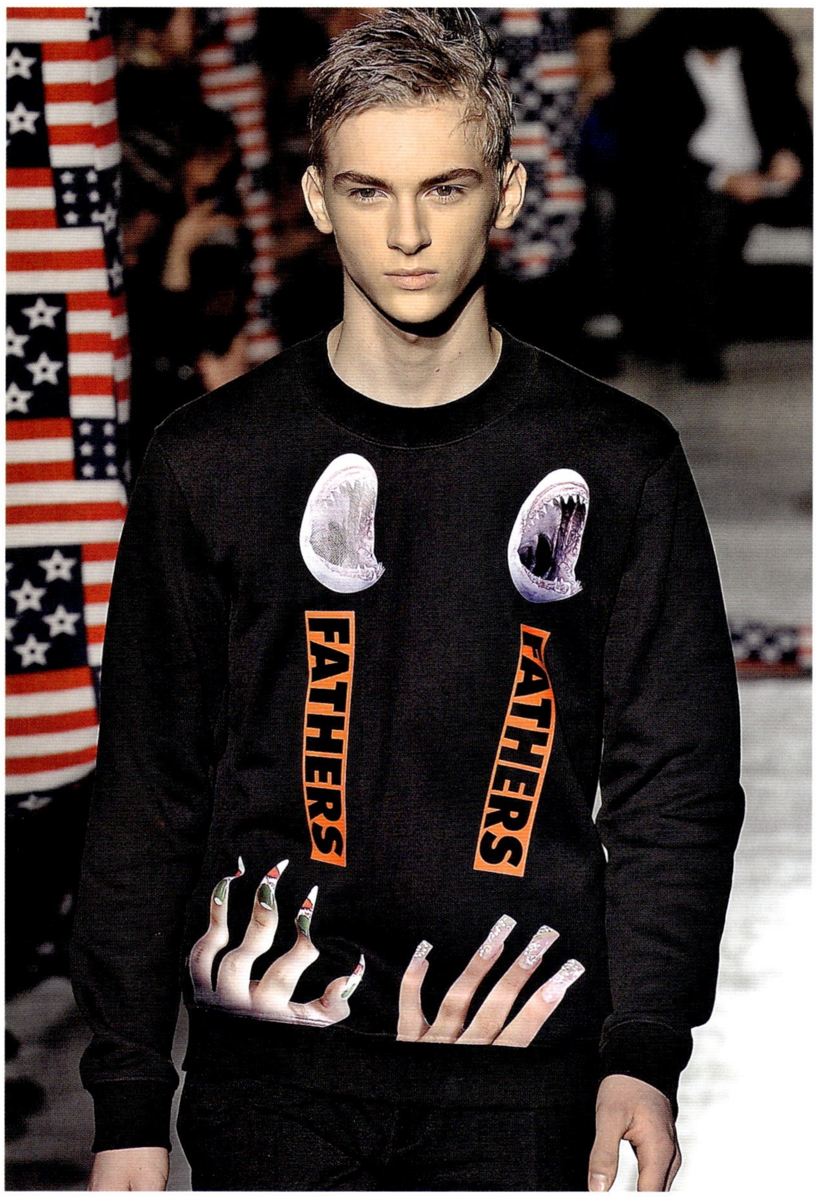

∧ *VAMPIRE FANGS* INSTALLATION | ART BASEL MIAMI | STERLING RUBY, 2012

< MEN'S COLLECTION | RAF SIMONS & STERLING RUBY, 2014

> MEN'S COLLECTION | RAF SIMONS & STERLING RUBY, 2014

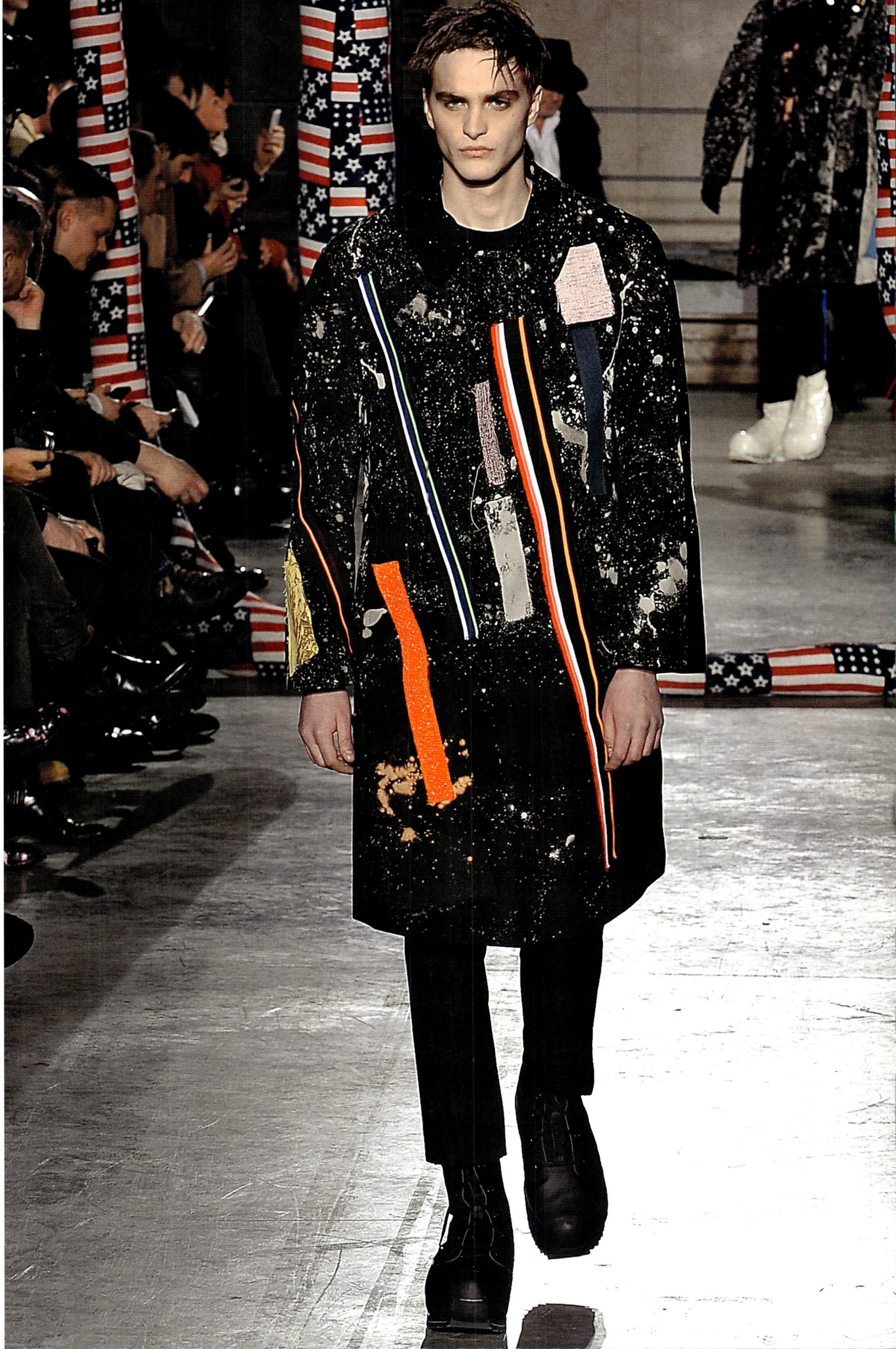

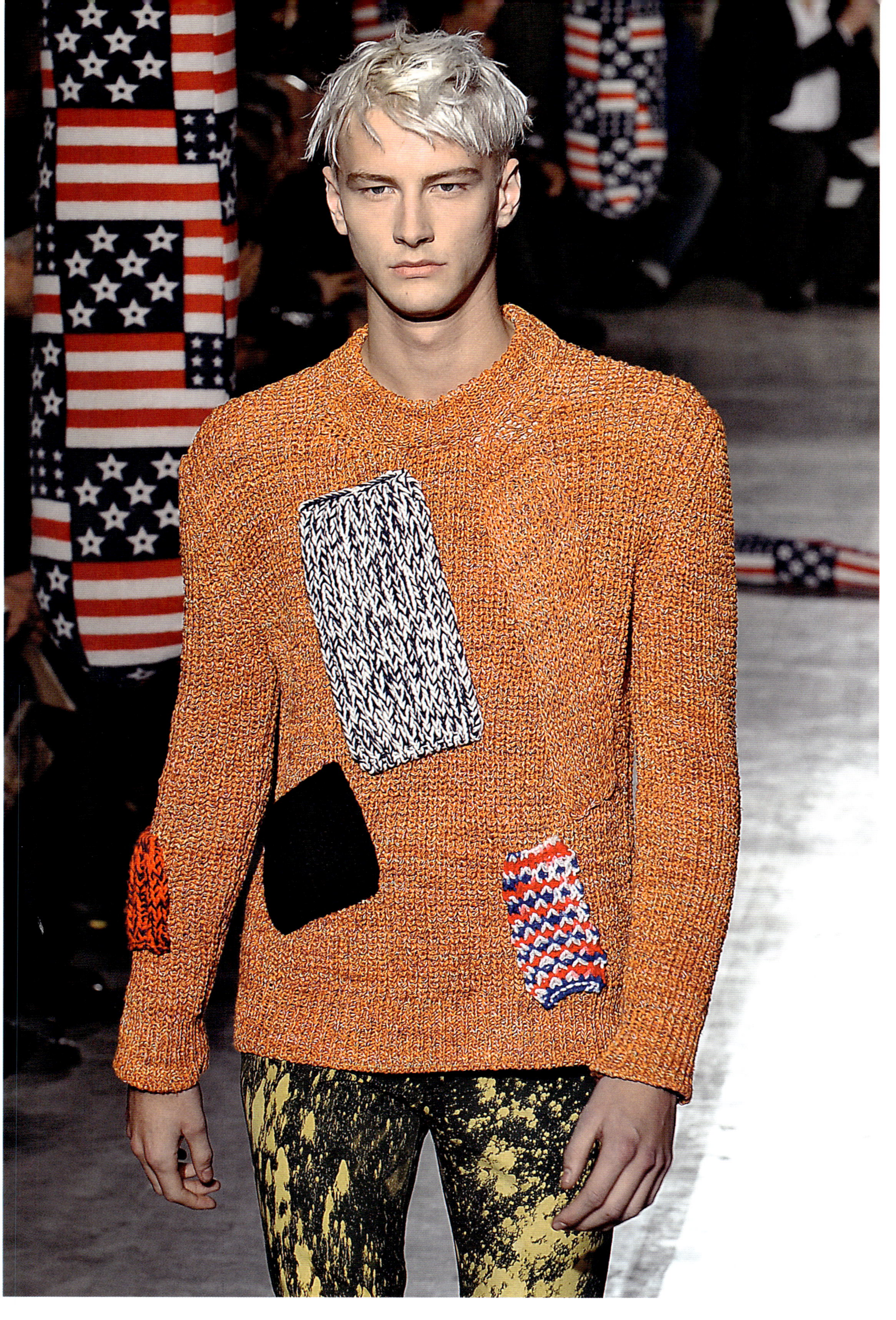

MEN'S COLLECTION | RAF SIMONS & STERLING RUBY, 2014

MEN'S COLLECTION | RAF SIMONS & STERLING RUBY, 2014

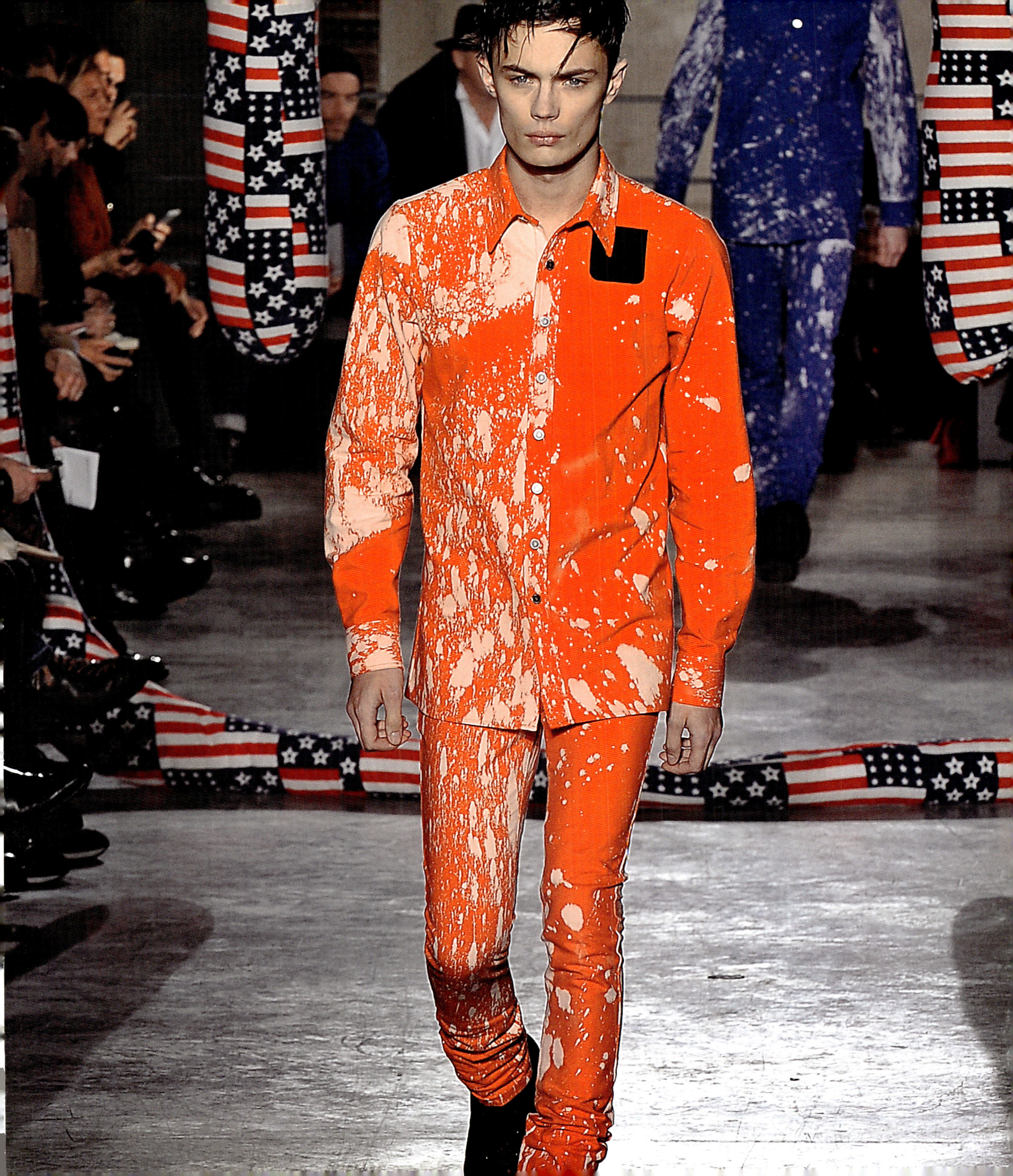

TIM ROELOFF

TS VERSACE

GIANNI VERSACE'S aggressively sexy garments, best super-modeled by the trinity of Christy Turlington, Naomi Campbell, and Linda Evangelista, were appreciated by the fashion-ravenous, yes, but also by theatergoers who'd seen his costumes for ballets and operas, and by museum curators as well. His work was displayed in 1985 at the Victoria & Albert Museum. In 1992 Gianni Versace (1946–1997) debuted a $1 million "Versace Signatures" exhibition at the Fashion Institute of Technology (FIT), which two years later traveled to the Kunstgewerbemuseum in Berlin.

After his devastating death, Versace's label soldiered on under the creative direction of his sister, Donatella Versace (b. 1955). Having been with the house since 1979, Ms. Versace continued to honor the spirit of her brother's designs while ushering the label into the 21st century.

For Fall/Winter 2008–09, Donatella Versace collaborated with Holland-born, Berlin-based collage artist Timotheus Paulus Roeloffs (b. 1965). "I have long been a fan and enthusiast where art is concerned," Versace said, adding, "Gianni was a true pioneer in that he blurred the boundaries between fashion and art—and fashion and music, and ballet, and celebrity, too."[70] An aficionada of Roeloffs's work—most famous for appearing prominently in the renowned Berlin art-squat Tacheles—and wanting to honor her brother's love of the once-divided German city, Versace commissioned twelve Roeloffs pieces to be used on her dresses. Roeloffs, however, was given strict parameters by the company's corporate offices: no alcohol bottles, sex, or politics, all themes pervasive in his artwork. Roeloffs's work explores themes of chaos and "societies in transformation,"[71] like that of East Berlin before and after 1989, juxtaposing provocative imagery (zebras in flagrante delicto; female nudes with animal heads) with political tropes in photomontages.

Versace did provide him with inspiring resources, however, among them 1960s wallpaper books belonging to her late brother and vintage imagery from the fashion house. The final works he created featured decaying urban environments, Icarus flying toward the forbidden sun, phrases like "Berlin has it all," and fragments of Versace advertising.

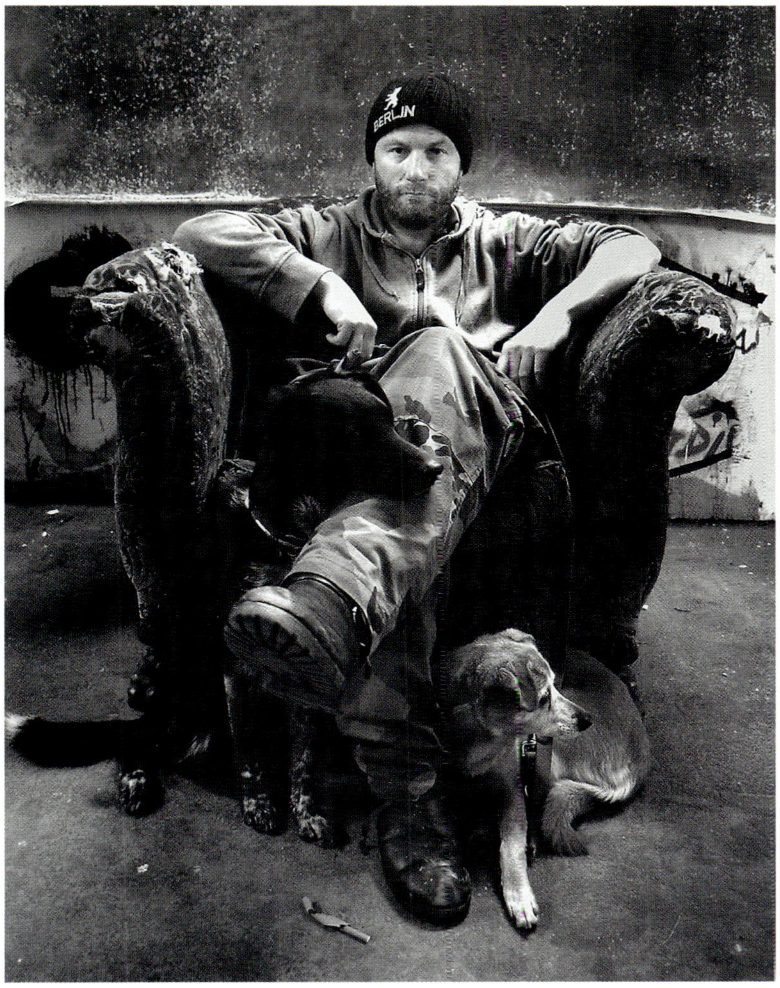

TIM ROELOFFS

Donatella Versace picked four of his pieces to be digitally printed on blindingly bright canary yellow, deep purple, and hot magenta satin minidresses. In order to capture the 3-D effect of Roeloffs's hand-cut collages, embroidery was added on top of the floral parts of the prints.

The collaboration between Tim Roeloffs and Donatella Versace is one of the most hands-off partnerships described in this volume. Throughout the entire project, the two never met. It was quite literally a case of her people calling his people, with intermediaries arranging all the details. Perhaps because of this, there's a certain incongruity to the designs, a visual abruptness that in less expert hands could be jarring, but that is instead, with each half of this loosely coupled duo riffing on the work of the other, actually able to conjure a sense of freshness and opposites-attract possibility.

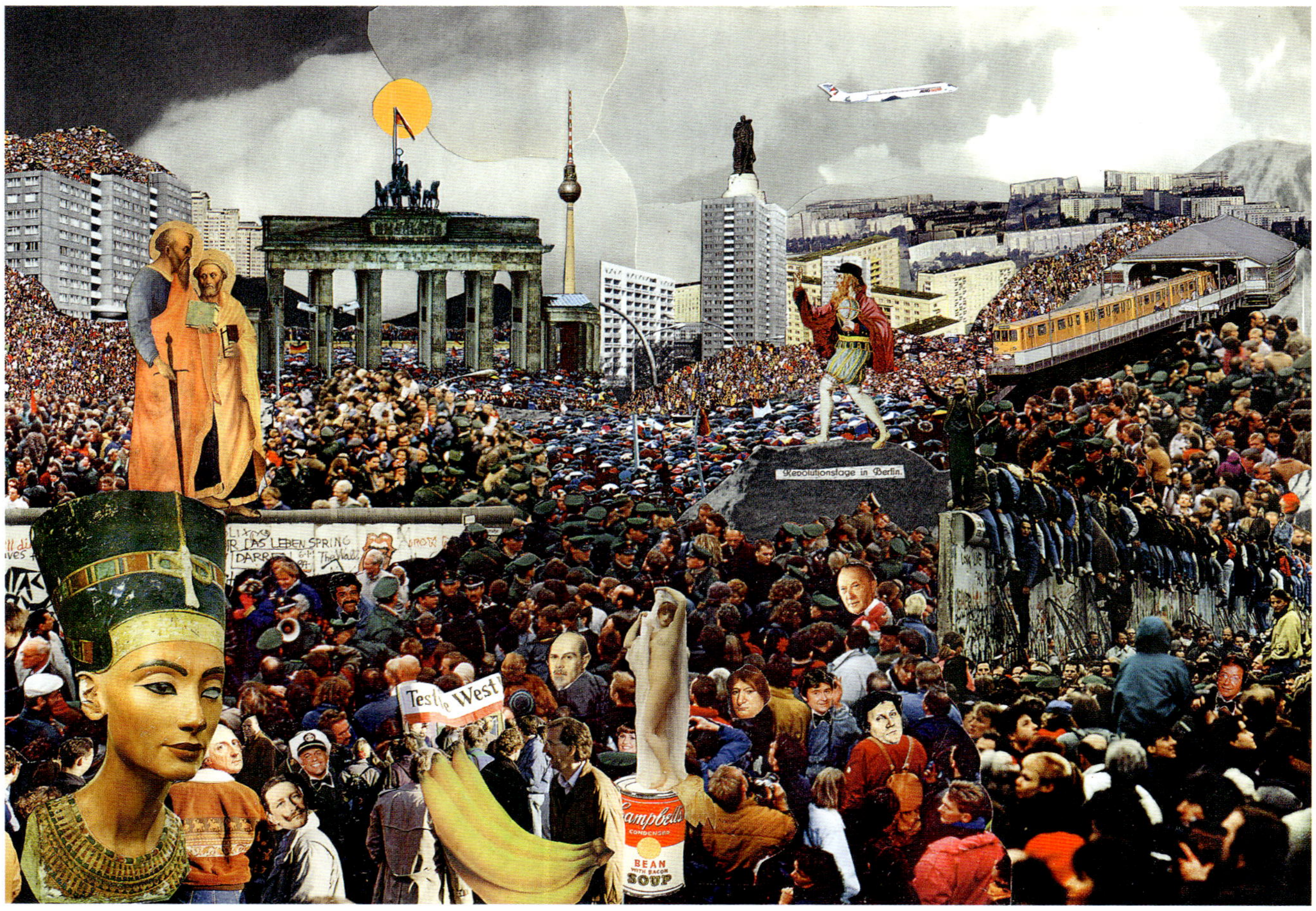

NOV. 9TH, 1988: BERLINERS CELEBRATE THE FALL OF THE WALL | COLLAGE | TIM ROELOFFS, CIRCA 2005

VERSACE DRESS | TIM ROELOFFS, 2008

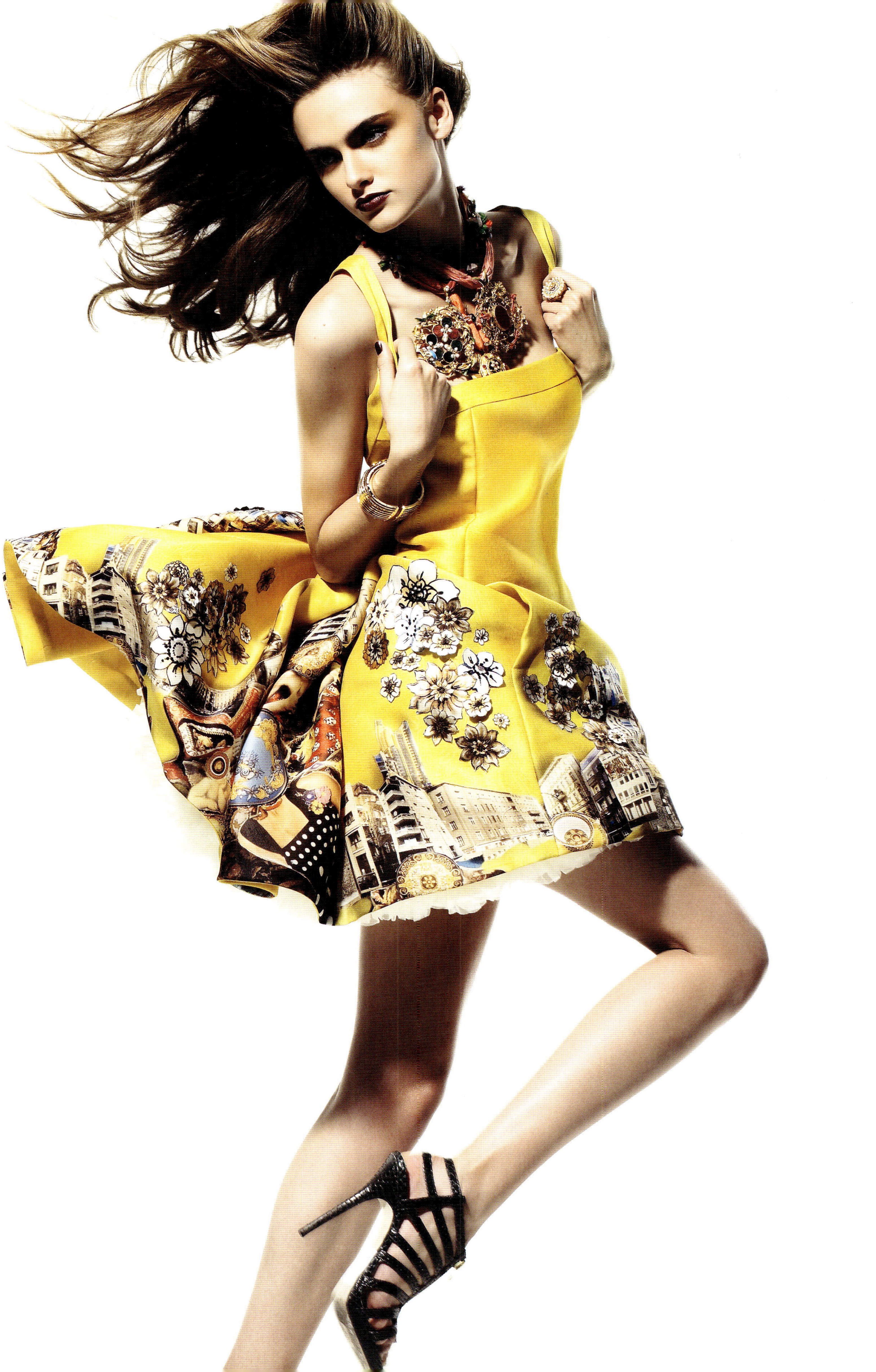

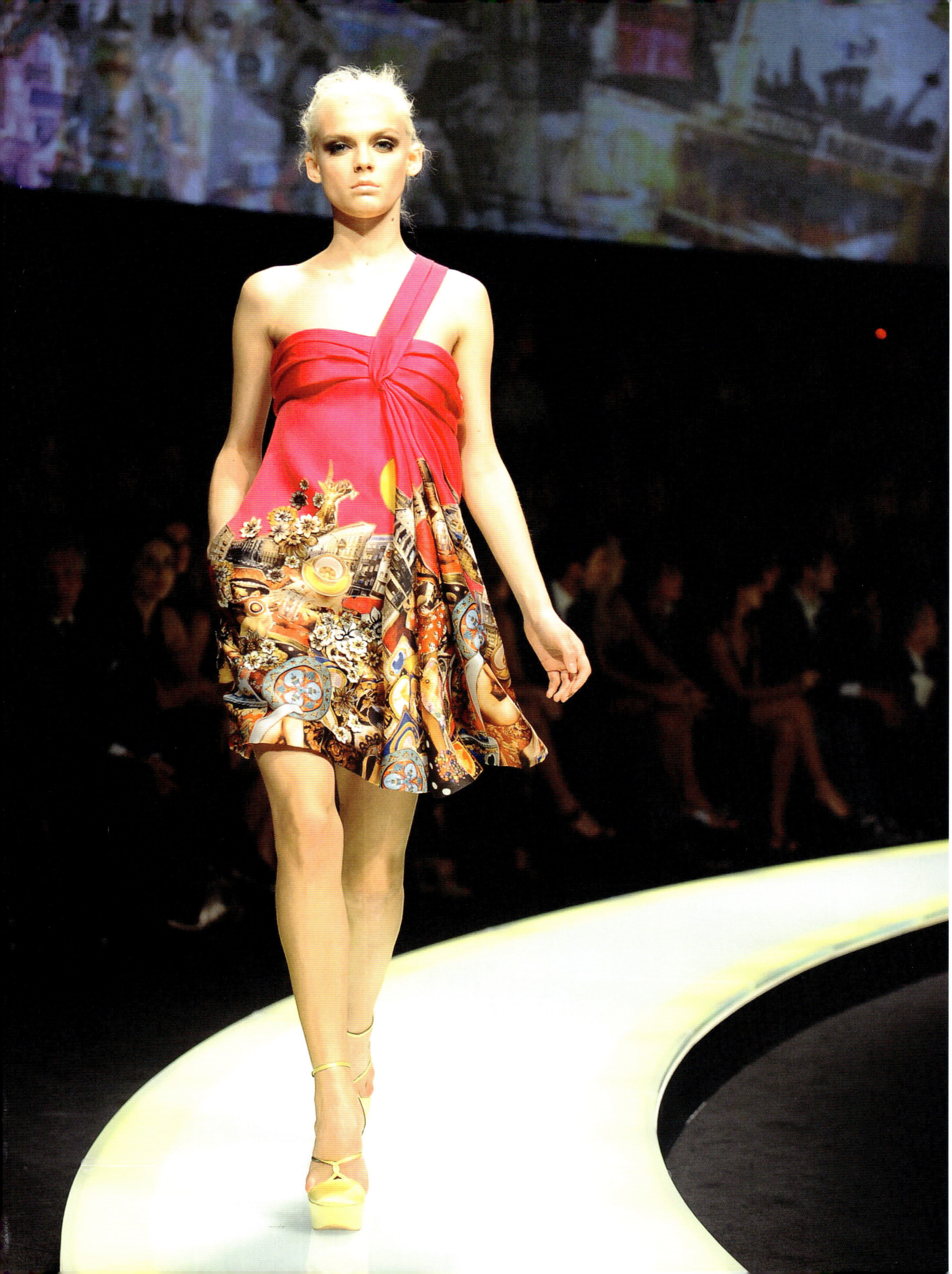

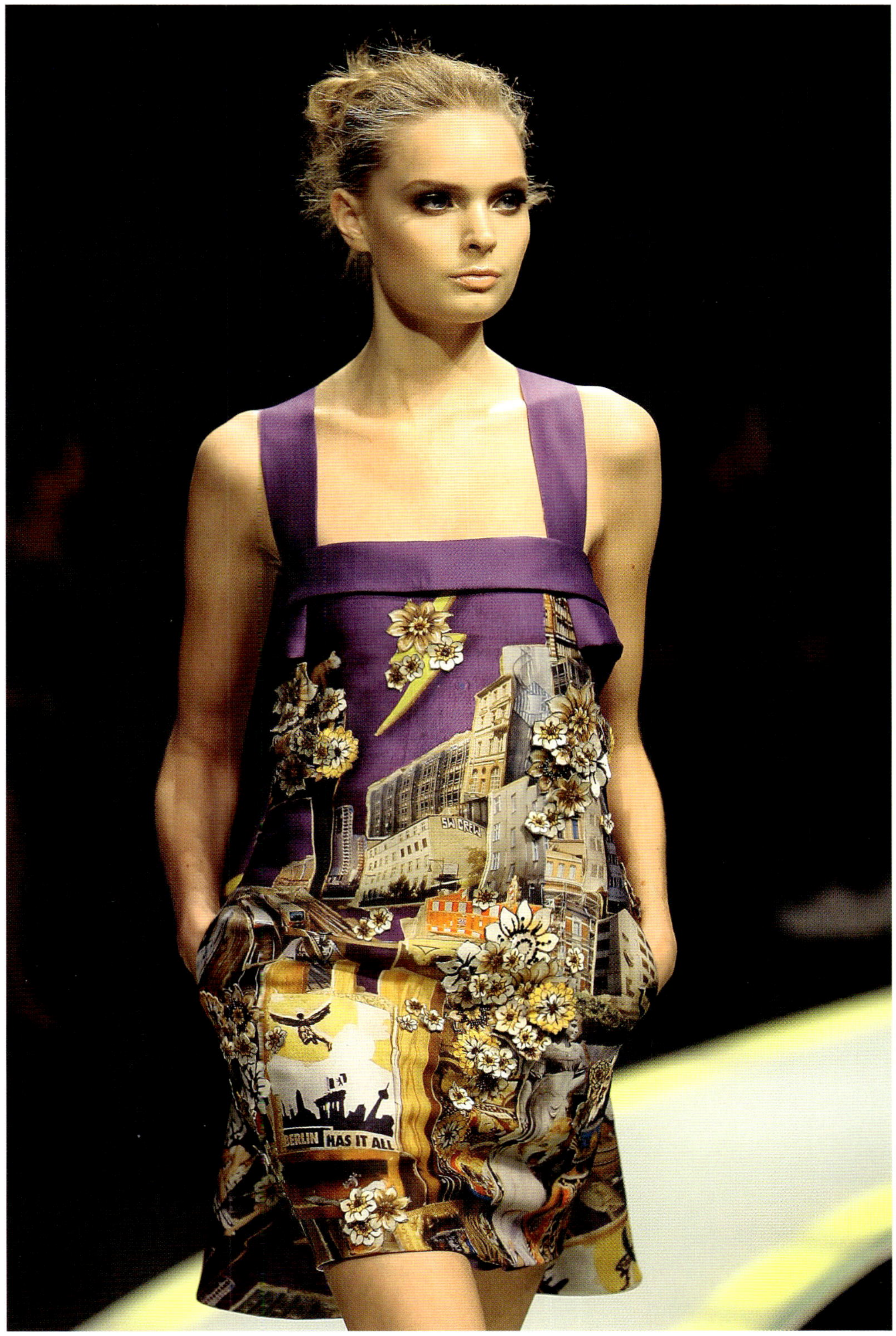

VERSACE DRESS | TIM ROELOFFS, 2008

VERSACE DRESS | TIM ROELOFFS, 2008

THE CHAPMAN BROTH

ERS LOUIS VUITTON

GO AHEAD. LOOK.

Be shocked. Dismayed. Display the highest form of moral outrage. For as long as possible. And then watch those explosive feelings dissipate under the weight of reality. Realize that the sculptural mannequins used in the Chapman Brothers' work are just that: resin and fiberglass. The real threat of the art duo's work is the impending realization of how benign and banal it actually is. Summarizing the Young British Artist movement they are a part of, Jake Chapman ruminates: "In the YBA 'paradigm' the true misanthropic element lies in the fact that much of the work was intended to generate boredom rather than euphoric entertainment."[72] In that light, the Chapman Brothers' collaboration with Louis Vuitton was unsuccessful, as it did not evoke ennui but excitement.

As it was Louis Vuitton's first artistic collaboration for menswear, the fashion press was ecstatic. Global coverage, sales, and name recognition had followed Louis Vuitton's womens wear collaborations with Stephen Sprouse, Takashi Murakami, Richard Prince, and Yayoi Kusama, under the creative direction of Marc Jacobs. In Fall/Winter 2013–14, Louis Vuitton's fashion and art collaborations were no longer for ladies alone. Kim Jones (b. 1979), men's style director of Louis Vuitton, asked longtime friend Iakovos "Jake" Chapman (b. 1966) and older brother Konstantinos "Dinos" (b. 1962) to collaborate on his Bhutan-inspired collection. The pair produced their most user-friendly work, albeit for them that meant illustrations of a flying eyeball in a hellish garden (an allusion to Diana Vreeland's interior decorating scheme), zombie owls, and a vivisected teddy bear. Jones put the creepy yet adorable monsters on tuxedos, smoking jackets, velvet slippers, and massive embroidered man-bags that Dinos Chapman cheekily thinks should be used to "carry a lot of money around."[73]

Jake Chapman's bond with fellow Brit Kim Jones made the collaboration easy. "It's been a nice working relationship. We'd get the Eurostar to meet Kim in Paris."[74] While likely exaggerated, the ongoing working relationship between the brothers, which began in 1991, is more contentious. In their tome *Flogging a Dead Horse*, Dinos definitively states, "We enjoy squabbling." Jake echoes the sentiment, explaining, "We're much too pessimistically bound to yearn for creative symbiosis. . . . It's not a love-in."[75] Yet, despite their sibling status, the

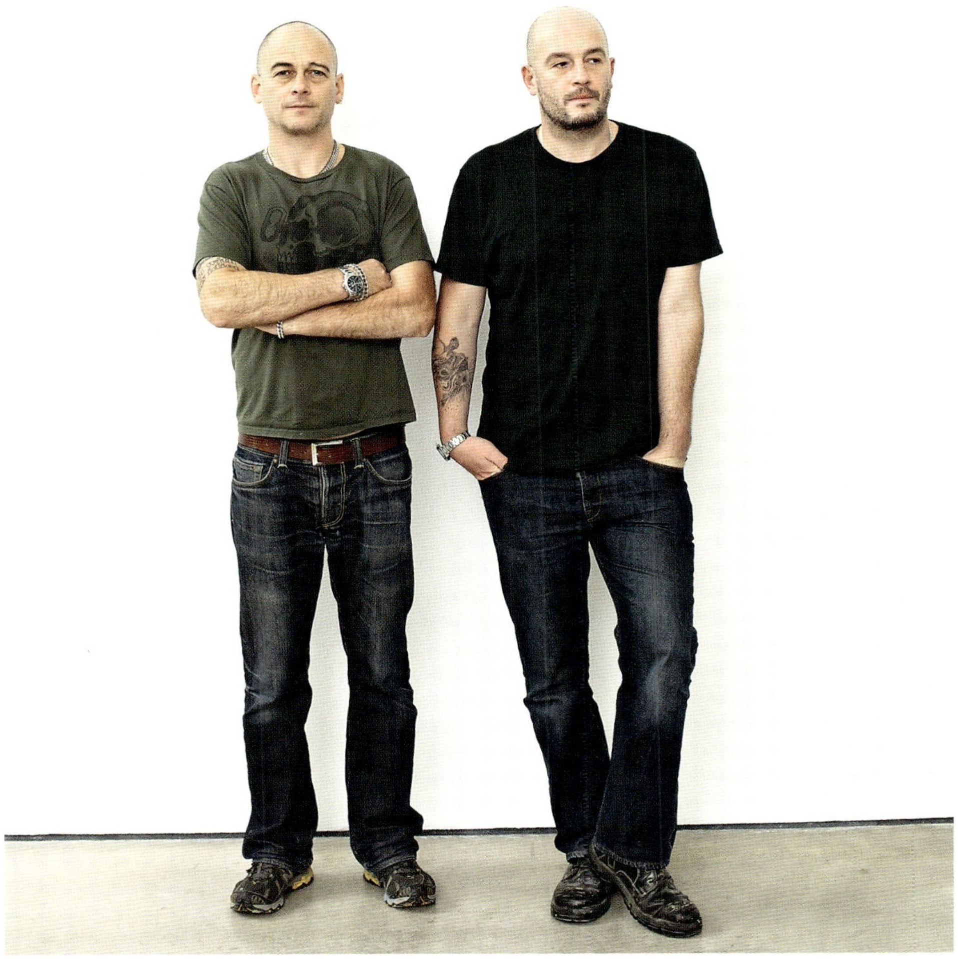

DINOS AND JAKE CHAPMAN

pair has been making it work for over twenty years. While the Chapman Brothers did create a saccharine catwalk backdrop for Stella McCartney's Spring/Summer 2009 collection, the collaboration with Kim Jones was the pair's real entrance into fashion.

The Chapman Brothers view their artwork and their collaboration with Louis Vuitton as complementary: "The people who are buying the bags are the kind of people who would buy our work. So I don't think it's a new market; it's part of the same market. . . . You've got the sculptures, you should really have the bag."[76] Chapman's ideology illustrates 18th-century philosopher Denis Diderot's namesake effect. Following the impulse purchase of a sumptuous scarlet dressing gown, Diderot fell into a frenzy of consumption purchasing equally divine items for every aspect of his life. Had Diderot been born 275 years later, the infamous dressing gown that started it all would likely have been one designed together by the Chapman Brothers and Kim Jones for Louis Vuitton.

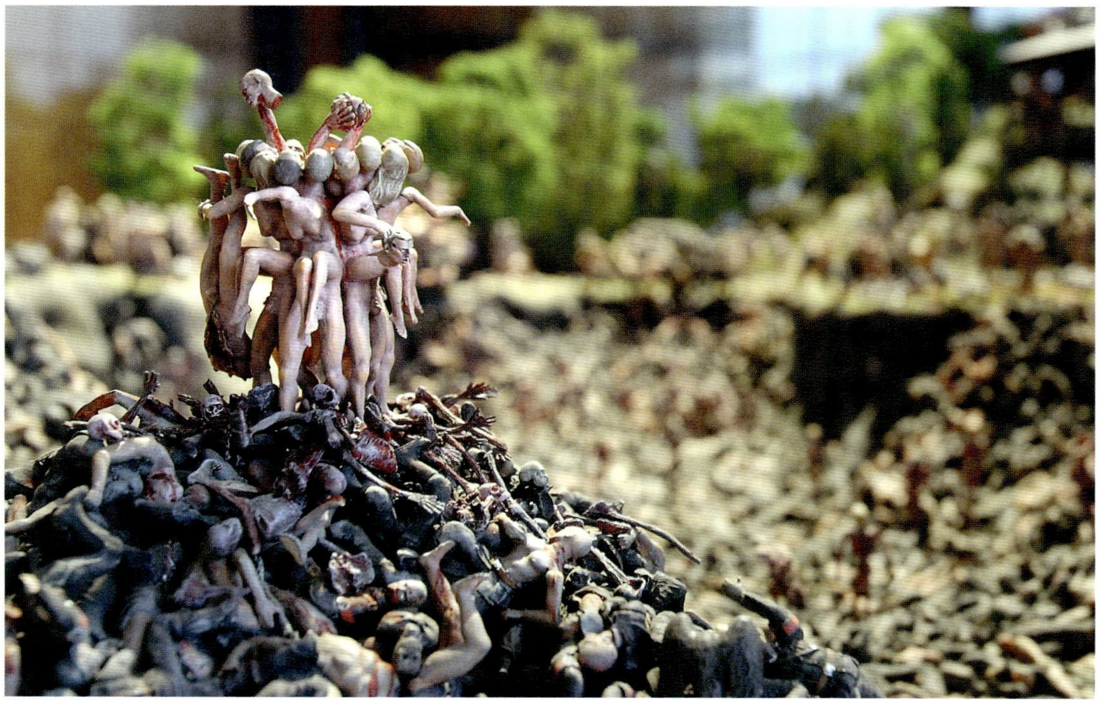

/\ *HELL* (DETAIL) | 9-PIECE SCULPTURAL INSTALLATION | JAKE AND DINOS CHAPMAN, 2000

> PANTS WITH CHAPMAN BROTHERS' *GARDEN IN HELL* TEXTILE | LOUIS VUITTON, 2013

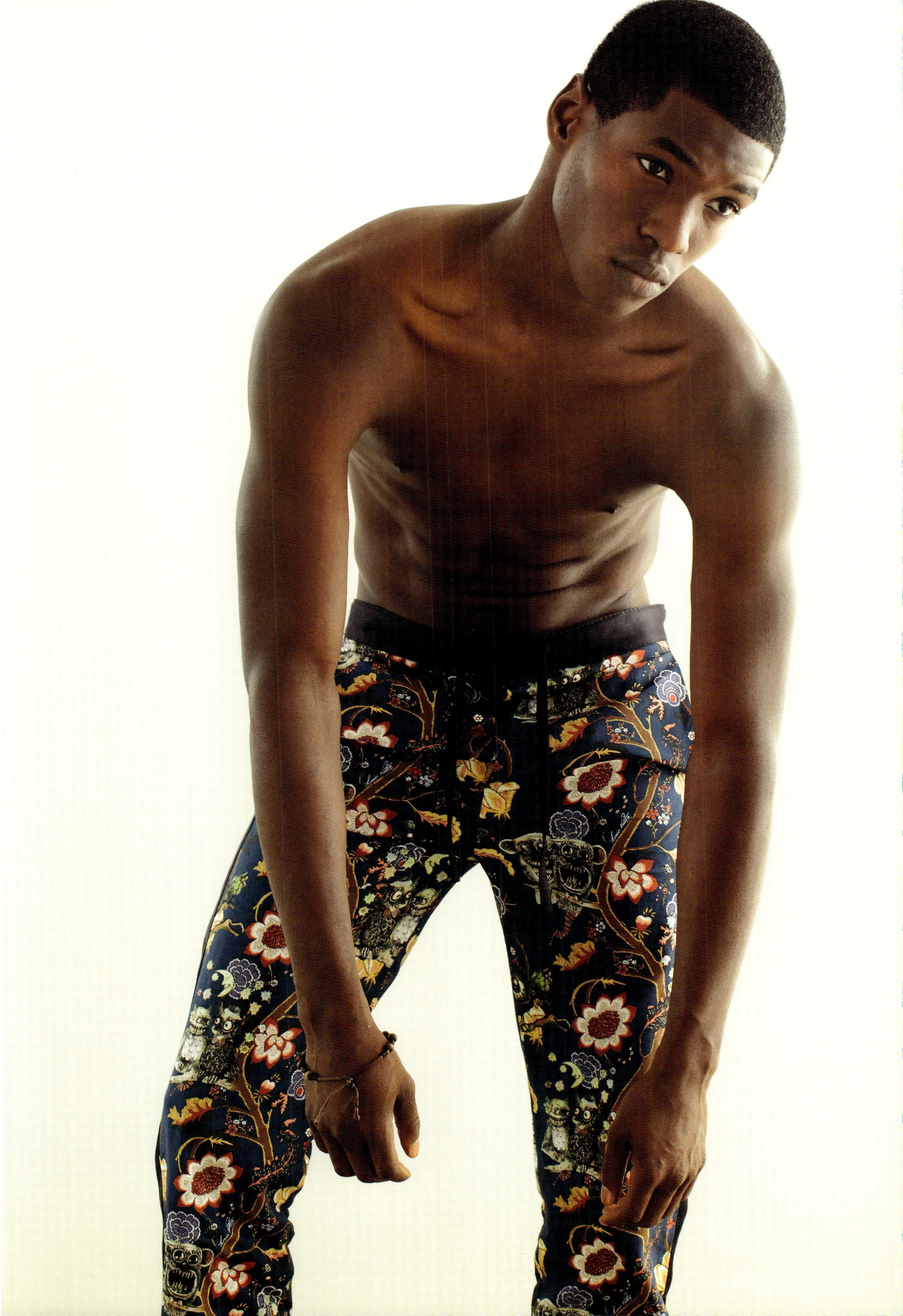

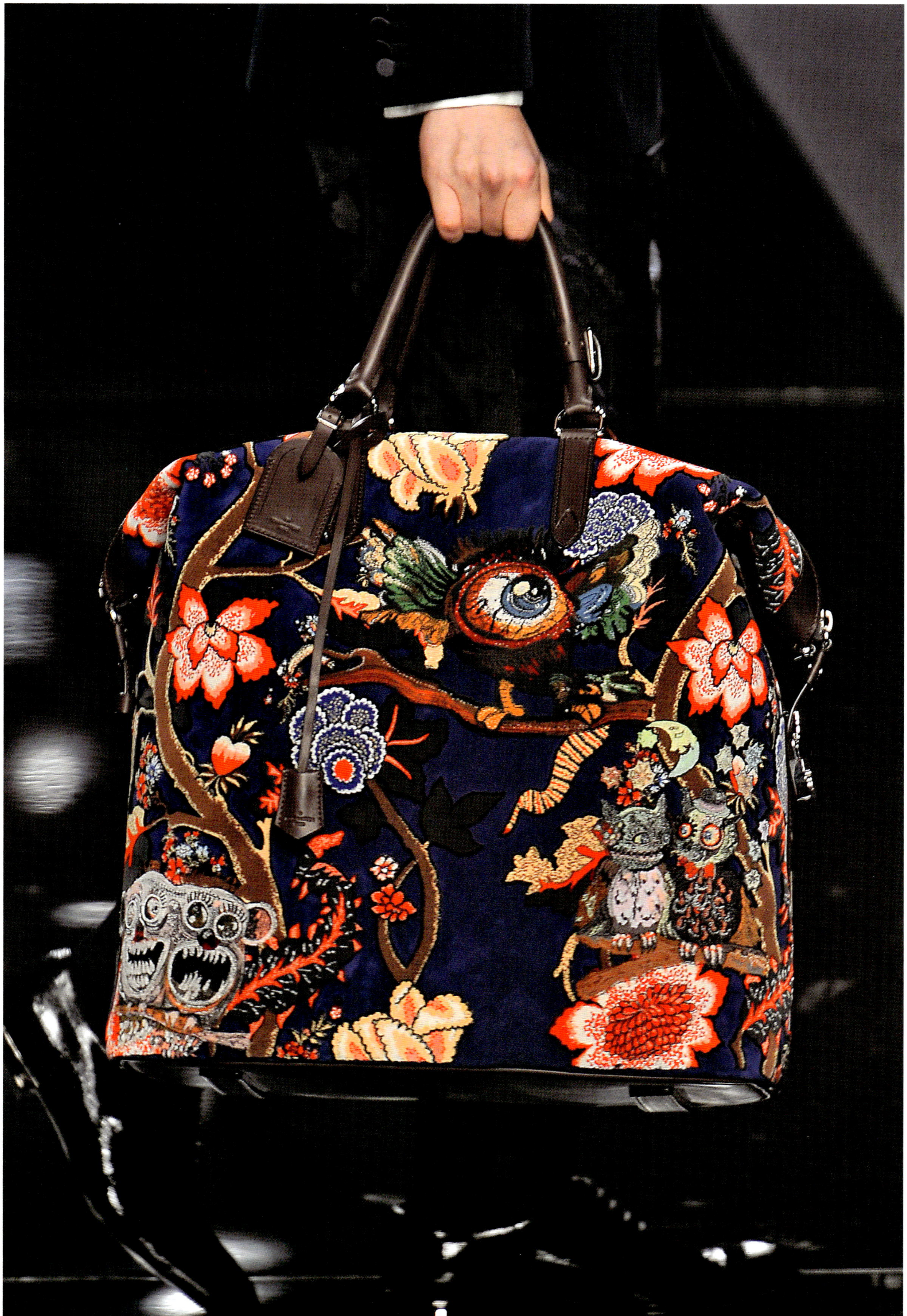

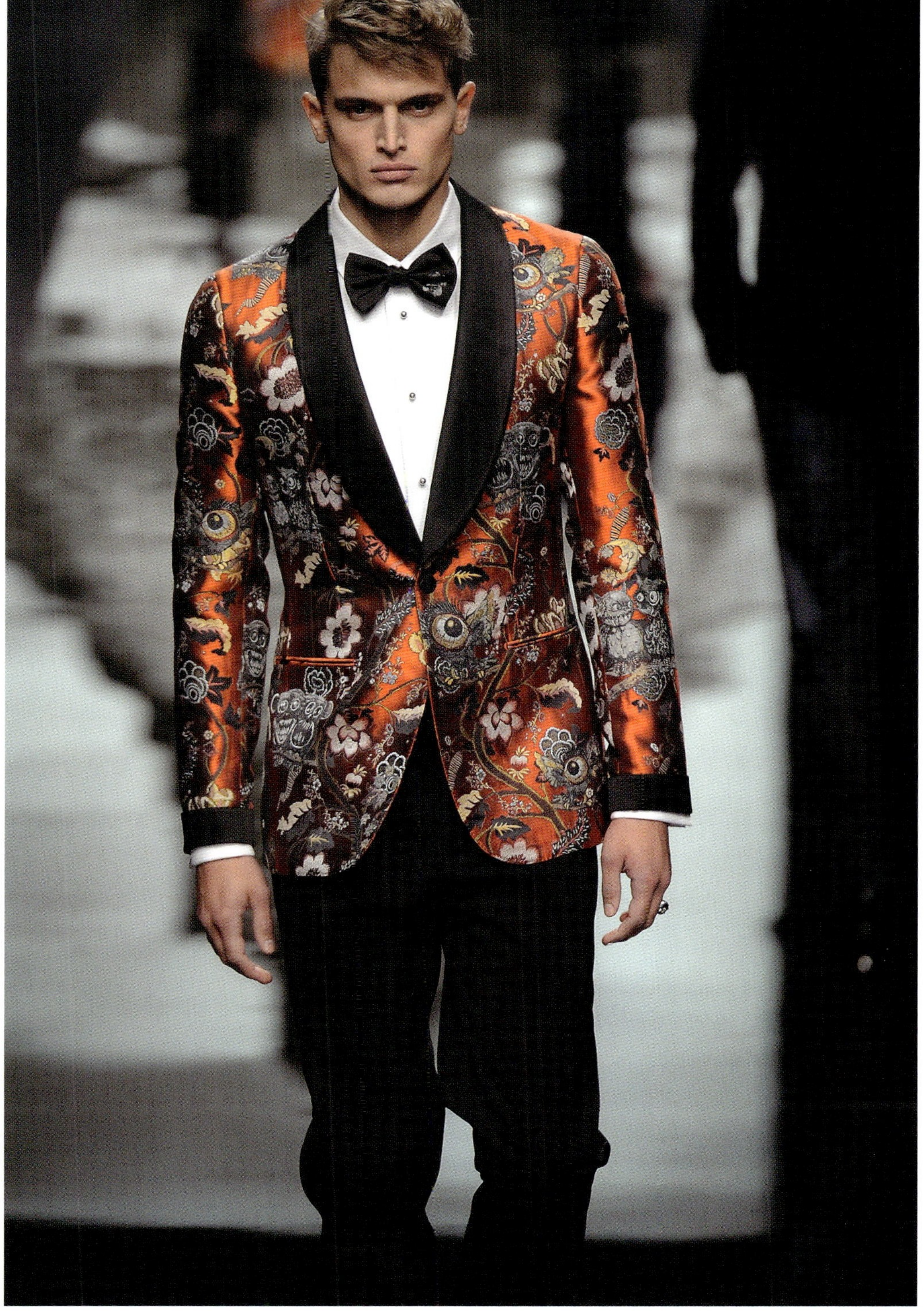

TOTE WITH CHAPMAN BROTHERS' *GARDEN IN HELL* TEXTILE | LOUIS VUITTON, 2013

TUXEDO JACKET WITH CHAPMAN BROTHERS' *GARDEN IN HELL* TEXTILE | LOUIS VUITTON, 2013

SWEATER WITH CHAPMAN BROTHERS DETAIL | LOUIS VUITTON, 2013

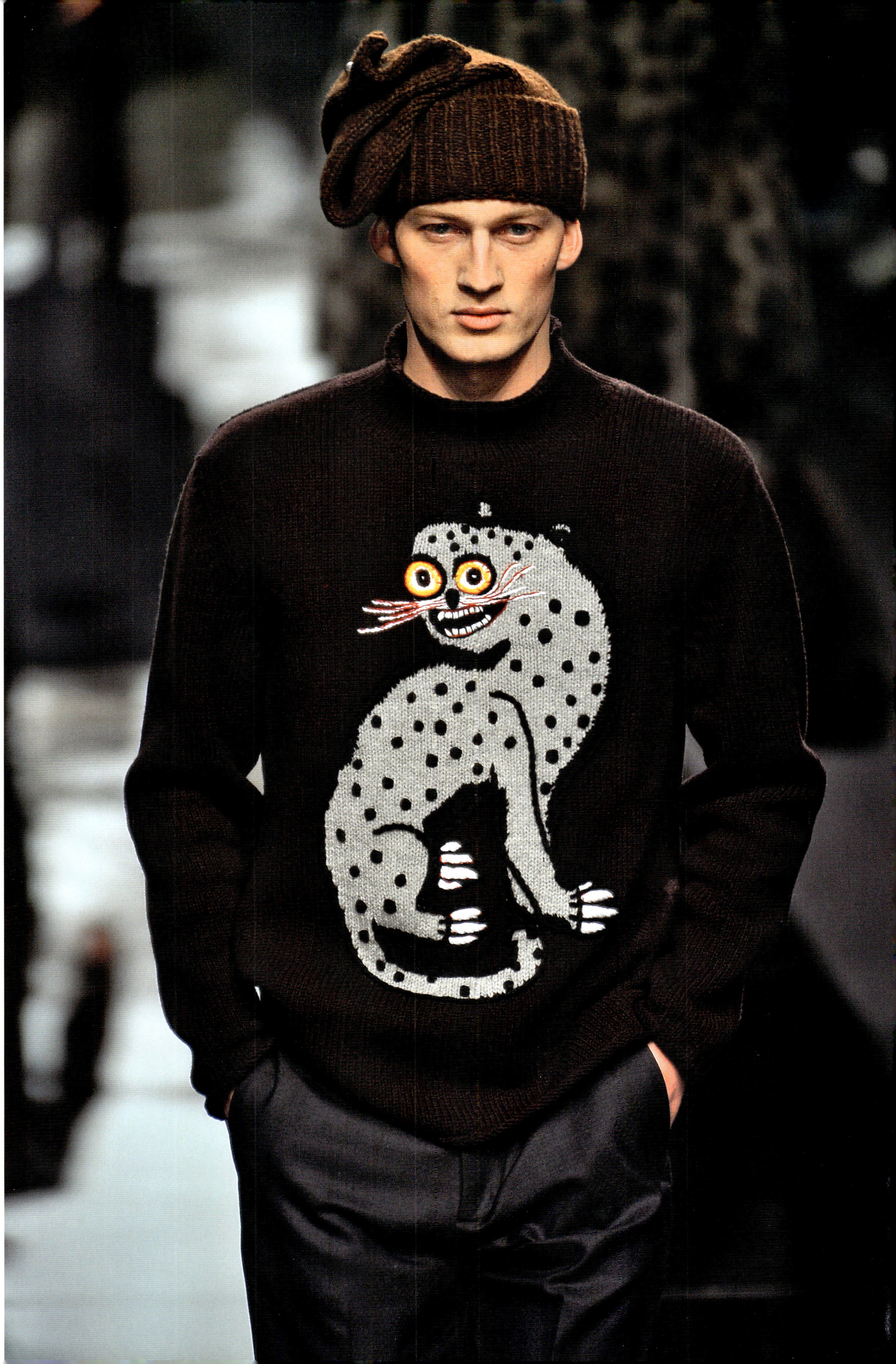

TIM BURTON

TIM WALKER

THE FANTASTICAL

worlds of childhood tales often encompass the sinister. To hit the high notes of pure delight, evil must be introduced and conquered, something filmmaker Tim Burton (b. 1958) has always understood. Burton's "family" films, like *The Nightmare Before Christmas* (1993) and *The Corpse Bride* (2005), deal with themes of death and other scary and weird elements that have been ever present in children's literature. While Burton's interpretations may heighten their bizarre details, the original texts on which he based his *James and the Giant Peach* (1996), *Charlie and the Chocolate Factory* (2005), and *Alice in Wonderland* (2010) all incorporate imaginative, and sometimes disturbing, otherworldly elements that border on hallucinogenic.

Fashion photographer Tim Walker (b. 1970) has garnered fame for his ability to create similar, though sweeter, imagery for publications like *Vogue*, *Love*, and *W*. In 1995, Walker awoke editorial opulence that had been a sleeping beauty since Diana Vreeland's 1971 departure from American *Vogue*. His photos dazzle with intricate, playful unrealities full of couture and, often, enormous props. Yet, after a decade indulging his wild whims, Walker's work began to take a Tim Burton–esque turn: "My lemoncurd-and-honey vision got darker."[77] After all, "sweetness can't genuinely exist without a darkness."[78]

Thus two brilliant creatives adept at crafting narrative-filled fanciful imagery found themselves walking close at hand. Walker and Burton were brought together not only by a shared vision of the world (or other worlds), but also by the Museum of Modern Art's then-impending retrospective of Tim Burton's career.

For British *Vogue*'s December 2008 issue, Walker and Burton collaborated on "Tales of the Unexpected." The shoot references Roald Dahl's novel *Charlie and the Chocolate Factory* (which was Burtonized in 2005), along with allusions to others of Dahl's various tales. Musician Devonté "Dev" Hynes played a clashing, dashing Willy Wonka in an eclectic ensemble of Vivienne Westwood MAN. Model Karen Elson gleefully mucked about with giant eyes, an ode to Dahl's *The Twits*, in an Yves Saint Laurent dress. Tim Burton and his longtime partner, actress Helena Bonham Carter, are themselves models, appearing as though they've accidentally blown themselves up while concocting revolting recipes in the wake of having crashed Wonka's glass elevator.

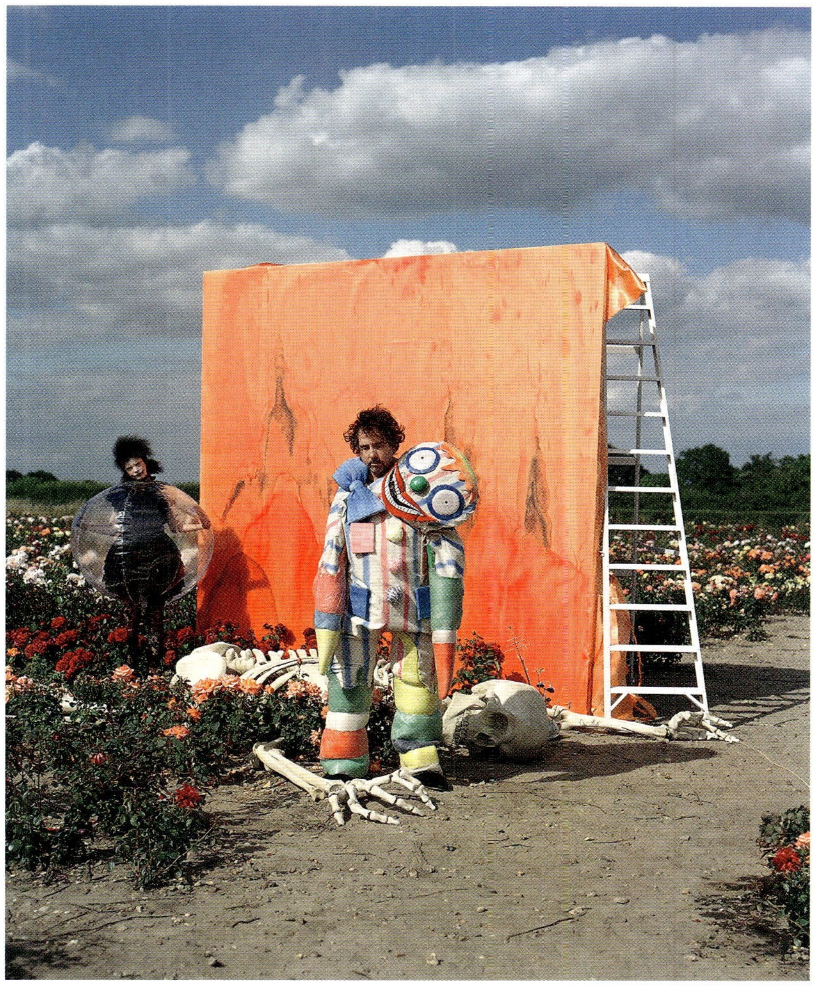

TIM BURTON IN *TRICKS AND TREATS*, TIM BURTON AND TIM WALKER FOR *HARPER'S BAZAAR*, 2009

Tim Burton and Tim Walker came together again for Halloween 2009, offering stateside *Harper's Bazaar* readers more tricks than treats. Polish supermodel Malgosia Bela joined models Sophie Srej and Evelina Mambetova along with Burton and a larger-than-life skeleton in the Cants of Colchester rose field. Bela, clad in Nina Ricci, danced with a skeletal devil—although not in the pale moonlight, as Walker never uses a flash. The wardrobe of Edward Scissorhands was upgraded with the help of Rodarte and shoe god Nicholas Kirkwood's creations for the cult brand. Burton later holds the skeleton's head in a sack; whether the present is for a good or bad little boy is anyone's guess.

The media hype, including the spreads by Burton and Walker done in anticipation of Burton's MoMA exhibition (November 22, 2009, to April 26, 2010) worked, drawing over 800,000 visitors, the third-largest crowd in the museum's history.

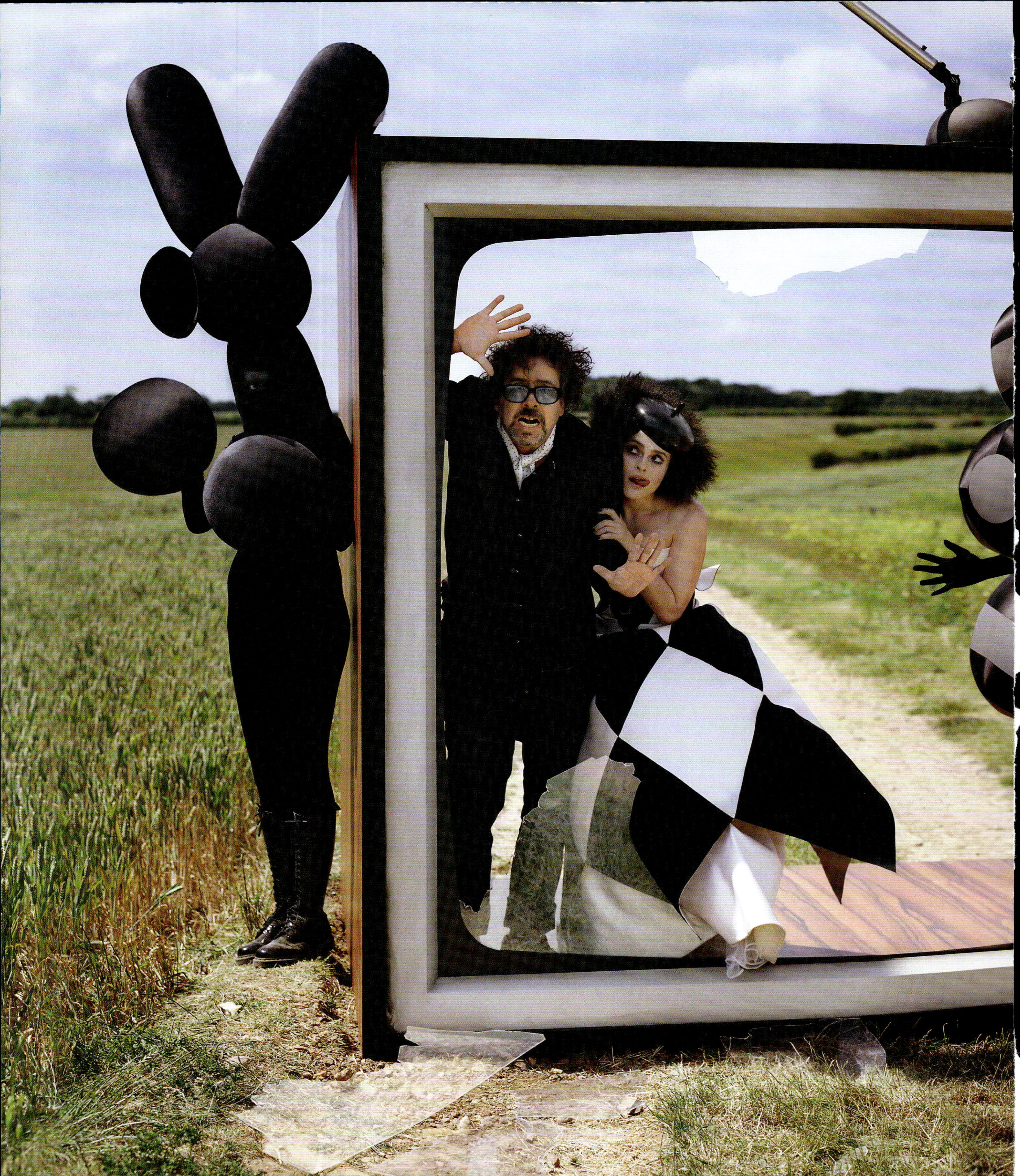

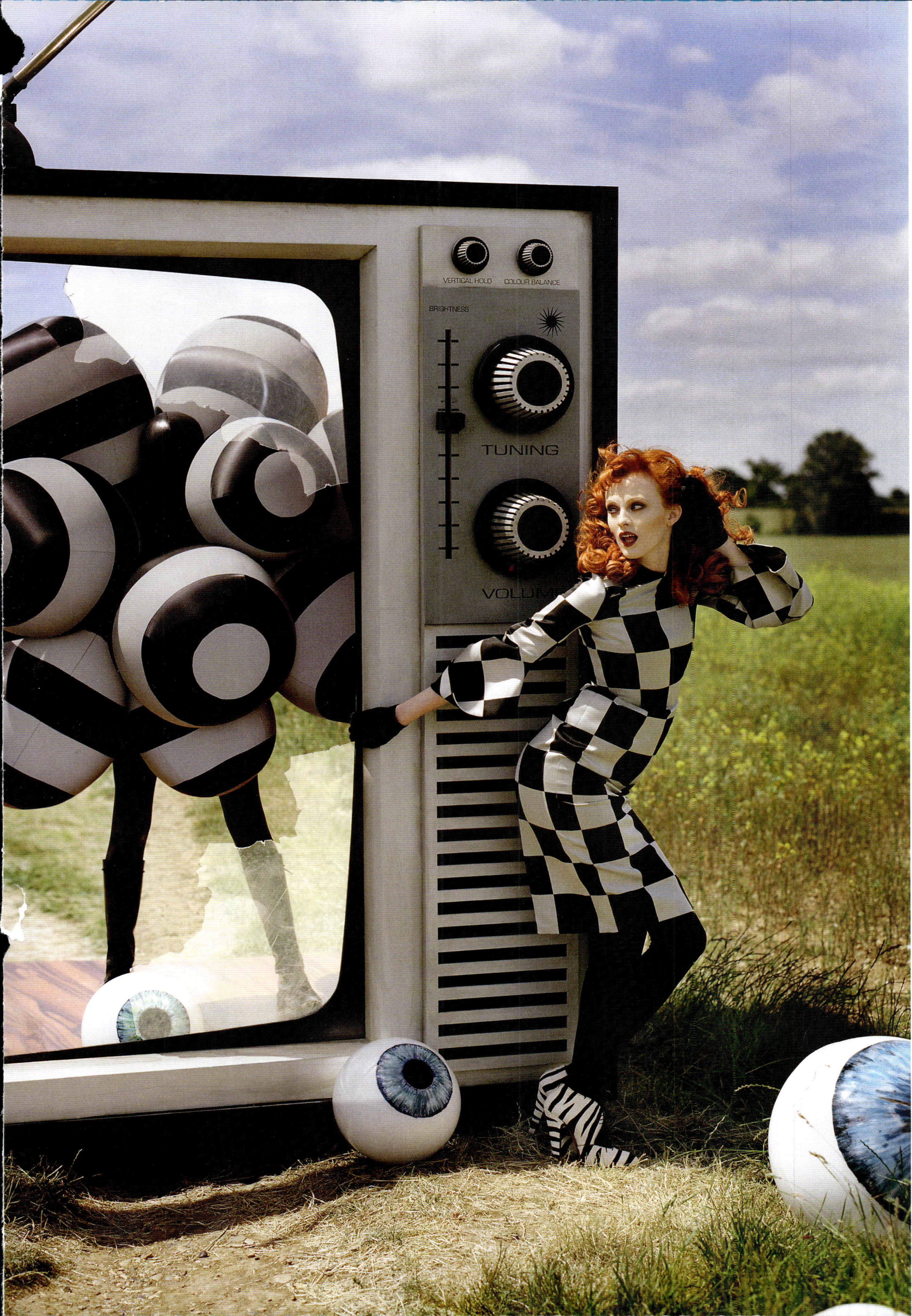
VERTICAL HOLD
COLOUR BALANCE
BRIGHTNESS
TUNING

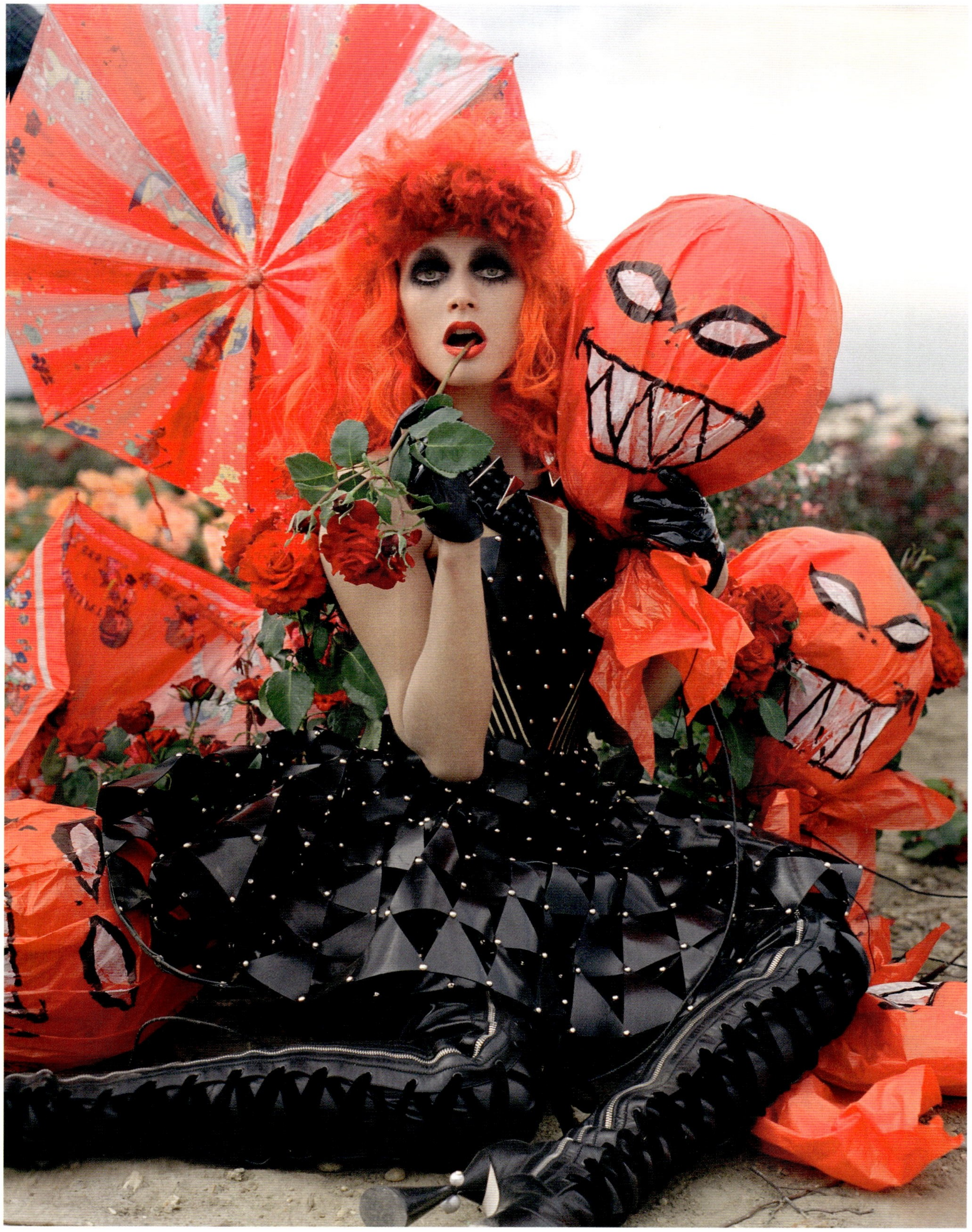

< TIM BURTON, HELENA BONHAM CARTER, AND KAREN ELSON IN *TALES OF THE UNEXPECTED* | TIM BURTON AND TIM WALKER FOR *BRITISH VOGUE*, 2008

^ *TRICKS AND TREATS* | TIM BURTON AND TIM WALKER FOR *HARPER'S BAZAAR*, 2009

> *TALES OF THE UNEXPECTED* | TIM BURTON AND TIM WALKER FOR *BRITISH VOGUE*, 2008

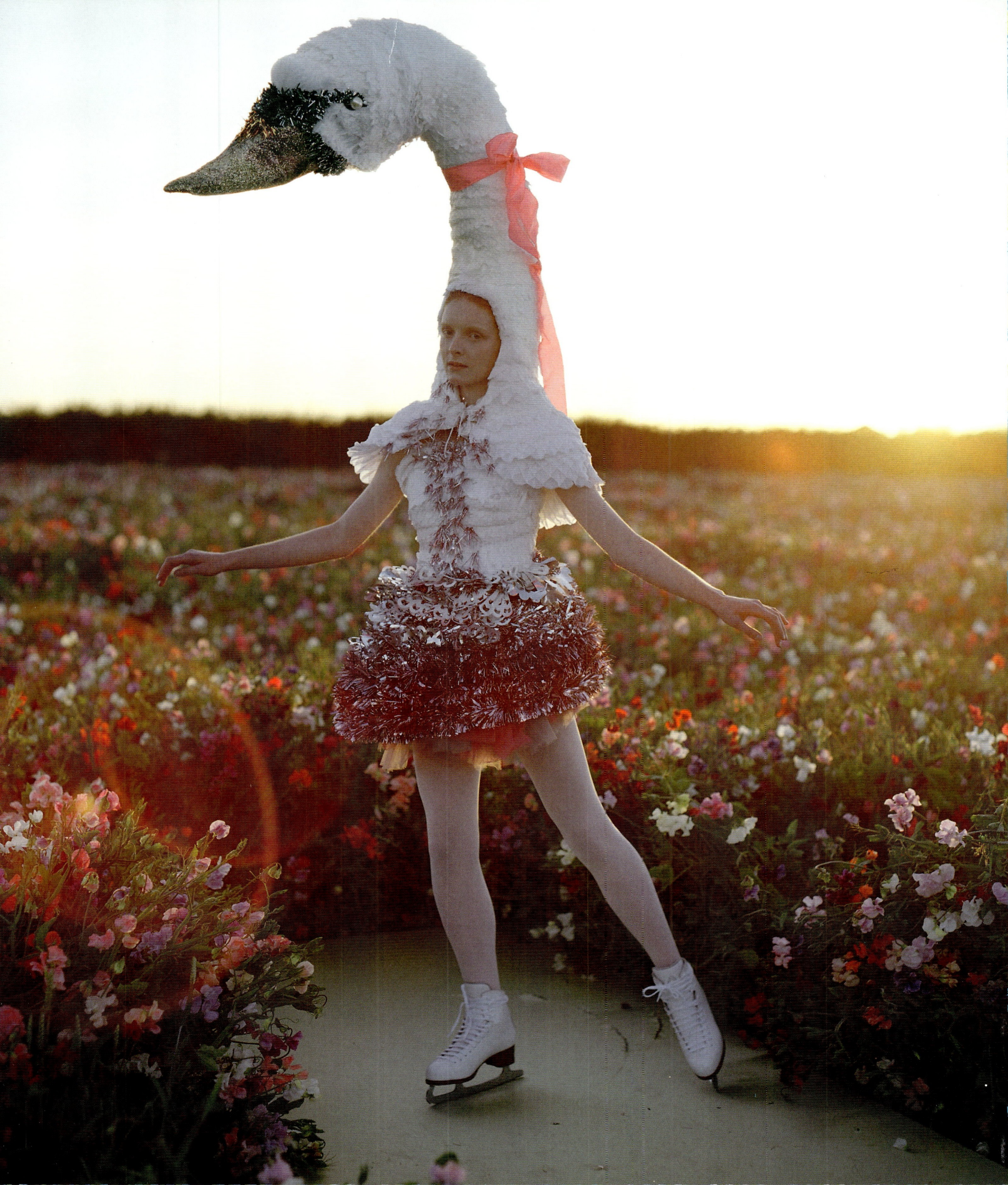

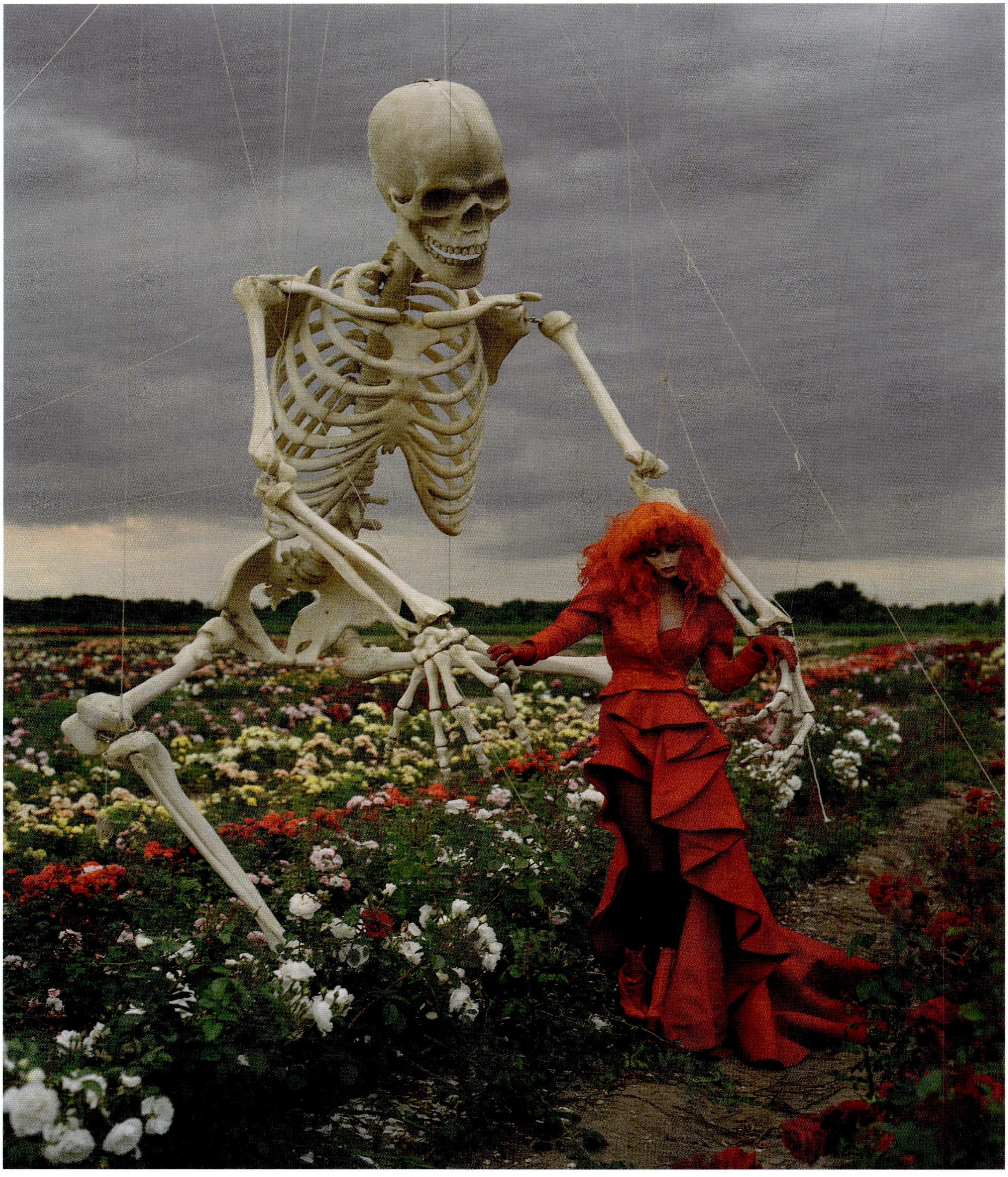

TRICKS AND TREATS | TIM BURTON AND TIM WALKER FOR *HARPER'S BAZAAR*, 2009

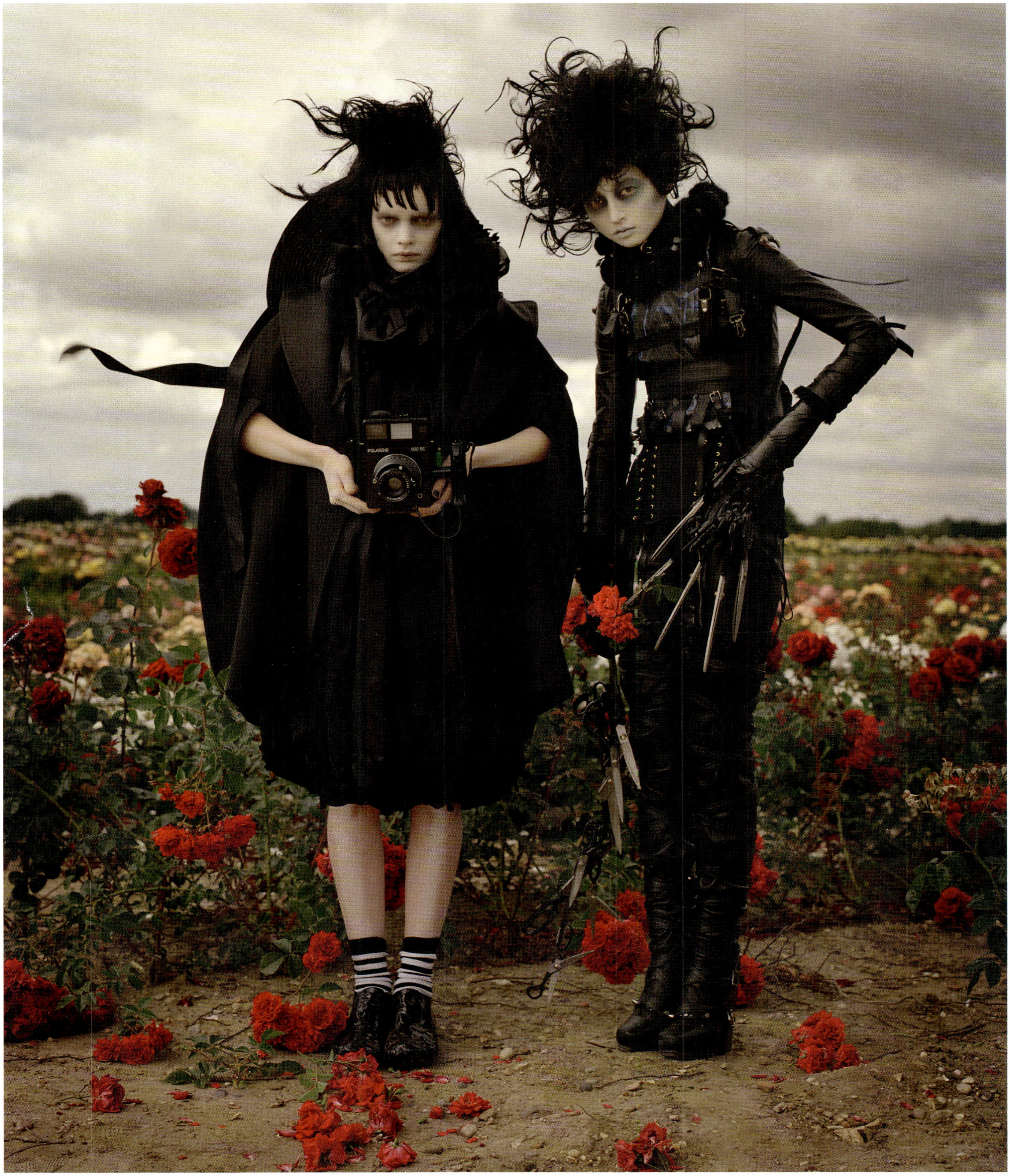

TRICKS AND TREATS | TIM BURTON AND TIM WALKER FOR *HARPER'S BAZAAR*, 2009

KEITH HARING + VI

VIENNE WESTWOOD

WHEN BRITISH DESIGNER Dame Vivienne Westwood (b. 1941) collaborated with New York street artist Keith Haring (1958–1990), she brought a literally underground sensation onto the Parisian catwalk. Born in Pennsylvania, Haring moved to New York in 1978, leaving the Ivy School of Professional Art in Pittsburgh for the School of Visual Arts. The emergence of New York graffiti culture energized Haring, who began "tagging" in 1980, drawing upwards of forty illustrations a day. He tagged from the South Bronx downtown to 14th Street, using empty advertising frames as canvas. Over the next five years, Haring made over five thousand neo-hieroglyphic drawings in the city's subway system.

In 1982, Haring's work was exhibited prestigiously above ground in SoHo and the 57th Street Galleries, as well as at Documenta 7 in Germany. As such, Haring's work was divided along class lines: available to the upper crust and the lower echelon. Haring made no distinction, asserting, "Art is about something being seen, whether it is absorbed by the eyes of people in the subways or of people in galleries."[79] Or on the catwalk!

For Autumn/Winter 1983–84, the London and Paris fashion crowd became privy to the New York sensation when Vivienne Westwood collaborated with Keith Haring. After Kim Hastreiter (b. 1951), the quirky, ever-relevant editor in chief of *Paper* magazine, profiled Haring, Vivienne Westwood contacted her for an introduction, and Hastreiter facilitated a meeting. Westwood flew over and Haring presented her with two large sheets covered in drawings. Westwood turned them into textiles, covering T-shirts, coats, and jackets in Haring's "New Wave Aztec" designs for her Witches collection.[80] Westwood later reminisced to *i-D* magazine, recalling Haring's work as an "esoteric sign language" made up of "space-invader type images."[81]

Westwood and Haring's partnership made sense. Westwood came to prominence with punk fashion, based on the DIY aesthetic of teens coming of age in dilapidated post-WWII England; Haring's rise stemmed from his DIY egalitarian approach to art in the dirtiest parts of a sleepless city.

Cool kids from the fashion and art world attended the Paris fashion show, including Haring's friend and renowned artist Jean-Michel Basquiat; fashion icon Anna Piaggi; and shutterbug Bill Cunningham. Haring's pal Madonna later sported pieces from the collection for three separate photo shoots.

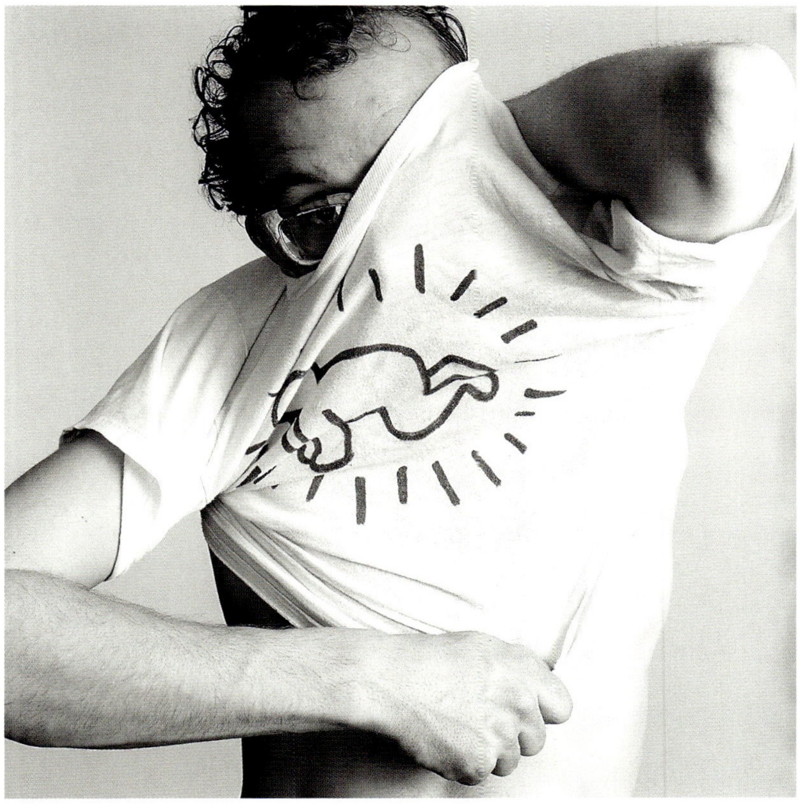

KEITH HARING

This was not the first or last time Haring's work appeared on clothing. In 1978, he hawked original silk-screened T-shirts for cash. In 1986, Haring opened the Pop Shop, an affordable store that sold his work on magnets, pins, and T-shirts. Youngsters lucky enough to run into Haring might even leave with his work on their jeans or sneakers. The artist personally turned everyday wear into original art.

While Keith Haring made a one-off dress for the incomparable Grace Jones's 1986 music video "I'm Not Perfect (But I'm Perfect for You)," his only other apparel collab was with Stephen Sprouse for Fall 1988. Haring's other collaborative work was varied: he designed Swatch watches from 1985 to 1986, and Absolut Vodka ads. He nonchalantly remarked, "There isn't much difference between the people I have to deal with in the art market or in the commercial world."[82]

Following Haring's death in 1990, the Keith Haring Foundation has repeatedly paired up with fashion designers (e.g., Jeremy Scott, Patricia Field, and Nicholas Kirkwood) to keep Haring's art alive and ever present. For those who can't shell out for designer duds, Haring's work can still be publically viewed around Brooklyn's Woodhull Hospital, NYC's Carmine Street, the Harlem River park along FDR Drive, and other locations and museums around the world, just the way Haring would have wanted it.

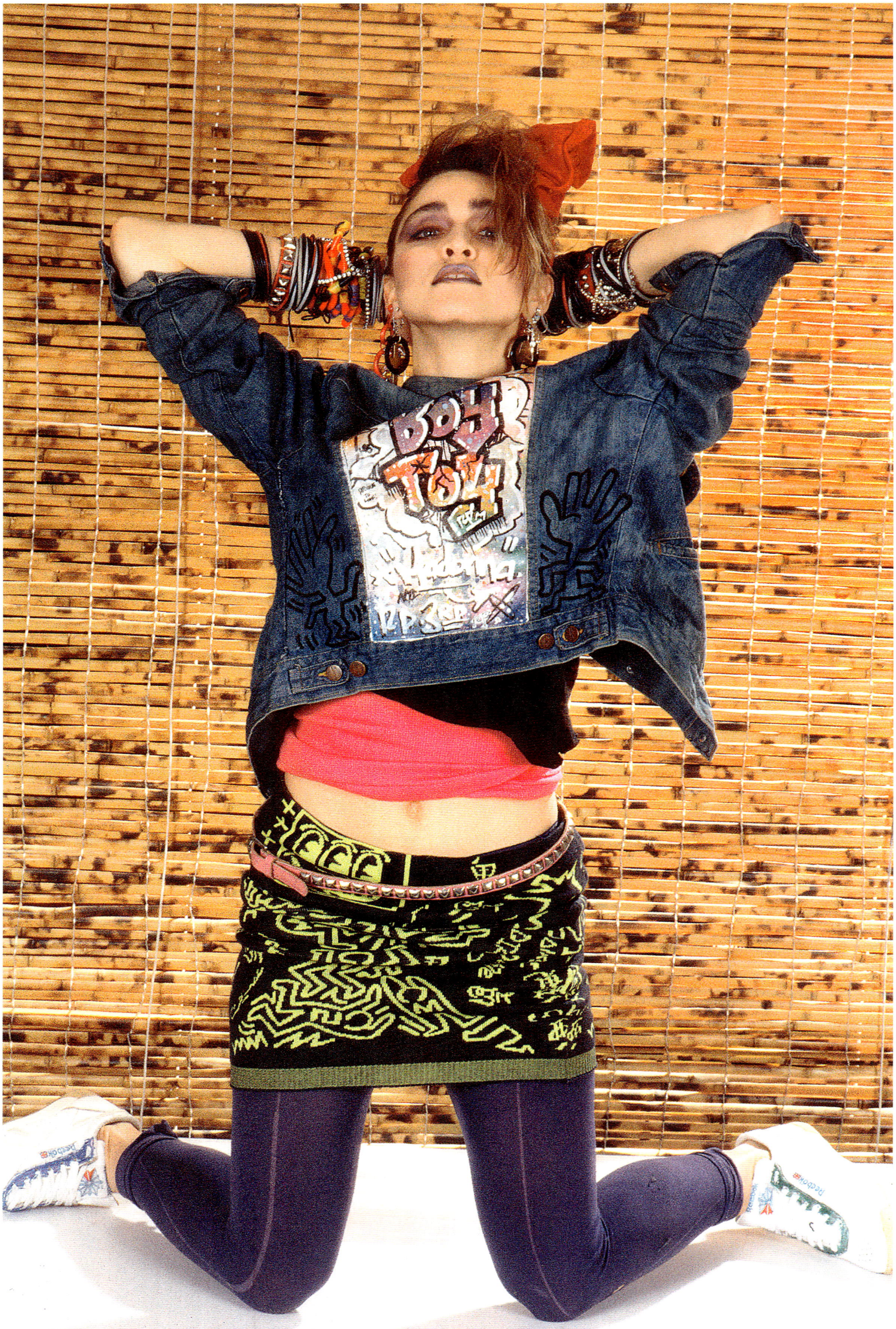
BOY TOY

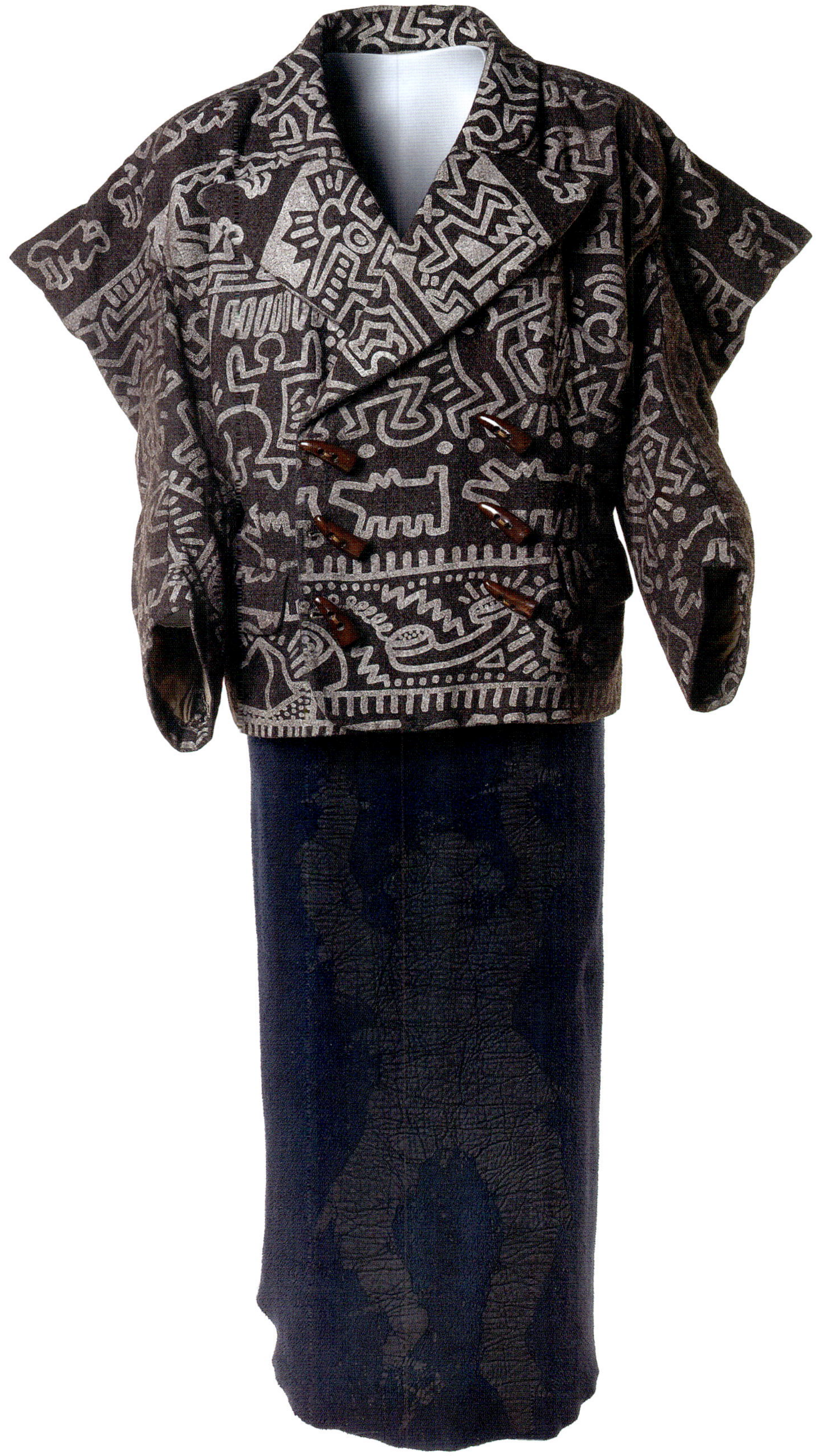

MADONNA IN DEVIL SKIRT WITH KEITH HARING TEXTILE | VIVIENNE WESTWOOD, 1983

WITCHES JACKET WITH KEITH HARING TEXTILE | VIVIENNE WESTWOOD, 1983

EPILOGUE: ZEVS

"THE ART WORLD

is increasingly intertwined with fashion and luxury due to the frequency of trends and big brand names." —Zevs[83]

Zevs is the bad-boy id of French artist Christophe Aguirre Schwarz (b. 1977), who has, since the beginning of the 21st century, raised the pulse of the art and fashion worlds through Liquidated Logo street taggings and provocative Visual Attacks graffiti interventions, two series of street art that provide merciless commentary on fashion's commercialism and omnipresent iconography. For the purposes of our book, Zevs's work positions itself as an insightful (and visual y intoxicating) counterpoint to the largely harmonious art and fashion collaborations that fill the preceding pages.

Christophe Aguirre Schwarz began his art career in the 1990s as a masked Parisian graffiti artist. He and fellow taggers André (Saraiva) and the anonymous artist known only as Invader are credited with giving credence to the French street art scene and increasing its visibility. Schwarz's pseudonym, "Zevs," comes from a regional train with the code name "Zeus" that nearly crushed him while he was tagging in the Paris metro. In Greek mythology, Zeus is the father of gods and men—a sort of mythological superhero; it is a fitting identity for Schwarz to adopt as he battles the "gods" of the fashion world.

Zevs first garnered widespread public attention in 2001 with his "bombings" of fashion advertisements pervasive on and above the streets of Paris. Termed "Visual Attacks," the artist applied bu let-like circles of dripping red paint that bled on and between the eyes of models pictured in Benetton, Gap, Yves Saint Laurent, and Rochas ads. The effect is brutal and repulsive, yet engaging. The models in the ads are transformed from dominant purveyors of all things desirable about the fashion brand into, at best, passive fashion victims and, at worst, self-infected zombies succumbing to and feeding upon the lure of fashion's commercialism.

Zevs's most iconic work began in the mid-2000s with his Liquidated Logos—a concept and technique that re-created the logos of fashion, financial, and consumer brands with dripping paint, giving the effect of logos melting and slowly disintegrating. According to Zevs, "The logo is the keystone of a brand's identity—it interacts with a person's emotions, serving as an

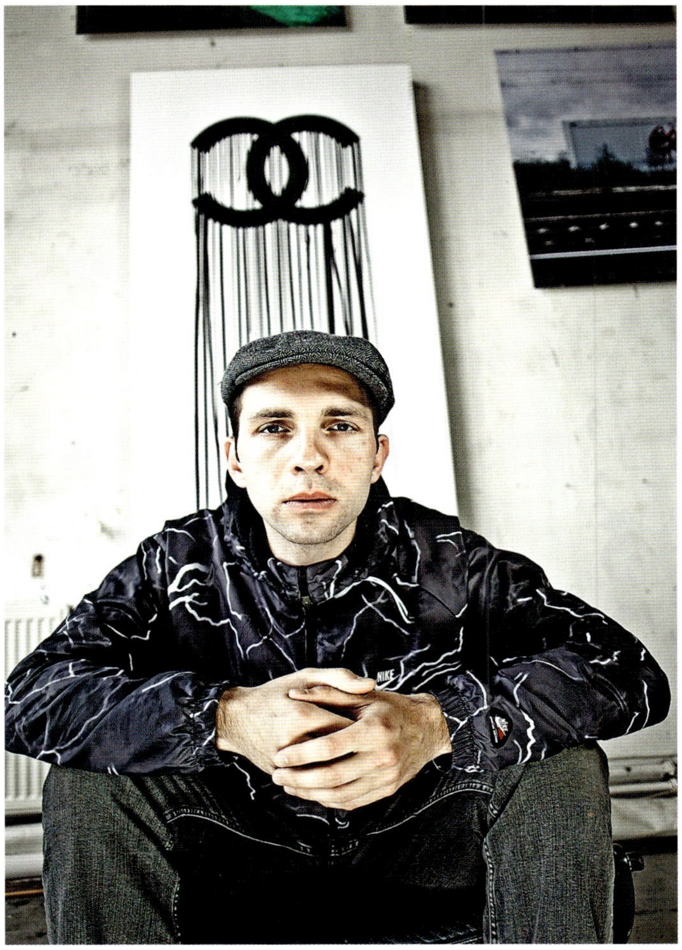

CHRISTOPHE AGUIRRE SCHWARZ, BETTER KNOWN AS ZEVS

extremely efficient and fast 'silent seller.' Logos are meant to be seen, and so when the logos of Chanel or Louis Vuitton are liquidated, it is an attack on a network of signs of identification, social codes, significations, and emotions. By suggesting an opposing force, liquidation recalls overconsumption, the tyranny of advertising, and the slang of the appearances."[84]

In 2009, Zevs's first solo show of Liquidated Logo paintings opened at the Art Statements gallery in Hong Kong. To inaugurate the exhibition's arrival, Zevs tagged a dripping black Liquidated Chanel logo onto the façade of Hong Kong's Giorgio Armani boutique. Zevs was subsequently arrested and briefly imprisoned for the act, an event that reignited the debate begun with his Visual Attacks: Is the work of Zevs vandalism or art?

Zevs remains a keen observer and ferocious critic of the fashion world's influential role in contemporary culture and art. He continues to incorporate the iconography of the fashion world into paintings, sculpture, photography, and site-specific installations that are exhibited internationally in cities including Moscow, New York, São Paulo, and Tokyo.

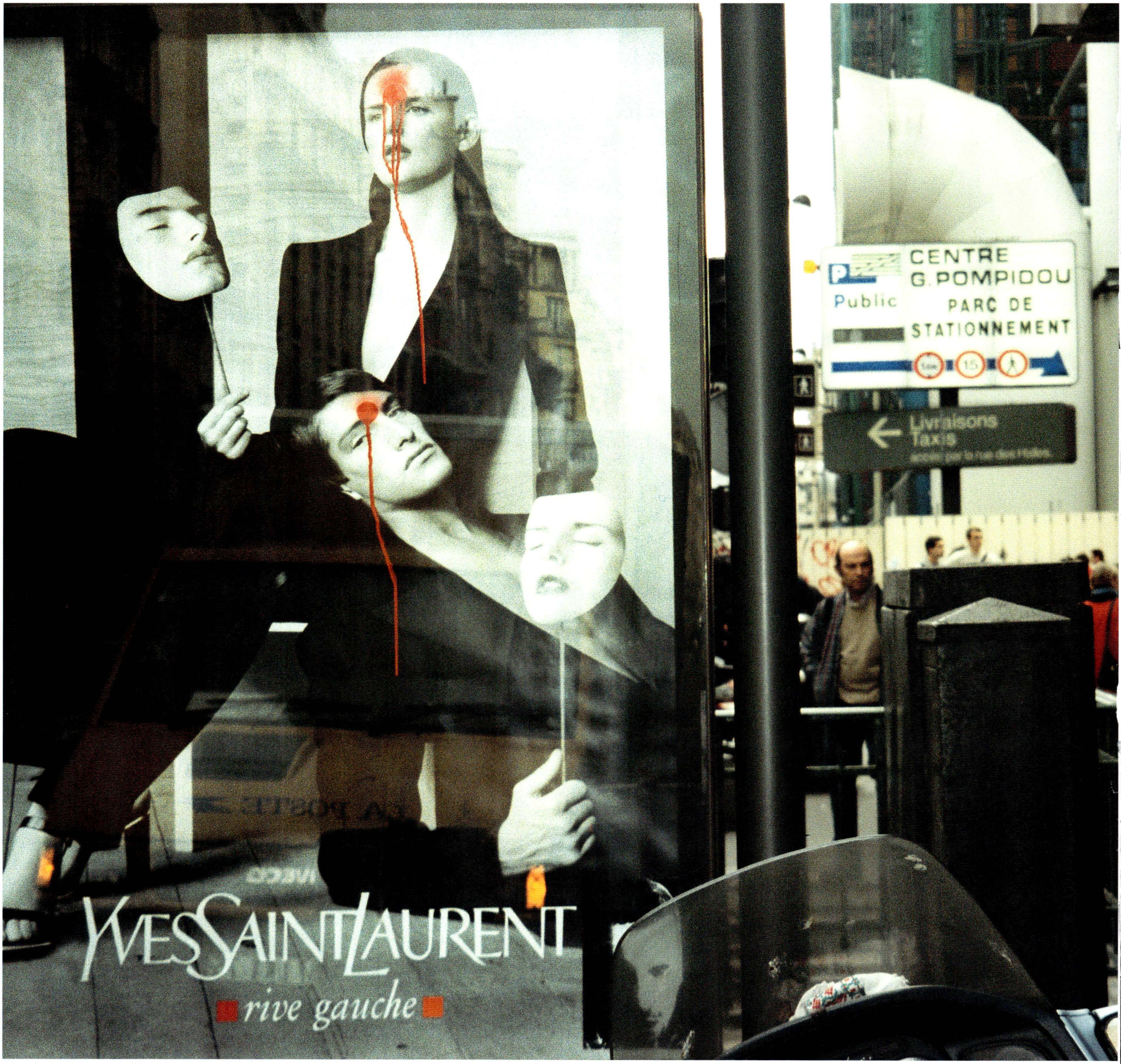
YVES SAINT LAURENT
rive gauche
P
Public
CENTRE
G.POMPIDOU
PARC DE
STATIONNEMENT
15
Livraisons
Taxis

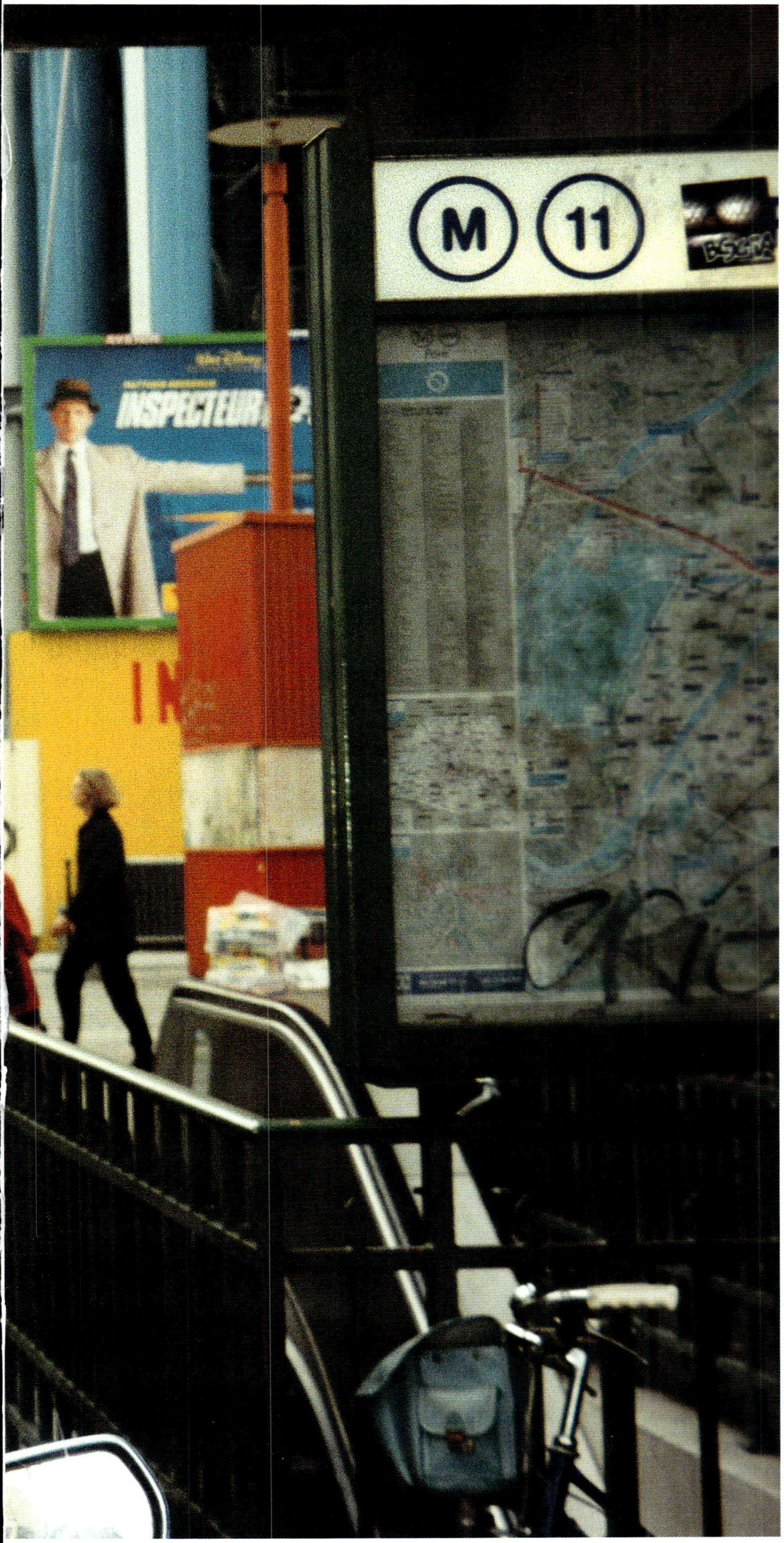

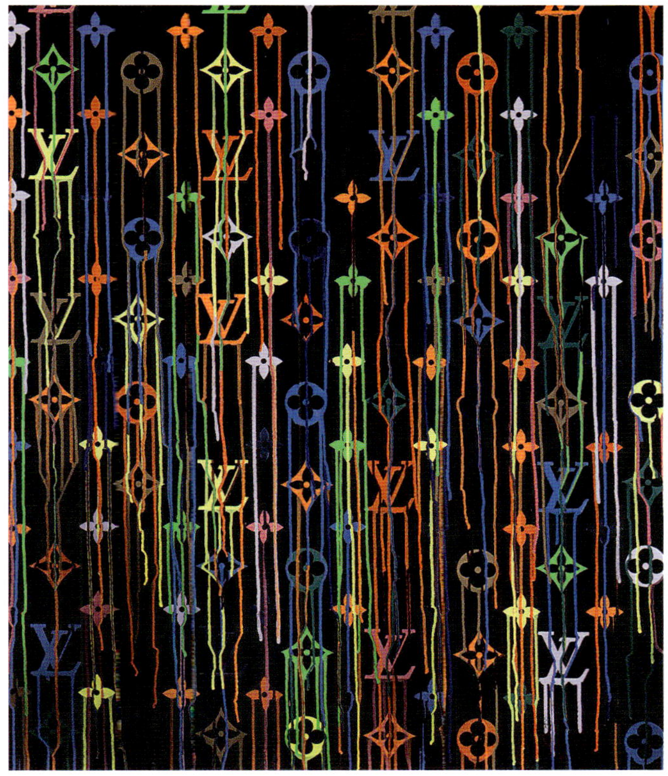

VISUAL ATTACK–YVES SAINT LAURENT–PARIS | PAINT ON SIDEWALK POSTER | ZEVS, 2001

LIQUIDATED LOUIS VUITTON MURAKAMI MULTICO–BLACK | LIQUITEX ON CANVAS | ZEVS, 2011

BIBLIOGRAPHY

A Space Called Public website. http://www.aspacecalledpublic.de.

Absalom, Rebekah. "Artist Textiles: Picasso to Warhol 2014 Exhibition." The Clothes Maiden. http://www.theclothesmaiden.com/2014/01/artist-textiles-picasso-to-warhol-2014.html.

Adams, Rebecca. "Prada Marfa Closing? Texas Lawmakers Attempting to Shut Down Beloved Installation." *Huffington Post*, September 18, 2013. http://www.huffingtonpost.com/2013/09/18/prada-marfa-closing-texas-_n_3948470.html.

Alexander, Ella. "To the Stage." *Vogue UK*, June 7, 2011.

Alexander McQueen official website. "Damien Hirst and Alexander McQueen Collaboration," August 2013. http://www.alexandermcqueen.com/experience/en/alexandermcqueen/archive/damien-hirst-alexander-mcqueen-collaboration.

Alive Not Dead. "Rodarte in Hong Kong." April 10, 2010. http://www.alivenotdead.com/letswowwowwow/RODARTE-IN-HONG-KONG-profile-993299.html.

Andy Warhol Museum website. "Billy Kluver and Andy Warhol: Silver Clouds." http://www.warhol.org/education/resourceslessons/Billy-Kluver-and-Andy-Warhol--Silver-Clouds.

——. "Early Work." http://www.warhol.org/collection/art/earlywork.

AnOther website. "Rodarte × Maggie Cheung: In Pictures." March 29, 2010.

Armstrong, Lisa. "The Perfect: Dior Andy Warhol Handbag." *Telegraph*, September 27, 2013.

Artnet website. "Richard Anuszkiewicz." http://www.artnet.com/artists/richard-anuszkiewicz/biography.

Artsy website. "About Yasumasa Morimura." https://artsy.net/artist/yasumasa-morimura.

Aspden, Peter. "Lunch with Jeff Koons." *Financial Times*, August 21, 2009.

Axelrod, Nick. "Cindy Sherman Wears Chanel." *Women's Wear Daily*, August 31, 2010.

Baggini, Julian. "The Simpsons as Philosophy." *BBC News*, May 19, 2006. http://news.bbc.co.uk/2/hi/uk_news/magazine/4995624.stm.

Bailey, Glenda, Stephen Gan, and Elizabeth Hummer. *Harper's Bazaar Greatest Hits*. New York: Abrams, 2011.

Barneys New York website. "Over the Rainbow: Raymond Meier's Color-Drenched Windows at Barneys New York." March 27, 2011. http://thewindow.barneys.com/raymond-meier-windows.

Beaton, Cecil. *The Glass of Fashion*. London: Weidenfeld and Nicolson, 1954.

Becker, Wolfgang, et al. Haring. Helsinki: Amos Anderson Art Museum, 2000.

Belcove, Julie. "The Bazaar World of Dalí." Harper's Bazaar, December 19, 2012.

Belloni, Emanuela, ed. Translated by Lars Håkan Svensson and Vibeke Emond. Keith Haring. Malmö, Sweden: Malmö Konsthall and Charta, 1994.

Bender, Marylin. The Beautiful People. New York: Coward-McCann, 1967.

Benedict, Tyler. "Armstrong's Damien Hirst Butterfly Bicycle Gets Animal Rights Folks All A-Flutter." *Bike Rumor*, July 27, 2009. http://www.bikerumor.com/2009/07/27/armstrongs-damien-hirst-butterfly-bicycle-gets-animal-rights-folks-all-a-flutter/.

Bergstein, Mary. "The Artist in His Studio: Photography, Art, and the Masculine Mystique." *Oxford Art Journal* 18, no. 2 (1995).

Betz Hull, Margaret. "Postmodern Philosophy Meets Pop Cartoon: Michel Foucault and Matt Groening." *Journal of Popular Culture* 34, no. 2 (2000).

Bierend, Doug. "Welcome to 1960s Paris Where Futuristic Bubbles Ferry Floating Models." CNN website, February 25, 2014. http://www.cnn.com/2014/02/25/world/welcome-to-1960s-paris.

Biography website. "Gianni Versace." http://www.biography.com/people/gianni-versace-9517836#related-video-gallery.

Blanks, Tim. "Fall 2013 Menswear: Louis Vuitton." *Style.com* website, January 17, 2013. http://www.style.com/fashionshows/review/F2013MEN-LVUITTON.

——. "Fall 2013 Ready-to-Wear: Christian Dior." *Style.com* website, March 1, 2013. http://www.style.com/fashionshows/review/F2013RTW-CDIOR.

——. "Raf Simons Opens His Atelier—and Shares His Label—to Artist Sterling Ruby for the Most Complete Designer/Artist Collaboration Yet." *Style.com* website, December 16, 2013. http://www.style.com/style-file/2013/12/raf-simons-opens-atelierand-shares-labelto-artist-sterling-ruby-complete-designerartist-collaboration-yet.

——. "Spring 2012 Ready-to-Wear: Mary Katrantzou." *Style.com* website, September 9, 2011. http://www.style.com/fashionshows/review/S2012RTW-MKATRANTZOU.

Bliven Model Art. "Stella McCartney Jeff Koons." http://blivenmodelart.com/stella-mccartney-jeff-koons.

Blouin Artinfo website. "Andy Warhol." http://www.blouinartinfo.com/artists/andy-warhol-69.

——. "Bottega Veneta's Tomas Maier on Fashion, Art and Emerging Talent." October 9, 2013. http://www.blouinartinfo.com/news/story/956495/bottega-venetas-tomas-maier-on-fashion-art-and-emerging-talent.

——. "John Chamberlain." http://www.blouinartinfo.com/artists/john-chamberlain-89.

Blum, Dilys E., curator. Teacher packet. *The Art & Fashion of Elsa Schiaparelli* (September 28–January 4, 2003). Philadelphia Museum of Art.

Bolton, Andrew. *Alexander McQueen: Savage Beauty*. New York: Metropolitan Museum Press, 2011.

Bonami, Francesco, Peter De Potter, Collier Schorr, and Raf Simons. *Raf Simons: Redux*. Milan, Italy: Fondazione Pitti Discovery, 2005.

Boodro, Michael. "Art and Fashion: A Fine Romance." Art News, September 1990.

BootLeg Productions. "*Bottega Veneta* AOC S'11 with Alex Prager." Vimeo video. 2011. http://vimeo.com/20258250.

Bottega Veneta. "Art of Collaboration." http://www.bottegaveneta.com/experience/us/pages/our-world/art-of-collaboration.

——. "The Art of Collaboration: Spring/Summer 2011–Alex Prager." http://www.bottegaveneta.com/experience/us/art-of-collaboration/spring-summer-2011-alex-prager.

Bowles, Hamish. "Christian Dior/Fall 2013 RTW Review." *Vogue*, March 1, 2013.

Bramlett, Lizzie. "LaCoste." Vintage Fashion Guild (website). http://vintagefashionguild.org/label-resource/lacoste.

Brand, Jan, and José Teunissen, eds. *Fashion and Imagination: About Clothes and Art*. Arnheim: ArtEZ Press, 2009.

Breslin, Tale. "Filip Pagowski, A Retrospective." Life + Times, May 30, 2012.

Brooks, Katherine. "Damien Hirst Fiasco: Artist Kills 9,000 in the Name of Art." Huffington Post, October 16, 2012. http://www.huffingtonpost.com/2012/10/16/damien-hirst-kills-9000-b_n_1970627.html.

Browne, Alix. "A Stroke of Genius." *New York Times T Magazine*, March 28, 2012.

Brubach, Holly. "But Is It Art?" *New York Times*, November 17, 1996.

Buck, Joan Juliet. "Raf Simons, Force of Nature: Dior's Creative Director Collaborates with the Artist Robert Longo to Turn Fashion into Art." *Harper's Bazaar*, September 2013.

Bumpus, Jessica. "Autumn/Winter 2013–14 Ready-to-Wear: Christian Dior." *Vogue UK*, March 1, 2013.

Burley, Isabella. "Peter Saville on Brand Tribalism." *Dazed Digital*, 2014. http://www.dazeddigital.com/fashion/article/18015/1/peter-saville-on-brand-tribalism.

——. "Raf Simons × Sterling Ruby AW14." *Dazed Digital*, January 16, 2014. http://www.dazeddigital.com/fashion/article/18464/1/raf-simons-x-sterling-ruby-aw14.

Business of Fashion (BoF) website. "Kim Jones." http://www.businessoffashion.com/kim-jones.

Callaway, Nicholas, ed. *Issey Miyake: Photographs by Irving Penn*. New York: New York Graphic Society, 1988.

Cameron, Dan. "Self Determination." *Vogue*, July 1994.

Camhi, Leslie. "People Are Talking About: Grand Gestures." *Vogue*, November 2005.

Canale Moda. "Vivienne Westwood: The Legendary 'World's End' Collection, 1984 in Paris." YouTube video, posted by Fashion Channel—Milano. https://www.youtube.com/watch?v=N2pCmDncngc.

Carter, Lee. "Galliano Who? Raf Simons Reclaims Christian Dior's Artistic Past." Blouin Art Info website, June 13, 2013. http://www.blouinartinfo.com/news/story/914551/galliano-who-raf-simons-reclaims-christian-diors-artistic-past.

Cavanagh, Alice. "Raf Simons and Sterling Ruby's Rocker, Art-Infused Show." *New York Magazine*, January 16, 2014.

Cernek, Susan. "Exclusive: A Tour of the Coach Archives (Vintage Handbag Lovers, You're Gonna Want to Spend Some Quality Time Here)." *Glamour* blog, September 9, 2012. http://www.glamour.com/fashion/blogs/dressed/2012/09/exclusive-a-tour-of-the-coach.html.

Chan, Sewell. "Haring's 'Crack Is Wack' Mural Is Being Restored." *New York Times*, September 5, 2007.

Chandès, Hervé, Raymond Meier, and Kazuko Sato. *Issey Miyake: Making Things*. Zurich: Scalo Publishing, 1998.

Charles-Roux, Edmonde. *Chanel: Her Life, Her World—And the Woman Behind the Legend She Herself Created*. New York: Alfred A. Knopf, 1975.

Cheape, Hugh. *Tartan*. Edinburgh: National Museum of Scotland, 1991.

Choi, Mary H. K. "House of Style: Rise of the Supermodel." MTV Style website, July 24, 2012. http://style.mtv.com/2012/07/24/house-of-style-rise-of-the-supermodel/.

Cindy Sherman official website. "Biography." http://www.cindysherman.com/biography.shtml.

Clark, T. J. *Farewell to an Idea: Episodes from a History of Modernism*. New Haven: Yale University Press, 1999.

——. "Jackson Pollock's Abstraction" In *Reconstructing Modernism*, edited by Serge Guilbaut. Cambridge, Mass.: MIT Press, 1990.

Coach website. "Company Profile." http://www.coach.com/online/handbags/genWCM-10551-10051-en-/Coach_US/CompanyInformation/Investor-Relations/CompanyProfile.

Cohn, Hana. "The 50 Best Artist Collaborations in Fashion." *Complex*, April 4, 2013.

Colette Gallery website. "Keith Haring and Fashion." April 2013. http://en.colette.fr/content/keith-haring-2.

Collins, Lauren. "Viva Donatella!" *New Yorker*, September 24, 2007.

Comenas, Gary. "Andy Warhol Chronology." Warhol Stars website. http://www.warholstars.org/andy_warhol_1928-1959.html

Compton, Nick. "Bottega Veneta: The Dream Weavers' Tale." *Telegraph*, March 1, 2014.

Conley, Kevin, and Max Vadukul. "Pret-a-Danser." *New Yorker*, September 22, 1997.

——. "A Dangerous Mind." *Vogue*, May 2011.

Conway, Megan. "The New Imagist." *Black Book*, December 2011.

Craik, Jennifer, and Sharon Peoples. "Exhibition Review: Vivienne Westwood: 34 Years in Fashion." *Fashion Theory* 10, no. 3 (2006).

Crow, Thomas. *Modern Art in the Common Culture*. New Haven: Yale University Press, 1996.

Damien Hirst official website. "Damien Hirst Collaboration with Alexander McQueen Announced." August 13, 2013. http://www.damienhirst.com/news/2013/mcqueen.

——. "Read More about the Artist." February 1, 2012. http://www.damienhirst.com/biography/read-more-about-the-artist.

David Tucker official website. "Salvador Dalí in *Vogue*." August 8, 2012. http://www.davidtucker.me/blog/salvador-dali-vogue.

Day, Patrick Kevin. "Matt Groening Ends Life in Hell." *LA Times*, June 20, 2012.

De Buck Gallery website. "Artist Biography: Zevs." http://debuckgallery.com/artists/1/zevs/biography.

Dellinger, Jade. "The Pop Shop (1986–2005)." Keith Haring official website. http://www.haring.com/!/selected_writing/keith-haring-art-and-commerce#.U2KlYa21bgg.

Design Museum website. "Christian Dior." http://designmuseum.org/design/christian-dior.

Devine, T. M. *The Scottish Nation: 1700–2000*. Harmondsworth, UK: Penguin, 2001.

Diderot, Denis. "Regrets for My Old Dressing Gown, or A Warning to Those with More Taste than Fortune" (1769), translated for Marxists.org by Mitchell Abidor. Originally published in *Oeuvres Complètes* IV (Paris: Garnier Fréres, 1875). https://www.marxists.org/reference/archive/diderot/1769/regrets.htm.

Dior, Christian. *Christian Dior & I*. Translated by Antonia Fraser. New York: E. P. Dutton & Company, Inc., 1957.

Dior website. "Christian Dior and the World of Art." http://www.dior.com/couture/en_us/the-house-of-dior/the-story-of-dior/christian-dior-and-artists.

——. "Dior Does Warhol." http://www.dior.com/magazine/en_us/News/Dior-Does-Warhol.

——. "The Persistence of Memory." http://www.dior.com/magazine/en_us/News/The-Persistence-of-Memory.

Dominus, Susan. "Why Isn't Maggie Cheung a Hollywood Star?" *New York Times*, November 14, 2004.

Donovan, Carrie. "Much Ado about the Japanese." *New York Times Magazine*, July 31, 1983.

Drake, Alicia. *The Beautiful Fall: Fashion, Genius, and Glorious Excess in 1970s Paris*. New York: Back Bay Books, 2006.

Duka, John. "Notes on Fashion." *New York Times*, March 29, 1983.

Dunbar, Alexander, and Dr. Roy Strong, eds. *Fashion 1900–1939*. Catalog for the Scottish Arts Council Exhibit. London: Idea Books, 1975.

Dystant, Lena. "Designer Peter Saville on Joy Division and Distorting the Lacoste Croc." *Selectism* website, December 11, 2013. http://www.selectism.com/2013/12/11/peter-saville-on-joy-division-lacoste-croc-interview

Egan, Jennifer. "James Is a Girl." *New York Times*, February 4, 1996.

Eisner, Lisa, and Román Alonso. "La Dolce Diva." *New York Times*, August 17, 2003.

English, Bonnie. "Sartorial Deconstruction: The Nature of Conceptualism in Postmodernist Japanese Fashion Design." Dissertation, Griffith University, Queensland, Australia. http://www98.griffith.edu.au/dspace/bitstream/handle/10072/45481/77770_1.pdf.

——. *Japanese Fashion Designers*. Oxford: Berg, 2011.

Etherington, Rose. "Peter Saville Wins London Design Medal 2013." *Dezeen* website, September 16, 2013. http://www.dezeen.com/2013/09/16/peter-saville-wins-london-design-medal-2013/

Fabrikant, Geraldine. "The Media Business; Vogue Tries a More Relaxed Look." *New York Times*, October 31, 1988.

Famous Logos "Lacoste Logo." http://www.famouslogos.net/lacoste-logo.

Fang, Charlene, and Zoe Li. "Wing Shya: 'I See Beauty in Everything.'" CNN website travel section, April 28, 2011. http://travel.cnn.com/hong-kong/play/wing-shya-i-see-beauty-everything-755880.

Fashion News Live. "Melvin Sokolsky Chats with Rocco Leo Gaglioti at Spring Summer 2008 LA Fashion Week." YouTube video. August 10, 2013. https://www.youtube.com/watch?v=LXXeCbE7YRk.

Felipe Oliveira Baptista website. "Exhibition: Felipe Oliveira Baptista." http://www.felipeoliveirabaptista.com/main.html.

Femina website. "Les Polos Lacoste réinterprétés par Peter Saville en vente cet automne." August 12, 2013. http://www.femina.ch/polo-lacoste-logo-réinterprété.

Filip Pagowski official website. "Filip Pagowski." http://www.filippagowski.com.

Flaherty, Erin "Alexander McQueen: Misogyny or Artistry?" *Allure Daily Beauty Reporter* blog, March 11, 2009. http://www.allure.com/beauty-trends/blogs/daily-beauty-reporter/2009/03/backstage-alexander-mcqueen-mi.html.

Flanner, Janet. "Comet." *New Yorker*, June 18, 1932.

Foundació Gala-Salvador Dalí website. "Biography." https://www.salvador-dali.org/dali/en_biografia.html.

Foxx, Marc. "Sterling Ruby." *Artforum*, December 2006.

Foxy Production. "Sterling Ruby, *The Masturbators*." http://www.foxyproduction.com/exhibitions/226/pr.

Francis, Mark, with Margery King, and Hilton Als, eds. *The Warhol Look: Glamour, Style, Fashion*. New York: Bullfinch Press, 1997.

Frankel, Susannah. "Stella's Very Grown-Up Collection." *Independent* website, October 3, 2008. http://www.independent.co.uk/life-style/fashion/news/stellas-very-grownup-collection-949707.html.

——. *Visionaries: Interviews with Fashion Designers*. London: Victoria and Albert Museum, 2001.

Freshness website. "Comme des Garçons Play × Converse Jack Purcell." February 14, 2011. http://www.freshnessmag.com/2011/02/14/comme-des-garcons-play-x-converse-jack-purcell.

——. "Comme des Garçons Play × Converse Pro Leather Collection," May 22, 2013. http://www.freshnessmag.com/2013/05/22/comme-des-garcons-play-x-converse-pro-leather-collection.

Freund, Alex, and Lisa Mosko. "Interview: Rodarte." *Gravure*, November 17, 2013.

Furniss, Ann. "Donatella Versace: 'I'm not a believer in the natural look.'"

Independent website, February 8, 2010. http://www.independent.co.uk/life-style/fashion/features/donatella-versace-im-not-a-believer-in-the-natural-look-1892132.html.

Fury, Alex. "Bagheads: Chapman Brothers and Designers [sic] Kim Jones Gives a Dark Twist to Classic Louis Vuitton Luggage." *Independent*, September 7, 2013.

Gablik, Suzi. "Report from New York: The Graffiti Question." *Art in America* 70 (October 1982).

Galperina, Marina. "A Rare Look at Keith Haring's Original 'Crack Is Wack' Mural." *Animal New York* website, June 17, 2014. http://animalnewyork.com/2014/keith-haring-painting-crack-wack-mural.

Gawker website. "PETA Take Aim at Hirst, Armstrong." July, 24, 2009. http://gawker.com/506656/peta-takes-aim-at-hirst-armstrong.

Geczy, Adam, and Vicki Karaminas. *Fashion and Art*. London: Berg, 2012.

GH36 website. "Tim Roeloffs." http://gh36.de/wordpress/?p=9077.

Gladstone, Valerie. "Sharks, Butterflies and Controversy: Damien Hirst at the Tate Modern." *New York Times*, May 8, 2012.

Golbin, Pamela, ed. *Louis Vuitton/Marc Jacobs*. New York: Rizzoli, 2012.

Goodnough, Robert. "Pollock Paints a Picture." *Art News* 50, no. 3 (May 1951).

Graham, Mhairi. "Jackson Pollock." *AnOther* website, November 15, 2012. http://www.anothermag.com/current/view/2337/Jackson_Pollock.

Grimes, William. "Jacques Kaplan, 83, Bold Furrier, Dies." *New York Times*, July 22, 2008.

Gross, John. "New York: The Mutual Admiration of Fashion and Surrealism Over the Years." *New York Times*, December 13, 1987.

Gross, Michael. "Fashion: Valentino and Versace Stage a Designer Duet in New York." *New York Magazine*, September 14, 1992.

Gruen, John. *Keith Haring: The Authorized Biography*. London: Thames and Hudson, 1991.

Grundy, Gareth. "Peter Saville on His Album Cover Artwork." *Guardian*, May 28, 2011.

Guggenheim Museum website. "Jackson Pollock." http://www.guggenheim.org/new-york/collections/collection-online/artwork/3486.

Hager, Reinhard. "Tim Roeloffs." *Galerie Gerling* website, 2005. http://www.galerie-gerling.com/Tim-Roeloffs.html.

Hainley, Bruce. "All the Rage: The Art/Fashion Thing." *Artforum* 34 (March 1996).

Hammarlund, Beth. "String Theory: Meeting of the Minds." *L'étoile*, October 12, 2012.

Hane, Mikiso. *Japan: A Short History*. London: Oneworld Publishing, 2013.

Haring, Keith. *Future Primeval. New York*: Abbeville Press, 1990.

——. *The Keith Haring Journals*. New York: Viking, 1996.

Harper's Bazaar website. "Bazaar Over the Years." http://www.harpersbazaar.com/fashion/fashion-photography/bazaar-140-lookbook#slide-8.

Harper's Bazaar. "Four American Painters." April 1944.

——. "The Simpsons Go to Paris with Linda Evangelista." October 14, 2009.

Harriman, Margaret Case. "Profiles: A Dream Walking." *New Yorker*, July 1, 1939.

Harris, Rachel. "Issey Miyake Guest Artist Series no. 1 Yasumasa Morimura," *FIDM Museum* blog, June 29, 2012. http://blog.fidmmuseum.org/museum/2012/06/issey-miyake-guest-artist-series-no-1-yasumasa-morimura.html.

——. "Issey Miyake Pleats Please," *FIDM Museum* blog, May 26, 2011. http://blog.fidmmuseum.org/museum/2011/05/issey-miyake-pleats-please.html.

Harrison, Martin. "Seeing Fashion." Melvin Sokolsky website. http://www.sokolsky.com/#/conversation/seeing-fashion.

Hastreiter, Kim. "Funny How Things Turn Out." Keith Haring website. http://www.haring.com/!/selected_writing/funny-how-things-turn-out#.U2KlbK21bgg.

Hautaniemi, Conor. "Bottega Veneta Spring–Summer 2011." Produced by Legs Media. Vimeo video, posted by HAUT. http://vimeo.com/73168819.

Hawkins, Richard. "Sterling Ruby: Long Live Amorphous Law." *Flash Art* 34, no. 250 (October 2006).

Hearst website. "*Harper's Bazaar*." http://www.hearst.com/magazines/harpers-bazaar.

Heller, Steven. "Henry Wolf, Graphic Designer and Photographer, Dies at 80." *New York Times*, February 16, 2005.

Hiott, Brian. "William Eggleston and the Rise of Color Photography." *Hyperion* 5, no. 1 (May 2010).

Hirst, Damien. *A Thousand Years* (1990). Damien Hirst official website. http://www.damienhirst.com/a-thousand-years.

——. *For the Love of God* (2007). http://www.damienhirst.com/for-the-love-of-god.

——. *Mother and Child (Divided)* (1993). http://www.damienhirst.com/mother-and-child-divided-1.

——. *Nessus* (2009). http://www.damienhirst.com/nessus.

Hoffman, Ellen. "H&M and Jeff Koons Announce Collaboration—Mark Your Calendars!" *Refinery29* website, June 12, 2014. http://www.refinery29.com/2014/06/69486/jeff-koons-hm-collaboration.

Holzman, Harry, and Martin S. James. *The New Art—The New Life: The Collected Writings of Piet Mondrian*. New York: Da Capo, 1993.

Homes, A. M. "Uneasy Pieces." *Vanity Fair*, September 2010.

Honigman, Ana Finel. "Valerie Steele on Dance and Fashion." *AnOther* website, February 27, 2014. http://www.anothermag.com/current/view/3424/Valerie_Steele_on_Dance_and_Fashion.

Horyn, Cathy. "Amid New Looks, A New Way to See." *New York Times*, March 4, 2012.

——. "Binky and Sheba, Meet Rei." *New York Times*, March 11, 2011.

——. "Gang of Four." *New York Times*, February 24, 2008.

——. "Hands and Minds: Raf Simons and Sterling Ruby." *New York Times* blog, January 17, 2014. http://runway.blogs.nytimes.com/2014/01/17/hands-and-mind-raf-simons-and-sterling-ruby.

——. "Much to Applaud, With Footnotes." *New York Times* blog,

February 23, 2008. http://www.nytimes.com/2008/02/23/fashion/shows/23FASHION.html.

——. "The Real Cindy Sherman." *Harper's Bazaar*, February 2012.

——. "Sarah Burton: New Creative Director at McQueen." *New York Times* blog, May 27, 2010. http://runway.blogs.nytimes.com/2010/05/27/sarah-burton-new-creative-director-at-mcqueen/.

——. "Sarah Burton's First Collection for McQueen." *New York Times* blog, October 5, 2010. http://runway.blogs.nytimes.com/2010/10/05/sarah-burtons-first-collection-for-mcqueen.

Iacovelli, Cinzia. "Melvin Sokolsky." *Vogue Italia* website. http://www.vogue.it/en/encyclo/photography/s/melvin-sokolsky.

i-D website. "Wing Shya." http://i-d.vice.com/en_gb/topics/216/wing-shya.

Irwin, William, Mark T. Conard, and Aeon J. Skoble, eds. *The Simpsons and Philosophy: The D'oh! of Homer*. Chicago: Open Court, 2001.

Issac, Tina. "Free People: In Paris, Celebrating Women Who Go Their Own Way: Cindy Sherman and Les Femmes de Chloé." *Style.com* website, September 29, 2012. http://www.style.com/culture/parties/2012/fashionweek-092912_chloe_anniversary_sherman_gagosian

Jackson Pollock 1951. Exhibition catalog. New York: Betty Parsons Gallery, November 28¬–December 16, 1951.

Jacobs, Mark. "The Talk; Scissor Sisters." *New York Times*, August 28, 2005.

Janowitz, Tama. "Warhol's Bazaar Years." *Harper's Bazaar*, February 1, 2007.

Johnson, Ken. "Art in Review: Aipad Photography Show New York." *New York Times*, March 19, 2010.

Jones, Amelia. "'Clothes Make the Man': The Male Artist as a Performative Function." *Oxford Art Journal* 18, no. 2 (1995).

Karmel, Pepe. *Jackson Pollock: Interviews, Articles, and Reviews*. New York: Museum of Modern Art, 1998.

Kawamura, Yuniya. "The Japanese Revolution in Paris Fashion." *Fashion Theory* 8, no. 2 (2004).

Keith Haring Foundation Archives website. "Pop Culture." http://keithharing-foundationarchives.wordpress.com/pop-culture.

Kendall, Elizabeth. "Mark Morris: Breaking Away." *Vogue*, March 1985.

Kennedy, Randy. "John Chamberlain, Who Wrested Rough Magic From Scrap Metal, Dies at 84." *New York Times*, December 21, 2011.

Killip, Teofilo. "A History of BAPE Collaborations." *Complex* website, August 19, 2013. http://www.complex.com/style/2013/07/every-bape-collaboration/bape-comme-des-garcons.

Kim, Min-Jung. "Dress Designed by Yasumasa Morimura for Pleats Please Issey Miyake." Powerhouse Museum Collection Database online. November 2008. http://www.powerhousemuseum.com/collection/database/?irn=384449.

Kimmelman, Michael. "A Warhol Footnote." *New York Times*, October 24, 1993.

Kismaric, Susan, and Eva Respini. "Fashioning Fiction in Photography Since 1990." In *Fashion and Imagination: About Clothes and Art*, edited by Jan Brand and José Teunissen. Arnhem, Netherlands: ArtEZ Press, 2009.

Knox, Kristin. *Alexander McQueen: Genius of a Generation*. London: A&C Black, 2010.

Krause-Wahl, Antje. "Between Studio and Catwalk–Artists in Fashion Magazines." *Fashion Theory* 13, no. 1 (2009).

Krauss, Rosalind. *The Originality of the Avant-Garde and Other Modernist Myths*. Cambridge, Mass.: MIT Press, 1986.

Krementz, Jill. "Jill Krementz Covers Picasso to Koons at MAD." *New York Social Diary* website, September 2011. http://www.nysocialdiary.com/node/1907476.

Kyoto Costume Institute. *Dress* (Spring/Summer 1997). Rei Kawakubo for Comme des Garçons. Accession Number AC9412 96-32-8A.

——. *Dress "Mondrian"* (Autumn/Winter 1965). Yves Saint Laurent. Accession Number: AC5626 87-18-1.

LACMA website. "Rodarte: Fra Angelico Collection (December 17, 2011–February 5, 2012)."http://www.lacma.org/art/installation/rodarte-fra-angelico-collection.

Lacoste official website. Press kit. http://www.lacoste.com/library/contents/press/pdf/LACOSTE_presskit_en.pdf.

Laferla, Ruth. "Don't Say We Didn't Tell You." *New York Times*, August 25, 2005.

Lam, Wendy. "JOYCE Presents Rodarte × Maggie Cheung Collection." *Nitrolicious* website, March 30, 2010. http://nitrolicious.com/?s=Rodarte+x+Maggie+Cheung.

Lambert, Eleanor. *World of Fashion*. New York: R. R. Bowker Company, 1976.

Lau, Susie. "Between the Salted Egg and the Golden Egg." *StyleBubble* website, March 20, 2010. http://www.stylebubble.co.uk/style_bubble/2010/03/between-the-salted-egg-and-the-golden-eggs.html.

LeFevre, Camille. "Dress Meets Dancing Body." MNArtists website, January 25, 2013. www.mnartists.org.

Levy, Ariel. "Brand-New Bag." *New Yorker*, April 25, 2011.

Liebowitz, Meyer. "Furs Are Hand Painted." *New York Times*, June 26, 1963.

Lipsky-Karasz, Elisa. "The King of Everlasting Style." *Harper's Bazaar*, September 16, 2011.

Llorca, Juan Carlos. "Texas Brands Prada Marfa 'Store' an Illegal Ad." *Dallas News*, September 24, 2013.

Lobenthal, Joel. "Psychedelic Fashion." Berg Fashion Library website, 2005.

Lönnqvist, Bo. *Maktspel i Kläder: om det osynligas kulturella anatomi*. Stockholm, Sweden: Schildts, 2008.

Lord, Richard. "A Skewed View." *South China Morning Post*, April 22, 2012.

LOVE website. "Keith Haring Gets Fashionable at Colette." April 16, 2013. http://www.thelovemagazine.co.uk/article/327/keith-haring-gets-fashionable-at-colette.

Luhring Augustine Gallery website. "Yasumasa Morimura." http://www.luhringaugustine.com/artists/yasumasa-morimura.

Lunde, Carl. *Anuszkiewicz*. New York: Abrams, 1971.

Lutyens, Dominique. "Thou Shalt Be a Bit Rude." *Guardian Weekend*, June 2001.

MacSweeney, Eve. "Yoko Rising." *Vogue*, August 2006.

Madsen, Axel. *Chanel: A Woman of Her Own*. New York: Henry Holt, 1990.

Maillet, Géraldine. "Fashion Close Up: Mary Katrantzou." *Fascineshion* website. http://www.fascineshion.com/en/fashion-close-up/mary-katrantzou/278.

Manchester, Elizabeth. Summary for *Untitled* #126. Tate Online Catalog (2000–2001). https://www.tate.org.uk/art/artworks/sherman-untitled-126-t07185/text-summary.

Martin, Douglas. "Nancy White, 85, Dies; Edited *Harper's Bazaar* in the '60s." *New York Times*, May 29, 2002.

Martin, Richard. "'The New Soft Look': Jackson Pollock, Cecil Beaton, and American Fashion in 1951." *Dress* 7 no. 1, 1981.

——. *Versace*. New York: Universe Publishing, 1997.

Mary Katrantzou official website. "Biography." http://www.marykatrantzou.com/biography.

——. "Mary Katrantzou Central Saint Martins MA AW 2008." YouTube video, posted by Tatoumik. May 12, 2008. http://www.youtube.com/watch?v=ruA5mQXF1Pk.

Matthew Marks Gallery website. "Nan Goldin." http://www.matthewmarks.com/new-york/artists/nan-goldin.

Mattick, Paul. "The Avant-Garde in Fashion." In *Art in Its Time: Theories and Practices of Modern Aesthetics*. London: Routledge, 2003.

McDermott, Catherine. *Vivienne Westwood*. Translated by Stephan Collins. Stockholm, Sweden: B. Wahlströms, 1999.

McManis, Sam. "Homer's Odyssey: Berkeley Course Uses 'The Simpsons' to Discuss Philosophy." *SFGate* website, March 16, 2003. http://www.sfgate.com/living/article/Homer-s-odyssey-Berkeley-course-uses-The-2627809.php.

Mellor, David. *Cecil Beaton: A Retrospective*. New York: New York Graphic Society, 1986.

Melvin Sokolsky official website. "About Melvin Sokolsky." http://www.sokolsky.com/#/about.

Menkes, Suzy. "The Collections: London: Designers: No More Rock 'n' Roll." *New York Times*, February 19, 2004.

——. "Emotion: Real or Surreal?" *New York Times*, March 1, 2013.

——. "The Flesh and Fabric of Surrealist Design." *The Age*, August 24, 1988.

Merce Cunningham Trust website. "Scramble, 1967." http://www.mercecunningham.org/index.cfm/choreography/dancedetail/params/work_ID/89.

Metro Galleries Website. Press release, April 2012. http://www.metropictures gallery.com/exhibitions/2012-04-28_cindy-sherman.

Metropolitan Museum of Art. *Autumn Rhythm* (Number 30) (1950). Jackson Pollock. Accession Number 57.92.

——. *Coat* (1963). Jacques Kaplan and Marisol. Accession Number 1979.570.1.

——. *Diablo* (1983). Vivienne Westwood. Accession Number 2006.253.42.

——. *Dress* (Spring/Summer 1997). Rei Kawakubo for Comme des Garçons. Accession Number 1998.516.1a,b.

——. *Ensemble* (1983). Vivienne Westwood. Accession Number 2006.253.45a-c.

——. *Hat* (Winter 1937–1938). Elsa Schiaparelli. Accession Number 1974.139.

——. *Mondrian* (1962). Sally Victor. Accession Number 2009.300.1320.

——. *Number 28* (1950). Jackson Pollock. Accession Number 2006.32.51.

Metropolitan Museum of Art website. "New Photography 2010: Alex Prager." http://www.moma.org/interactives/exhibitions/2010/newphotography/alex-prager.

Michault, Jessica. "Christian Dior Ready to Wear Fall 2013 Paris." *Nowfashion* website, March 1, 2013. http://nowfashion.com/christian-dior-ready-to-wear-fall-winter-2013-paris-3522#content.

Mitchell, Louise, ed. *Cutting Edge: Fashion from Japan*. Sydney, Australia: Powerhouse, 2005.

MOCA website. "Rodarte: States of Matter (March 4, 2011–June 5, 2011). http://www.moca.org/museum/exhibitiondetail.php?&id=442.

Mondrian, Piet. *The New Art, The New Life: The Collected Writings of Piet Mondrian*. Edited and translated by Harry Holtzman and Martin S. James. New York: Thames and Hudson, 1986.

Morimura, Yasumasa, and Donald Kuspit. *Daughter of Art History*: Photographs by Yasumasa Morimura. New York: Aperture, 2003.

Morris, Bernadine. "Anuszkiewicz Sets Legs into Motion." *New York Times*, May 29, 1965.

——. "Fabrics Designer Returns a Salute." *New York Times*, June 23, 1966.

Mower, Sarah. "Mary Katrantzou/Spring 2012 RTW." *Vogue*, September 20, 2011.

——. "Spring 2006 Ready-to-Wear: Stella McCartney." *Style.com* website. October 5, 2005. http://www.style.com/fashionshows/review/S2006RTW-SMCCARTN.

——. "Versace Fall 2008 Ready-to-Wear." *Style.com* website, February 21, 2008. http://www.style.com/fashion-shows/fall-2008-ready-to-wear/versace.

Muir, Gregor. *Lucky Kunst: The Rise and Fall of Young British Art*. London: Aurum Press, 2009.

Müller, Florence, and Farid Chenoune, eds. *Yves Saint Laurent*. Paris: Petit Palais/Musee des Beaux-Arts de la Ville de Paris, 2010.

Museu do Design e da Moda website. "Felipe Oliveira Baptista." 2013. http://www.mude.pt/exposicoes/felipe-oliveira-baptista_5.html.

Museum of Contemporary Art Chicago website. "Jeff Koons: Teacher Resource." http://mcachicago.org/archive/collection/Koons-txt.html.

Museum of Fine Arts Boston. *The Dragon, Paris* (1963). Melvin Sokolsky. No. 2007.480.

Museum of London. *Jacket* (1983). Vivienne Westwood. ID No. 2003.70.

Museum of Modern Art. *The Persistence of Memory* (1931). Salvador Dalí. Accession Number 162.1934.

Myers, Holly. "Shape Shifter." *Art Review* no. 6 (December 2006).

Naifeh, Steven, and Gregory White Smith. *Jackson Pollock: An American Saga*. New York: Clarkson N. Potter, Inc., 1989.

National Art Gallery. *Number 1, 1950* (Lavender Mist) (1950). Jackson Pollock. No. 1976.37.1.

Needleman, Deborah. "Editor's Letter: Heart and Soul." *New York Times T Magazine* blog, December 6, 2013. http://tmagazine.blogs.nytimes.com/2013/12/06/editors-letter-heart-and-soul.

New York Times. "Art Is Background for Off-Beat Pelts." September 21, 1960.

——. "Schiaparelli Sees Paris Style Mecca." December 11, 1940.

New York University website. "Cindy Sherman."http://www.nyu.edu/greyart/exhibits/odysseys/Sherman/body_sherman.html.

Nikkah, Roya. "Damien Hirst Condemned for Killing 9,000 Butterflies in Tate Show." *Telegraph*, October 14, 2012.

Nochlin, Linda. "Whose Millennium Is It Anyway? Beauty, Truth, and Justice at the Fin de Siècle." In *Culture and Humanity in the New Millennium: The Future of Human Values*. Edited by Sin-Wai Chan and Siu Tong Kwok. Hong Kong: Chinese University of Hong Kong, 2002.

Novovitch, Barbara. "Vandal Hated the Art, but, Oh, Those Shoes." *New York Times*, October 8, 2005.

Nowacki, Kim, Meghan Louttit, and Gabrielle Plucknette. "Classic Magazine Photographs: Then and Now." *New York Times*, August 18, 2011.

Nowness website. "Melvin Sokolsky: Magical Realism," July 16, 2011. http://www.nowness.com/day/2011/7/16/1541/melvin-sokolsky-magical-realism.

O'Brien, Glenn. "James Nares." *Interview*, November 23, 2008.

——. "Nan Goldin: In the Frame." *Harper's Bazaar*, October 19, 2011.

O'Connor, Francis Valentine, and Eugene Victor Thaw. *Jackson Pollock: A Catalogue Raisonné of Paintings, Drawings, and Other Works*. Volume 4. New Haven: Yale University Press, 1978.

O'Doherty, Brian. "'All Fur' Exhibition: Painted Pelts Displayed at the Allen Stone." *New York Times*, March 5, 1964.

O'Hagan, Sean. "Nan Goldin: 'I Wanted to Get High from a Really Early Age.'" *Guardian*, March 22, 2014.

O'Neill, Alistair. "Exhibition Review: Vivienne Westwood: 34 Years in Fashion." *Fashion Theory* 10, no. 3 (2006).

O'Neill, Claire. "Out with the Old and In with the Old-Inspired: Fresh Photos at MoMA." *Picture Show: Photo Stories from NPR* (blog). August 26, 2010. http://www.npr.org/blogs/pictureshow/2010/08/23/129381210/prager

Oliver, William. "Mary Katrantzou Womenswear A/W11." *Dazed Digital* website. http://www.dazeddigital.com/fashion/article/9721/1/mary-katrantzou-a-w11.

——. "Mary Katrantzou Womenswear S/S12." *Dazed Digital* website. http://www.dazeddigital.com/fashion/article/11500/1/mary-katrantzou-womenswear-s-s12.

Olley, Michelle. "Diary Entries by Michelle Olley Appearing in VOSS, Spring/Summer 2001." Metropolitan Museum of Art blog, September 18, 2000. http://blog.metmuseum.org/alexandermcqueen/michelle-olley-voss-diary/

Ominous, Anne. "Sex and Death and Shock and Schlock: A Long Review of the Times Square Show." *Artforum*, October 1980.

Paddle8 blog. "Andy Warhol in the World of Fashion." March 22, 2013.https://paddle8.com/blog/2013/03/22/andy-warhol-in-the-world-of-fashion.

——. "The Brushstroke by James Nares." May 1, 2013. http://paddle8.com/blog/2013/05/01/the-brushstroke-by-james-nares.

Pask, Bruce. "Perfect Pairing: Raf Simons's Colorful Collaboration with Sterling Ruby for Fall/Winter 2014." *New York Times T Magazine* blog, January 16, 2014. http://tmagazine.blogs.nytimes.com/2014/01/16/perfect-pairing-raf-simonss-colorful-collaboration-with-sterling-ruby-for-fallwinter-2014.

Paul Kasmin Gallery website. "James Nares." http://www.paulkasmingallery.com/artists/james-nares.

Pechman, Ali. "Some Like It Haute: Gaultier in the Galleries." *ARTnews*, November 7, 2013.

Petridis, Alexis. "Peter Saville: The UK's Most Famous Graphic Designer." *Guardian*, September 8, 2013.

Phelps, Nicole. "Bottega Veneta." *Style.com* website, September 24, 2010. http://www.style.com/fashionshows/review/S2011RTW-BVENETA.

Philadelphia Museum of Art. *Woman's Dinner Dress* (Summer 1946). Elsa Schiaparelli. Accession Number 1969-232-28.

Pinsky, M. I. *The Gospel According to the Simpsons: The Spiritual Life of the World's Most Animated Family*. Louisville: Westminster John Knox Press, 2001.

Pithers, Ellie. "Lacoste Collaborates with Peter Saville." *Telegraph*, November 29, 2013.

Politanoff, Evelyne. "Melvin Sokolsky: 'Fashion in a Bubble.'" *Huffington Post*, August 1, 2011. http://www.huffingtonpost.com/evelyne-politanoff/melvin-sokolsky-fashion-i_b_908860.html.

Porter, Charlie. "Paris Fashion Week: Men's, Report 1." *Financial Times*, January 16, 2014.

Prada, Miuccia, et al. *Prada*. New York: Abrams, 2010.

Prager, Alex, director. "Touch of Evil." *New York Times Magazine* website. Video gallery. December 6, 2011.

Premiere Heure website. "Wing Shya." http://www.premiere-heure.fr/directors/wingshya.

Presley, Ann, and Martha Jenkins. "The T-Shirt: Canvas for Signs of the Times." *International Journal of Fashion Design, Technology, and Education* 4, no. 2 (2011).

Prickett, Sarah Nicole. "Raf & Ruby." *New York Times T Magazine* blog. June 10, 2014. http://tmagazine.blogs.nytimes.com/2014/06/10/raf-simons-sterling-ruby-dior-hauser-wirth.

Pulimood, Steven. "2TRAPS SUPERMAX." 032c, Winter 2010–2011.

Ratcliff, Carter. "Joseph Beuys." *Vogue*, March 1980.

Reif, Rita. "Fur Coats and Carpets on Exhibit at a Gallery." *New York Times*, March 4, 1964.

Reilly, Maura. "James Nares at Paul Kasmin." *Art in America*, October 1999.

Remsen, Nicholas. "How Much Is That Sculpture in the Window?" *Style.com* website, September 4, 2013. http://www.style.com/stylefile/2013/09/how-much-is-that-sculpture-in-the-window.

——. "Photoshop Fantastic: Mary Katrantzou's Printed Wonderlands." Blouin Artinfo website, March 15, 2013. http://www.blouinartinfo.com/news/story/879448/photoshop-fantastic-mary-katrantzous-printed-wonderlands.

Ribas, João. "Sterling Ruby: Sincerely Hostile." *Flash Art* 42, no. 271 (March–April 2010).

Richardson, Nigel. "Marfa, Texas: Tales of the Unexpected." *Telegraph*, February 2, 2014.

Rodman, Selden. *Conversations with Artists*. New York: Capricorn, 1961.

Rose, Barbara. "Zeitgeist: in Berlin: 'The Spirit of the Times.'" *Vogue*, February 1983.

Rosenzweig, Phyllis. *The Fifties: Aspects of Painting in New York*. Washington: Hirshhorn Museum and Sculpture Garden, 1980.

Ross, Christine. *The Aesthetics of Disengagement: Contemporary Art and Depression*. Minneapolis: University of Minnesota Press, 2006.

Ross, Josephine. *Beaton in Vogue*. London: Thames and Hudson, 1986.

——. *Society in Vogue: The International Set Between the Wars*. New York: Vendome Press, 1992.

Russel, John. "Salvador Dalí, Pioneer Surrealist, Dies at 84." *New York Times*, January 24, 1989.

Ryzik, Melena. "Watch Out for the Horses on Your Way to the Train." *New York Times*, March 24, 2013.

Saint Laurent, Yves, et al. *Yves Saint Laurent*. New York: Clarkson N. Potter, Inc., 1983.

Sarto, Christina. "Le provocazioni di Zevs, l'artista che manipola le griffe." Translated into English for the De Buck Gallery. http://www.debuck-gallery.com/news/60/le-provocazioni-di-zevs-l-artista-che-manipola-le-griffe. Originally published in Italian in *Sette*, October 2, 2013.

Sauers, Jenna. "'Is He For or Against Women?' Alexander McQueen and the Female Form." *Jezebel* website, February 15, 2010. http://jezebel.com/5472257/is-he-for-or-against-women-alexander-mcqueen-and-the-female-form.

Save Prada Marfa website. http://www.savepradamarfa.com.

Saville, Peter. "The Lacoste Collector Polo No. 8." YouTube video, posted by DigitalPriv. http://www.youtube.com/watch?v=XzxrcHVqz00&noredirect=1.

Schapiro, Meyer. *Modern Art: 19th and 20th Centuries*. New York: George Braziller, 1978.

Schreiber, Sonja. "Wiedereröffnung: Berliner Kunstgewerbemuseum mit großer Modegalerie." *LesMads* website, November 20, 2014. http://www.lesmads.de/2014/11/wiedereroeffnung-berliner-kunstgewerbemuseum-mit-grosser-modegalerie.html.

Schwartz, Barry. "Melvin Sokolsky: A Specific Palette." *Photo Media Online* website, March 4, 2010. http://www.photomediaonline.com/features-stories/people-and-places/item/428-melvin-sokolsky-a-specific-palette.html.

Sebra, Matthew. "This Just In: Coach × James Nares Limited Edition Tote Collection." *GQ* blog, April 19, 2012. http://www.gq.com/style/blogs/the-gq-eye/2012/04/this-just-in-coach-x-james-nares-limited-edition-tote-collection.html.

Seno, Alexandra A. "Rodarte Sisters Talk About What's Next in Fashion." *Wall Street Journal*, April 16, 2010.

Shanes, Eric. *Andy Warhol*. New York: Parkstone International, 2005.

Sherman, Cindy. *Cindy Sherman: The Complete Untitled Film Stills*. New York: Museum of Modern Art, 2003.

Simons, Jade. "Bottega Veneta 'New Exposure' Photography Competition." *Vogue Paris*, May 29, 2013. Translated by Charlotte Collins. http://en.vogue.fr/fashion/fashion-news/diaporama/bottega-veneta-new-exposure-photography-competition/13565.

Sims, Josh. "Comme Undone." *i-D*, November 2004.

Singer, Sally. "Rodarte in Conversation with Sally Singer." Video. February 22, 2010. Cooper-Hewitt website. http://www.cooperhewitt.org/2010/02/22/cooper-hewitt-rodarte-in-conversation-with-sally-singer.

Sischy, Ingrid. "In the Artist's Studio: Cindy Sherman." *Vanity Fair*, March 2012.

Small, Michael. "Drawing on Walls, Clothes, and Subways, Keith Haring Earns Favor with Art Lovers High and Low." *People*, December 5, 1983.

Smith, Herbert. "Badges, Buttons, T-Shirts and Bumperstickers: The Semiotics of Some Recursive Systems." *Journal of Popular Culture* 21, no. 4 (Spring 1988).

Smith, Joan. "McQueen Had a Sinister View of Women's Bodies." *Independent*, February 14, 2010.

Smith, Roberta. "Art in Review: Nick Cave—Soundsuits." *New York Times*, November 3, 2006.

Sokolsky, Melvin, and Martin Harrison. *Melvin Sokolsky: Seeing Fashion*. Santa Fe, N.M., and Milan, Italy: Arena Editions, 2000.

Söll, Änne. "Pollock in Vogue: American Fashion and Avant-garde Art in Cecil Beaton's 1951 Photographs." *Fashion Theory* 13 (2009).

Soloman, Deborah. "Nan Goldin: Scenes from the Edge." *Wall Street Journal*, October 9, 1996.

Sooke, Alastair. "Miuccia Prada Interview: Fondazione Prada, Milan." *Telegraph*, May 5, 2009.

Sowray, Bibby. "Miuccia Prada." *Vogue UK*, April 18, 2012.

Spector, Nancy. "Jackson Pollock." Guggenheim Museum Online Collections website. www.guggenheim.org/newyork/collections.

Spindler, Amy M. "Fashion/Review: In London, Blueblood Meets Hot Blood." *New York Times*, March 5, 1996.

——. "Gianni Versace, 50, the Designer Who Infused Fashion with Life and Art." *New York Times*, July 16, 1997.

——. "In London, the Scene Has Final Say." *New York Times*, March 4, 1997.

——. "Patterns; A Trade Show Challenges the Runway; A Ghost Apart; Tina Chow, the Collector." *New York Times*, September 21, 1993.

Steele, Valerie, et al. *Japan Fashion Now*. New Haven: Yale University Press, 2010.

Stella McCartney official website. "About Stella." http://www.stellamccartney.com/experience/us/stellas-world/about-stella.

Stoppard, Lou, et al. "Collections: Christian Dior: Live Panel Discussion." SHOWStudio website, March 1, 2013. http://showstudio.com/collection/christian_dior_paris_womenswear_a_w_2013.

Stuart, Amanda Mackenzie. *Empress of Fashion: A Life of Diana Vreeland*. New York: Harper Luxe, 2012.

Studeman, Kristin. "On Our Radar: Coach × James Nares." *Style.com* website, April 18, 2012. http://www.style.com/stylefile/2012/04/on-our-radar-coach-x-james-nares.

Style.com website. "Rodarte Gets in the Mood for Maggie Cheung," March 22, 2010. http://www.style.com/stylefile/2010/03/rodarte-gets-in-the-mood-for-maggie-cheung.

——. "Naomi Campbell, Cindy Crawford & Christy Turlington Sing Freedom! '90 at Versace- #TBT." YouTube video, posted by Style.com. http://www.youtube.com/watch?v=n1SpAepT8gM.

Sudjic, Deyan. *Rei Kawakubo and Comme Des Garçons*. New York: Rizzoli, 1990.

Sundsbø, Sølve. "Damien Hirst × Alexander McQueen." *Style.com* website. Video. November 13, 2013. http://video.style.com/watch/damien-hirst-x-alexander-mcqueen-by-solve-sundsbo.

Sutton, Benjamin. "Watch This Beautiful Short Film for Rising Fashion Designer Rodarte Starring Maggie Cheung." *L Magazine* website, March 31, 2010. http://www.thelmagazine.com/TheMeasure/archives/2010/03/31/watch-this-beautiful-short-film-for-rising-label-rodarte-starring-maggie-cheung.

Svendsen, Lars. *Fashion: A Philosophy*. London: Reaktion Books, 2006.

Swarovski website. "Rodarte."http://www.brand.swarovski.com/Content.Node/ourinitiatives/fashion/newyorkfashionweek/ss10/rodarte/startpagerodarte.en.html.

Sydney Morning Herald. "Writing's on the Wall for Artist Squat." January 27, 2009.

Tate Modern. *Lobster Telephone* (1936). Salvador Dalí. Reference No. T03257.

Taylor, Melissa. "Culture Transition: Fashion's Cultural Dialogue Between Commerce and Art." *Fashion Theory* 9, no. 4 (2005).

Temple, Emily. "An Interactive Map of Keith Haring's Work in NYC." *Flavorwire* website, March 17, 2012. http://flavorwire.com/270437/an-interactive-map-of-keith-harings-work-in-nyc.

THIS Visits. "THIS Visits: Alex Prager." Vimeo video, posted by Incase. http://vimeo.com/14966446.

Thomas, Dana. "Gunpowder and Fashion." *Newsweek*, January 7, 1999.

Tim Roeloffs official website. "New Catalog/ New Works." November 14, 2014. http://www.roeloffs1.com/blog/2014/11/new-catalog-new-works/.

Tim Walker official website. "Biography." http://timwalkerphotography.com/biography.

Time. "Business: Haute Couture." August 13, 1934.

Townsend, Chris. *Rapture: Art's Seduction by Fashion*. London: Thames & Hudson, 2002.

University of Arizona website. "The Collaborative Legacy of Merce Cunningham." February 14–March 22, 2011. http://www.collaborativelegacy.arizona.edu.

University of Edinburgh website. "Honorary Degree for Maggie Cheung." July 8, 2011. http://www.ed.ac.uk/about/edinburgh-global/news-events/news/cheungdegree-040711.

Urban Re/inventors website. "Timotheus Paulus Roeloffs' Artwork." http://www.urbanreinventors.net/gallery.php?artist=timotheus&issue=2.

Vaidyanathan, Rajini. "Six Ways Alexander McQueen Changed Fashion." *BBC News Magazine*, February 12, 2010.

Van, Alan. "Damien Hirst's 'In and Out of Love' Art Exhibit Is Butterfly Hiroshima Video." Newmediarockstars website. October 19, 2012. http://newmediarockstars.com/2012/10/damien-hirsts-in-and-out-of-love-art-exhibit-is-butterfly-hiroshima-video.

Vermorel, Fred. *Vivienne Westwood: Fashion, Perversity, and the Sixties Laid Bare*. New York: Overstock Press, 1996.

Vestoj: The Journal of Sartorial Matters website. "Expanding Fashion: Rei Kawakubo for Merce Cunningham in 'Scenario,' 1997." January 8, 2014. www.vestoj.com/current/?p=2384.

Vickers, Hugo. *Cecil Beaton: The Authorised Biography*. London: Phoenix, 1985.

Victoria & Albert Museum website. "Gianni Versace." http://www.vam.ac.uk/content/articles/g/gianni-versace/.

——. *Photograph* (1963). Melvin Sokolsky. Museum No. PH.732-1987.

——. *Shoe Hat* (1937–1938). Elsa Schiaparelli. Museum No. T.2-2009.

——. *The Mondrian Collection* (1965). Yves Saint Laurent. Museum No. T.369-1974.

——. *The Skeleton Dress; The Circus Collection* (1938). Elsa Schiaparelli and Salvador Dalí. Museum No. T.394&A-1974.

Vintage Fashion Guild website. "Venet, Philippe." http://vintagefashionguild.org/label-resource/venet-philippe.

Viralam, Geneva. "Yasumasa Morimura Artist Biography." Luhring Augustine Gallery website. http://www.luhringaugustine.com/artists/yasumasa-morimura.

Vivienne Westwood official website. "The Early Years." http://www.viviennewestwood.co.uk/w/the-story/the-early-years.

——. "Witches, AW 1983–84." http://www.viviennewestwood.co.uk/w/the-story/the-early-years.

Vogue. "Collaboration." October 1983.

——. "Karen Finley." November 1999.

——. "The Soft New Look." March 1, 1951.

——. "*Vogue*'s Own Boutique: Downy Feathers/Boots." September 15, 1965.

Voguepedia. "Anna Wintour." http://www.vogue.com/voguepedia/Anna_Wintour.

——. "Bonnie Cashin." http://www.vogue.com/voguepedia/Bonnie_Cashin.

——. "Bottega Veneta." http://www.vogue.com/voguepedia/Bottega_Veneta.

——. "Christian Dior (Brand)." http://www.vogue.com/voguepedia/Christian_Dior_(Brand).

——. "Donatella Versace." http://stage.static.vogue.com/voguepedia/Donatella_Versace.

——. "Karl Lagerfeld." http://www.vogue.com/voguepedia/Karl_Lagerfeld.

——. "Prada." http://www.vogue.com/voguepedia/Prada.

——. "Raf Simons." http://www.vogue.com/voguepedia/Raf_Simons.

——. "Raymond Meier." http://www.vogue.com/voguepedia/Raymond_Meier.

——. "Reed Krakoff." http://www.vogue.com/voguepedia/Reed_Krakoff.

——. "Sarah Burton." http://www.vogue.com/voguepedia/Sarah_Burton.

Volk, Annick, and Terry Jones. *Raf Simons*. New York: Taschen, 2013.

Wallpaper website. "Tim Roeloffs Collaboration." http://www.wallpaper.com/fashion/tim-roeloffs-collaboration/2115#2F1SjxVZcBFQOHQB.99.

Wang, Connie. "Caption This: Bottega Veneta by Alex Prager." *Refinery29* website, March 18, 2011. http://www.refinery29.com/caption-this-karolina-kurkova-in-bottega-veneta-by-alex-prager.

Warhol, Andy. *Andy Warhol Fashion*. San Francisco: Chronicle Books, 2004.

Warren, Virginia Lee. "Schiaparelli: Still Shocking." *New York Times*, March 23, 1966.

Waters, John. *Role Models*. New York: Farrar, Straus, and Giroux, 2010.

Watt, Judith. *Alexander McQueen: The Life and the Legacy*. New York: Harper Design Books, 2012.

Webster, Sally. "Fashion Moda: A Bronx Experience." Lehman College CUNY website. 1996. http://www.lehman.cuny.edu/vpadvance/artgallery/gallery/talkback/fmwebster.html.

Weisman, Zoe. "Re-model." *F Newsmagazine*, April 2006.

Westfall, Stephen. "Nan Goldin." *BOMB Magazine* 37 (Fall 1991).

White, Constance C. R. "Reviews/Fashion: Where Supermodels Still Reign." *New York Times*, November 2, 1995.

White, Palmer. *Elsa Schiaparelli: Empress of Paris Fashion*. New York: Rizzoli, 1986.

Whitney Museum of American Art. *Number 27*, 1950 (1950). Jackson Pollock. Accession Number 53.12.

Wilcox, Claire. *Vivienne Westwood*. London: Victoria and Albert Museum, 2004.

Wilder, Charly. "The Berlin Wall: How Today's Art Reflects 20 Years of Memories." *Esquire* blog, November 9, 2009. http://www.esquire.com/the-side/feature/berlin-wall-art-110909#slide-1.

Williams, Alex. "We Three Queens." *New York Magazine*, April 7, 2003.

Wilson, Elizabeth, and Lou Taylor. *Through the Looking Glass: A History of Dress from 1860 to the Present*. London: BBC Books, 1989.

Wilson, Eric. "Front Row: Little Prada in the Desert." *New York Times*, September 29, 2005.

——. "Obituary: Bernard Lacoste, James Freedman." *New York Times*, March 23, 2006.

——. "Sisters Sisters." *New York Times*, May 19, 2005.

Wing Shya. "Rodarte × Maggie Cheung Collection." YouTube video, posted by Joyce HK. March 23, 2010. https://www.youtube.com/watch?v=Ag4ac5QqbmQ.

Wing Shya official website. "Profile." http://www.wingshya.com.

Wiseman, Eva. "Prints and the Revolution: Fashion Designer Mary Katrantzou." *Guardian*, February 11, 2012.

Wood, Andrew. "The Simpsons as Social Science." San Jose State University syllabus. http://www.sjsu.edu/faculty/wooda/muse/intro.html.

Wood, Ghislaine. *The Surreal Body: Fetish and Fashion*. London: Victoria and Albert Museum, 2007.

Woods, Vicki. "Matthew Barney's Personality Parade." *Vogue*, January 1996.

Wren, Christopher S. "Clinton Calls Fashion Ads' 'Heroin Chic' Deplorable." *New York Times*, May 22, 1997.

Wroe, David. "Ich bin ein Beer-liner." *The Age*, July 26, 2008.

Women's Wear Daily. "Raf Simons Men's RTW Fall 2014." January 16, 2014.

Yablonsky, Linda. "Characters Welcome." *New York Times*, October 9, 2011.

Young, Meghan. "The Rodarte + Maggie Cheung Short Film by Wing Shya." TrendHunter (blog). March 26, 2010. http://www.trendhunter.com/trends/rodarte-maggie-cheung-short.

Zarrella, Katharine K. "Felipe Oliveira Baptista Reflects on a Decade of Design." *Style.com* website, October 17, 2013. http://www.style.com/stylefile/2013/10/felipe-oliviera-baptista-reflects-decade-design.

FOOTNOTES

[1] T. J. Clark, "Jackson Pollock's Abstraction," in *Reconstructing Modernism*, Serge Guilbaut, ed. (Cambridge, Mass.: MIT Press, 1990), 219.

[2] Paul Mattick, "The Avant-Garde in Fashion," in *Art in Its Time* (London: Routledge, 2003), 165.

[3] Linda Nochlin, "Whose Millennium Is It Anyway? Beauty, Truth, and Justice at the Fin de Siècle," in *Culture and Humanity in the New Millennium: The Future of Human Values*, Sin-Wai Chan and Siu Tong Kwok, eds. (Hong Kong: Chinese University of Hong Kong, 2002), 171–72.

[4] Andy Warhol and Simon Doonan, *Andy Warhol Fashion* (San Francisco: Chronicle Books, 2004), 10.

[5] Cecil Beaton, *The Glass of Fashion* (London: Weidenfeld and Nicolson, 1954), 1.

[6] Jean Paul Gaultier, press preview, Brooklyn Museum of Art, October 23, 2013.

[7] Christian Dior, *Christian Dior & I*, trans. Antonia Fraser (New York: E. P. Dutton, 1957), 227.

[8] "Jackson Pollock's Abstractions," *Vogue*, March 1, 1951: 159.

[9] Ibid.

[10] "Art: Chaos, Damn It!" *Time*, November 20, 1950.

[11] T. J. Clark, "Jackson Pollock's Abstraction," in *Reconstructing Modernism*, Serge Guilbaut, ed. (Cambridge, Mass.: MIT Press, 1990), 173.

[12] "Alex Prager for Fourth & Main," YouTube video, posted by FourthandMain1, April 24, 2012, https://www.youtube.com/watch?v=ocgrjdVcb4M.

[13] Jocelyn Phillips, *Collect Contemporary: Photography* (London: Thames & Hudson, 2012), 155.

[14] "Behind the Scenes: New Photography 2010: Alex Prager," YouTube video, posted by MoMAvideos, November 6, 2010, https://www.youtube.com/watch?v=pIASkq7T0H8.

[15] Elizabeth Manchester, "Summary for *Untitled #126*," Tate online catalog, November2000– October 2001), https://www.tate.org.uk/art/artworks/sherman-untitled-126-t07185/text-summary.

[16] Ali Pechman, "Some Like It Haute: Gaultier in the Galleries," *ARTNews*, November 7, 2013.

[17] Pierre Galante, *Mademoiselle Chanel*, trans. Eileen Geist and Jessie Wood (Chicago: Henry Regnery Company, 1973), 132.

[18] *Guest of Cindy Sherman*, film, directed by Paul Hasegawa-Overacker (as "Paul H-O") and Tom Donahue (2008, Filmlike).

[19] Nick Axelrod, "Cindy Sherman Wears Chanel," *Women's Wear Daily*, August 31, 2010.

[20] Nikki Columbus, ed., *James Nares* (New York: Skira Rizzoli, 2014), 37.

[21] "Art in Motion: Coach × James Nares," press release, Coach New York.

[22] Ellie Somerville, "Artist James Nares's Painterly Bags for Coach Are a Stroke of Genius," *Architectural Digest*, May 9, 2011.

[23] Filip Pagowski, personal interview, May 21, 2014.

[24] Christian Dior, *Christian Dior & I*, trans. Antonia Fraser (New York: E. P. Dutton, 1957), 229.

[25] Ibid., 237.

[26] This is a rough estimate. In 1955, *Glamour* reached 609,000 readers, according to Theodore Peterson in *Magazines in the Twentieth Century* (Urbana: University of Illinois Press, 1956), 255.

[27] Gary Comenas, "Andy Warhol Chronology: 1928–1959," Warhol Stars website, http://www.warholstars.org/andy_warhol_1928-1959.html.

[28] David E. Warner interview in "Episode 0018: Interview with Melvin Sokolsky; Canon Explorer of Light and Fashion & Advertising Photographer," Vimeo video, http://vimeo.com/6680829; and personal interview, July 22, 2014.

[29] Obituary: Jacques Kaplan, *Telegraph*, July 25, 2008.

[30] Meyer Liebowitz, "Furs Are Hand Painted," *New York Times*, June 26, 1963.

[31] Rita Reif, "Fur Coats and Carpets On Exhibition at a Gallery," *New York Times*, March 4, 1964.

[32] Brian O'Doherty, "'All Fur' Exhibition: Painted Pelts Displayed at the Allen Stone," *New York Times*, March 5, 1964.

[33] "*Vogue*'s Own Boutique of Suggestions, Finds, and Observations: Downy Feathers/Boots," *Vogue*, September 15, 1965: 81.

[34] Géraldine Maillet, "Fashion Close Up: Mary Katrantzou," *Fascineshion*, http://www.fascineshion.com/en/fashion-close-up/mary-katrantzou/278/.

[35] Gia Kourlas, "Comme Dancing," *Time Out New York*, October 9, 1997, http://www.timeout.com/newyork/dance/comme-dancing.

[36] Judith Thurman, "The Misfit," *New Yorker*, July 4, 2005: 62.

[37] John Waters, *Role Models* (New York: Farrar, Straus, and Giroux, 2010), 103.

[38] Gia Kourlas, "Comme Dancing," *Time Out New York*, October 9, 1997, http://www.timeout.com/newyork/dance/comme-dancing.

[39] Ibid.

[40] Jennifer Goggans, personal interview, May 14, 2014.

[41] Holly Brubach, "Style; Dance Partners," *New York Times*, October 5, 1997.

[42] Alicia Drake, *The Beautiful Fall: Fashion, Genius, and Glorious Excess in 1970s Paris* (New York: Back Bay Books, 2006), 320.

[43] Kim Nowacki, Meghan Louttit, and Gabrielle Plucknette, "Classic Magazine Photographs: Then and Now," *New York Times*, August 18, 2011.

[44] Tamsin Blanchard, "A Smack in the Face for the Gurus of Heroin Chic," *Independent*, May 23, 1997.

[45] Sean O'Hagan, "Nan Goldin: I Wanted to Get High from an Early Age," *Guardian*, March 22, 2014.

[46] Emily King, ed. *Designed by Peter Saville* (London: Frieze, 2003), 16.

[47] Alexis Petridis, "Peter Saville: The UK's Most Famous Graphic Designer," *Guardian*, September 8, 2013.

[48] Lena Dystant, "Designer Peter Saville on Joy Division & Distorting the Lacoste Croc," *Selectism*, December 11, 2013, http://www.selectism.com/2013/12/11/peter-saville-on-joy-division-lacoste-croc-interview.

[49] "Stella McCartney & Jeff Koons," *Andy Warhol's Interview* (German edition), trans. for me by Arezu Rahimi, http://archiv.interview.de/Stella-McCartney-Jeff-Koons.

[50] Ibid.

[51] *The Jeff Koons Show*, TV movie, directed by Alison Chernick (2004, FilmBuff).

[52] Judith Watt, *Alexander McQueen: The Life and the Legacy* (New York: Harper-Collins International, 2012), 127.

[53] Ann Gallagher, curator, "Damien Hirst at Tate Modern," YouTube video, posted by Tate, April 4, 2012, https://www.youtube.com/watch?v=YWSb9QMlLoQ.

[54] Noel Fielding, "Damien Hirst—The First Look Presented by Channel 4," YouTube video, Channel 4 UK, April 3, 2012, https://www.youtube.com/watch?v=KDjaAkD5J8g.

[55] Nick Cave, personal interview, June 7, 2014.

[56] Ibid.

[57] Ibid.

[58] Yasumasa Morimura, "About My Work," in *Daughter of Art History*: Photographs by Yasumasa Morimura (New York: Aperture 2003), 114.

[59] Susannah Frankel, ed., *Visionaries: Interview with Fashion Designers* (London: Victoria and Albert Museum, 2001), 50.

[60] Dana Thomas, "Gunpowder and Fashion," *Newsweek*, January 7, 1999.

[61] Alastair Sooke, "Miuccia Prada Interview: Fondazione Prada, Milan," *Telegraph*, May 5, 2009.

[62] "Elmgreen & Dragset: New Kids on the Block," YouTube video, posted by REcreativeUK, March 1, 2012, https://www.youtube.com/watch?v=z1ST7roufEs.

[63] Ibid.

[64] Sarah Mower, "Prada Fall 2014 RTW Review," Vogue.com, February 20, 2014, http://www.vogue.com/fashion-week/fall-2014/prada/review.

[65] Mary Tannen, "Dirty Looks," *New York Times*, May 28, 2006.

[66] Marilyn Bender, *The Beautiful People* (New York: Coward-McCann, 1967), 283.

[67] Suzy Menkes, "The Duchess of Windsor's Royal Style," in *Harper's Bazaar Greatest Hits*, Glenda Bailey, ed., (New York: Abrams, 2011), 290.

[68] *Dior & I*, documentary film, directed by Frédéric Tcheng (2014, Entertainment One).

[69] Cathy Horyn, "Hands and Minds: Raf Simons and Sterling Ruby," *New York Times*, January 17, 2014.

[70] Alix Browne, "Cuff Love," *New York Times*, October 3, 2008.

[71] Ruben Donsbach, "Kaleidoscopic City," www.roeloffs1.com/blog/wp-content/uploads/ 2013/05//ILF4_tim-roeloffs.pdf.

[72] Jake Chapman, Dinos Chapman, and FUEL, eds., *Flogging a Dead Horse* (New York: Rizzoli, 2011), 15.

[73] Alex Fury, "Bagheads: Chapman Brothers and Designers [sic] Kim Jones Give a Dark Twist to Classic Louis Vuitton Luggage," *Independent*, September 7, 2013.

[74] Isabella Burley, "Hell Awaits: Kim Jones vs. Jake Chapman," *Dazed Digital*, http://www.dazeddigital.com/fashion/article/17598/1/hell-awaits.

[75] Jake Chapman, Dinos Chapman, and FUEL, eds., *Flogging a Dead Horse* (New York, Rizzoli, 2011), 312.

[76] Alex Fury, "Bagheads: Chapman Brothers and Designers [sic] Kim Jones Give a Dark Twist to Classic Louis Vuitton Luggage," *Independent*, September 7, 2013.

[77] Marion Hume, "The Lost Explorer: Tim Walker's Flight of Fancy," *Telegraph*, August 2010.

[78] "Mulberry Presents Tim Walker in Conversation with Penny Martin," YouTube video, posted by Mulberry, January 25, 2013, https://www.youtube.com/watch?v=ulc14x8Gh5M.

[79] Suzi Gablik, "Report from New York: The Graffiti Question," *Art in America* 70 (October 1982): 85.

[80] Ibid.

[81] Claire Wilcox, *Vivienne Westwood* (London: Victoria and Albert Museum, 2004), 19.

[82] Jade Dellinger, "The Pop Shop (1986–2005)," Keith Haring official website, http://www.haring.com/!/selected_writing/keith-haring-art-and-commerce#.U2KIYa21bgg.

[83] Alex Greenberger, "Street Artist Zevs on Attacking Luxury Brands with Their Own Logos," *Artspace* (September 12, 2013).

[84] Ibid.

ART CREDITS

Page 21: Martha Holmes/Time Life Pictures/Getty Images/Jackson Pollock © 2015 The Pollock-Krasner Foundation/Artists Rights Society (ARS), New York. Page 23: Cecil Beaton/Vogue/© Condé Nast. Jackson Pollock © 2015 The Pollock-Krasner Foundation/Artists Rights Society (ARS), New York. Page 25: Cecil Beaton/Vogue/© Condé Nast. Jackson Pollock © 2015 The Pollock-Krasner Foundation/Artists Rights Society (ARS), New York. Page 29: © Mark Squires/Contour by Getty Images. Page 31: Top: © Bottega Veneta by Alex Prager; bottom: © Bottega Veneta by Alex Prager. Page 32: Alex Prager/Image courtesy Lehmann Maupin, New York and Hong Kong. Page 33: © Bottega Veneta by Alex Prager. Page 37: © Martin Schoeller/AUGUST. Pages 38–39: © Cindy Sherman/Image courtesy Metro Pictures, New York. Page 40 & 41: © Cindy Sherman/Image courtesy Metro Pictures, New York. Page 42: © Cindy Sherman/Image courtesy Metro Pictures, New York. Page 43: © Cindy Sherman/Image courtesy Metro Pictures, New York. Page 47: Elizabeth Blake/Image courtesy Paul Kasmin Gallery, New York. Page 48: Image courtesy James Nares and Paul Kasmin Gallery, New York. Page 49: © James Nares for Coach. Pages 50–51: © James Nares for Coach. Page 55: George Rose/Getty Images. Page 56: Top left: © Matt Groening for Comme des Garçons; top right: © Matt Groening for Comme des Garçons; bottom left: © Matt Groening for Comme des Garçons; bottom right: © Matt Groening for Comme des Garçons. Page 57: © Matt Groening for Comme des Garçons. Page 61: © Steve Wood/Corbis. Page 63: © firstVIEW. Andy Warhol © 2015 The Andy Warhol Foundation for the Visual Arts, Inc./Artists Rights Society (ARS), New York. Page 64: © firstVIEW. Andy Warhol © 2015 The Andy Warhol Foundation for the Visual Arts, Inc./Artists Rights Society (ARS), New York. Page 65: © firstVIEW. Andy Warhol © 2015 The Andy Warhol Foundation for the Visual Arts, Inc./Artists Rights Society (ARS), New York. Page 69: © Melvin Sokolsky. Page 71: © Melvin Sokolsky. Page 72: © Melvin Sokolsky. Page 73: © Melvin Sokolsky. Page 77: Fred W. McDarrah/Getty Images. Page 78: © Richard Anuszkiewicz/Albright-Knox Art Gallery/Licensed by VAGA, New York, NY/Image courtesy Art Resource, New York. Page 79: © Meyer Liebowitz/The New York Times/Redux. Page 83: © Christopher Felver/Corbis. Page 84: © Fairweather & Fairweather LTD/Artists Rights Society (ARS), New York/Image courtesy Waddington Custot Galleries. Page 85: © firstVIEW. Page 86: © firstVIEW. Page 87: © firstVIEW. Page 91: © Eric Ogden/Corbis Outline. Page 92: Left: © Fashion Anthology, Right: © Fashion Anthology. Page 93: © Jacques Moatti. Pages 94–95: © Timothy Greenfield-Sanders. Page 99: © Ed Alcock/Eyevine/Redux. Page 100: © Nan Goldin. Page 101: © Nan Goldin. Page 102: © Nan Goldin. Page 107: © David M. Benett/Getty Images. Page 108: Top: © Peter Saville/Joy Division/Factory Records; bottom: © Peter Saville for Lacoste. Page 109: Left: © Peter Saville for Lacoste, Right: © Peter Saville for Lacoste. Page 113: © Martin Schoeller/AUGUST. Page 114: © Richard Burbridge/Art + Commerce. Jeff Koons © Jeff Koons. Page 115: © Jeff Koons for Stella McCartney. Page 117: © firstVIEW. Jeff Koons © Jeff Koons. Page 121: © Craig McDean/Art + Commerce. Damien Hirst © Damien Hirst and Science Ltd., All Rights Reserved/DACS, London/Artists Rights Society (ARS), New York, 2015. Page 122: © 2015 Alexander McQueenTrading Ltd., All Rights Reserved. © Damien Hirst and Science Ltd., All Rights Reserved/DACS, London/Artists Rights Society (ARS), New York, 2015. Page 123: © 2015 Alexander McQueenTrading Ltd., All Rights Reserved. Damien Hirst © Damien Hirst and Science Ltd., All Rights Reserved/DACS, London/Artists Rights Society (ARS), New York, 2015. Pages 124–125: Photo © Solve Sundsbo/Art + Commerce/© 2015 Alexander McQueenTrading Ltd., All Rights Reserved. Damien Hirst © Damien Hirst and Science Ltd., All Rights Reserved/DACS, London/Artists Rights Society (ARS), New York, 2015. Page 129: © Raymond Meier/Trunk Archive. Nick Cave © Nick Cave. Page 130: © Raymond Meier/Trunk Archive. Nick Cave © Nick Cave. Page 131: © Raymond Meier/Trunk Archive. Nick Cave © Nick Cave. Page 132: © Raymond Meier/Trunk Archive. Nick Cave © Nick Cave. Page 133: © Raymond Meier/Trunk Archive. Nick Cave © Nick Cave. Page 137: © 2001, Yasumasa Morimura/Image courtesy the artist and Luhring Augustine, New York. Page 138: © Alex Sainsbury. Page 139: © Alex Sainsbury. Page 143: © Elmar Vestner/Image courtesy Galerie Perrotin, Paris. Page 144: © Luc Novovitch/Alamy. Page 145: © Al Argueta/Alamy. Page 149: © Wing Shya. Pages 150–151: © Wing Shya for Rodarte. Page 152: © Wing Shya for Rodarte. Page 153: © Wing Shya for Rodarte. Page 157: Photo Andre Roji, 1937/© 2015 Artists Rights Society (ARS), New York/ADAGP, Paris/Image courtesy Art Resource, New York. Piet Mondrian © HCR International for The Mondrian Trust. Page 158: amw/Interfoto/Mary Evans. Piet Mondrian © HCR International for The Mondrian Trust. Page 159: Irving Penn/© Condé Nast. Piet Mondrian © HCR International for The Mondrian Trust. Page 163: Photo George Platt Lynes/© Estate of George Platt Lynes/The Metropolitan Museum of Art/Art Resource, New York. Page 164: The Philadelphia Museum of Art/Art Resource, New York. Page 165: © Cecil Beaton/Sotheby's. Page 169: © Frazer Harrison/Getty Images. Page 170: Top: © Wilfredo Lee/AP Images. Sterling Ruby © 2015 Sterling Ruby; bottom: © firstVIEW. Page 171: © firstVIEW. Page 172: © firstVIEW. Page 173: © firstVIEW. Page 177: © Tim Roeloffs. Page 178: © Tim Roeloffs. Page 179: Kai Z. Feng/Trunk Archive. Tim Roeloffs © Tim Roeloffs for Versace. Page 180: PPS Vienna/ZUMAPRESS/Newsroom. Tim Roeloffs © Tim Roeloffs for Versace. Page 181: Alessandro Garofalo/REUTERS/Newscom. Tim Roeloffs © Tim Roeloffs for Versace. Page 185: © Paul Stuart/CAMERA PRESS/Redux. Page 186: © Peter Macdiarmid/Reuters. The Chapman Brothers © The Chapman Brothers/White Cube. Page 187: © Maciek Kobielski/Art Licensing. The Chapman Brothers © The Chapman Brothers for Louis Vuitton. Page 188: © firstVIEW. The Chapman Brothers © The Chapman Brothers for Louis Vuitton. Page 189: © Chris Moore/Catwalking/Getty Images. The Chapman Brothers © The Chapman Brothers for Louis Vuitton. Page 191: © firstVIEW. The Chapman Brothers © The Chapman Brothers for Louis Vuitton. Page 195: © Tim Walker/Art + Commerce. Pages 196–197: © Tim Walker/Art + Commerce. Page 198: © Tim Walker/Art + Commerce. Page 199: © Tim Walker/Art + Commerce. Page 200: © Tim Walker/Art + Commerce. Page 201: © Tim Walker/Art + Commerce. Page 205: © Robin Holland/Corbis Outline. Keith Haring © The Keith Haring Foundation. Page 206: © Michael Putland/Getty Images. Keith Haring © The Keith Haring Foundation. Page 207: © Museum of London. Keith Haring © The Keith Haring Foundation. Page 211: © Stephane Grangier/Corbis. Pages 212–213: Left: © Zevs/Image courtesy DeBuck Gallery, New York; right: © Zevs/Image courtesy DeBuck Gallery, New York.

INDEX

Page numbers in *italics* refer to photographs.